W9-DEK-575

LEARN TO PLAY WINNING

CHESS

HISTORY, RULES, SKILLS AND TACTICS

LEARN TO PLAY WINNING
CHESS
HISTORY, RULES, SKILLS AND TACTICS

JOHN SAUNDERS

HERMES HOUSE

This edition is published by Hermes House,
an imprint of Anness Publishing Ltd,
Blaby Road, Wigston, Leicestershire LE18 4SE

Email: info@anness.com

Web: www.hermeshouse.com;
www.annesspublishing.com

Anness Publishing has a new picture agency outlet
for images for publishing, promotions or advertising.
Please visit our website www.practicalpictures.com
for more information.

Publisher: Joanna Lorenz
Editorial Director: Helen Sudell
Project Manager: Susie Behar
Designer: Jo Hill
Art Director: Lisa McCormick
Photography: Andrew Perris
Editorial Readers: Jay Thundercliffe, Lindsay Zamponi
Production Controller: Steve Lang

ETHICAL TRADING POLICY
At Anness Publishing we believe that business should
be conducted in an ethical and ecologically sustainable
way, with respect for the environment and a proper
regard to the replacement of the natural resources
we employ.
As a publisher, we use a lot of wood pulp in high-
quality paper for printing, and that wood commonly
comes from spruce trees. We are therefore currently
growing more than 750,000 trees in three Scottish
forest plantations. The forests we manage contain more
than 3.5 times the number of trees employed each year
in making paper for the books we manufacture.
Because of this ongoing ecological investment
programme, you, as our customer, can have the
pleasure and reassurance of knowing that a tree is
being cultivated on your behalf to naturally replace
the materials used to make the book you are holding.
For further information about this scheme, go to
www.annesspublishing.com/trees

© Anness Publishing Ltd 2007, 2011

All rights reserved. No part of this publication may
be reproduced, stored in a retrieval system, or
transmitted in any way or by any means, electronic,
mechanical, photocopying, recording or otherwise,
without the prior written permission
of the copyright holder.

A CIP catalogue record for this book is available
from the British Library.

Designed and produced for Anness Publishing by
The Bridgewater Book Company Ltd.

PUBLISHER'S NOTE
Although the advice and information in this book are
believed to be accurate and true at the time of going
to press, neither the authors nor the publisher can
accept any legal responsibility or liability for any
errors or omissions that may have been made.

CONTENTS

INTRODUCTION

What is chess? A dictionary or an encyclopaedia will tell you that it is a game of skill played by two players taking turns to move pieces or figures on a chequered board. This is perfectly correct, and chess belongs to a vast family of other parlour games that people of all ages play. Like all such games, it has a number of rules to learn, and the primary aim of this book is to teach you these rules so that you can start playing. Let's begin by dispelling a myth: chess is not hard to learn or play. It might appear complicated at first sight, especially when you find that there are five different types of pieces on the board at the beginning of the game, all of which move in different ways. However, in this book you will find simple, structured guidance on how each individual piece moves and, by working through the examples, it won't be long before you have mastered the basic elements of the game. Once you have learned the rules, the book also introduces some basic strategies and tactics to inspire you from the start. This will prepare you for your first few chessboard battles, and also provide a ready reference for the early phase of your chess-playing career.

Another question worth asking is 'Why chess?' Why should you play chess – rather than snakes and ladders? Why does it take more than 250 pages to introduce chess to the reader? The reason is because chess is far more than 'a board game' in the sense that a Rolls-Royce is superior to 'a car'. Yes, chess is a board game, and many people learn it and play it as such all their lives. There is nothing wrong with that – in fact, it is one of its greatest virtues. However, chess can also be a game of depth, creativity and imagination, and it has fascinated millions of people for over 500 years. Unlike other board games, its mysteries have yet to be solved by the colossal computing power available in the 21st century, despite millions of dollars being expended in the attempt. Chess has not yet yielded all of its secrets.

Before laying out the rules of the game, this book looks at the wider world of chess: its history, top players, celebrated aficionados and cultural significance. No other board game can compete with chess in terms of longevity. The codification of most sports and games only dates to the 1800s, but chess is

Above: One of the chess world's great stars, a child prodigy and a winnner of the World Chess Championships, Bobby Fischer (b.1943) is seen here playing chess in Varna, Bulgaria in 1962.

more than 1,000 years old, and the rules, as played today, have remained completely unchanged for about 500 years. In this regard, it is one of the intellectual wonders of the world. There are records of matches by chess players from the 16th and 17th centuries, which demonstrate a highly sophisticated level of play. Nobody knows who made the final amendments to the rules in the 15th century, but to have created a game that has remained unchanged for half a millennium and is still growing in popularity is true genius.

Having absorbed something of the culture and history of the game and learnt the basic rules, the next step for you to take is to learn how to play winning chess. It is one thing to know how to play a game, and another to be able to win with any regularity.

Winning isn't everything – but it's definitely important. This part of the book offers guidance in easy stages from beginner to intermediate player, using practical, fully illustrated examples to help you advance to the next level.

At this stage, you might well discover, to your great delight, that you have already learned enough to beat your chess-playing friends with great regularity. If that is the summit of your ambition, congratulations – feel free to skip the rest of the introduction. If you are still reading, then consider that there remain thousands of competition chess players out there who play much better chess than you do. Although it is beyond the scope of this book to elevate you to master level, look upon it as a challenge and try some competition chess (on-line or otherwise). A second myth that must be dispelled is that all competition players are grandmasters. The truth is that many are not much good but simply love the game and its social side. You will find a comfortable niche whatever your level – and make friends.

There is a huge range of chess literature and learning aids available, and this book contains plenty of advice for further reading. Additionally, not only does it provide practical advice on the best way to improve your game but it also contains information on how to take your first steps in competitive chess.

So what is chess? It's fun – read the book and enjoy playing it.

Above: Rules and strategies are clearly explained and many are illustrated with diagrams that show the chess positions involved in each move. From simple to complex, you will be guided through a wide variety of chess scenarios step by step.

Below: Learning chess is a challenging but rewarding pastime, and one that can become a passion for many players.

Chapter One:

The History of Chess

Chess has one of the richest histories of all games or sports, in part due to its sheer antiquity. Something in the game has appealed to people of all ages and cultures, ranging from Middle Eastern peoples of the pre-medieval period (and even earlier), to the computer-game-playing teenagers of the 21st century. For at least the last 500 years, chess has been particularly popular among literate people who have often applied their skills to the task of writing about it, even to the point of recording each move of games they have played. Consequently, although its origins are somewhat obscure, chess has an extraordinarily well-documented history. At the beginning of the 21st century, chess is more popular than ever. It has been estimated that upwards of 600 million people in more than 120 countries know how to play chess.

Right: As you will learn, the king is the most important piece on the chessboard. The object of the game is to checkmate the opponent's king.

THE EARLY HISTORY OF CHESS

The one thing we can say with great certainty about chess is that it is a very, very old game. It has been established that a forerunner of modern chess emerged well over 1,000 years ago, while the modern game, with the rules of the game as played today, came into being about 500 years ago.

Indian invention

Board games in general date from at least 6,000 years ago, but the first chess derivative emerged around AD600 in India. In one myth associated with a very early form of chess in India, the invention of the game is credited to a Hindu saint called Sissa, who was a Brahman at the court of a king. One day the Indian king (rajah) Balhait summoned Sissa and requested that he create a game based on mental skill and oppose the teaching of games in which mere chance decided the outcome by the throw of dice. The king also told Sissa that this new game should be designed to enhance the mental qualities required to analyse and

reason. The Brahman later returned to the court of the king with a board (*ashtapada*) consisting of 8 x 8 = 64 squares with rules that were strikingly similar to the ones we use today. The game he devised was called *chaturanga*, which is a Sanskrit military term meaning 'army composed of four members' – thought to be made up of chariots, foot soldiers, horses and elephants.

It is unclear whether *chaturanga* was a game in the sense in which we use the word today, and some chess historians believe that it actually derived from a divination ceremony. However, it was extremely similar to the game we now call chess: like the modern game, it was played on a 64-square board; the two players had 16 pieces each, with starting positions much as they are today; at least two of them (the knight and rook) moved exactly as those pieces do in modern chess; and the players took it in turns to make a move. *Chaturanga* later became known as 'chess'.

Above: *Xiang qi* is native to China and is commonly called Chinese chess. The earliest indications reveal the game was played as early as the 4th century BC in China.

Right: In medieval times the game of chess was played on the same type of board with the same pieces and basic rules as today. However, there were several variations concerning the movement of certain pieces.

Este es otro iuego departido en á axviii. trebeios que an a seer en. Se mismo toque puesto en la segun casa del cauallo blanco. z entrara el

Above: The 12th-century Muslim leader Saladin was said to be a very bad chess player, though a great war tactician. Here, he is depicted playing chess with his sister.

Chess travels east and west

The game then started its travels, in two directions. It travelled east to China, where it became known as *xiang qi*, or Chinese chess. This form is significantly different from the game as known in the West, but it has survived to the present day and remains very popular in China and other Asian countries.

The game also travelled west from India to Persia in the late 7th century AD, where it came to be known as *chatranj*. The rules were extremely similar to modern chess. Like today's game, the idea was to trap the king. It too proved hugely popular, spreading across the Arab world for 900 years. From Persia and the Arab countries, the game travelled farther west via the Mediterranean and North Africa, and also travelled via the European mainland to Russia and northern Europe by the 11th century, at the time of the Norman Conquest.

The game played in medieval Europe was very similar to the game played by the Persians 600 years earlier. The Crusades may also have played a part in the development of chess, and one myth has the 12th-century Muslim leader Saladin teaching the game to King Richard I of England, although legend also tells us that Saladin was a notoriously bad player. Popular tournaments were held throughout the Middle Ages as ways of solving disputes across Europe. During this period the complexity of the game meant it was played almost exclusively by the nobility.

THE GAME OF CHATRANJ

The Arabs reached a high level of skill in the game they called *chatranj*. They studied the theory of the game, developed a notation for recording games and composed problems for solving.

Above: Today's chess is based on a version of *chaturanga* that was played in India around the 7th century AD. It is believed that the Persians created a more modern version of the game, called *chatranj*.

The chessboard below shows a composition for which the solution in *chatranj* is exactly the same as it would be in modern chess. Black is to move first and checkmate White in five moves. Even a good chess player will find this puzzle tough to crack. But the most astonishing thing about this puzzle is its age: it was composed more than a 1,000 years ago.

Above: Black to play and mate in five moves.

THE BEGINNINGS OF MODERN CHESS

By the 11th century, chess was a well-known game throughout Europe, but it was still some time before the game turned into what we now recognize as chess. The ancient game seems to have gradually evolved into modern chess. Some of the rule changes were so specific that it is tempting to imagine them being made by one person, but nobody knows quite how this came about. Two of the pieces underwent a fundamental change in the way they were moved: the piece now known as a queen became the most powerful piece on the board after being one of the least useful, while the modern bishop also gained extra power after being little better than a pawn in terms of relative strength. These changes, together with a number of other smaller adjustments, were evidently the product of some very agile brains. They had the effect of making chess more dynamic and subtle; games could reach a quick conclusion, in a handful of moves if one of the players was unwary, but could also go to great lengths and require a great deal of patience.

Below: In the 11th century, the chess piece known as the queen became the most important piece on the board. Here is a 12th-century Italian queen, carved from ivory.

Guides to chess

Although there were still some regional variations and parts of the world where the old form of chess persisted, the revamped game quickly supplanted the old and spread through Spain and Italy. Soon expert chess players in Spain, Portugal and Italy were writing practical guides on how to play the game. The first one

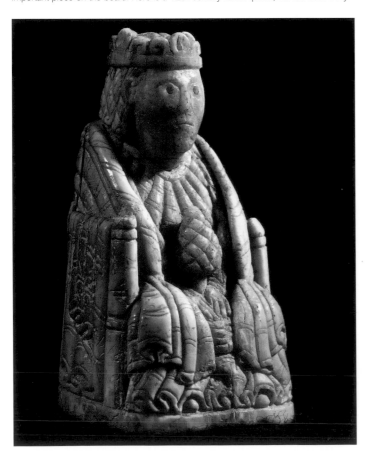

FIRST WORLD CHAMPION

♛ ♝ ♞ ♚

Ruy López de Segura (c.1530–1580), more commonly known as Ruy López, is sometimes accorded the title of first unofficial world champion. He was a priest from Badajoz in Spain and wrote one of the best-known early works on chess in 1561, called *Book of the Liberal Invention and Art of the Game of Chess*. His book included advice on chess openings, one of which came to be known by his name and is still played in high-level chess to this day. In his book, Ruy López introduced the word 'gambit', which derives from an Italian word describing the act of tripping up an opponent in wrestling. It is an apt term: chess players invariably use the word 'gambit' to describe a chess opening in which a player allows the opponent to capture a pawn in order to gain time to pursue an attack or get a grip on the game.

was a book by a Catalan player named Francesc Vicent, published in Valencia in 1495. This was soon followed by more chess books, which had tips for starting and ending the game (known by modern chess players as 'openings' and 'endgames'), as well as chess puzzles (or problems). It is clear from the advice in these books that play was already of a high order, with some of the principles of modern chess strategy already in place. Top players in different parts of the world were becoming known to each other. Two Italians, Paolo Boi (1528–1598) and Giovanni Leonardo Di Bona da Cutri (1542–1587) made trips to Spain, during which time they met the leading Iberian chess player, Ruy López, and beat him. With these successes, chess supremacy passed from Spain to Italy.

Far left: The growing popularity of chess as a recreational activity can be seen in its depiction in the art and artefacts of the 15th, 16th and 17th centuries. Here, a game of chess is portrayed on a 17th-century French mirror frame.

Left: Carved from ivory and dating from the 11th century, this chess piece belongs to the 16-piece Charlemagne chess set. The set includes two kings, two queens, four elephants, four knights, three chariots and one foot soldier.

Below: This 15th-century French miniature depicts Lancelot and Guinevere playing a game of chess. Chess has often been associated with the 'game of love'.

CHESS IN THE PRE-VICTORIAN ERA

Since the 1600s, the basic rules of chess have remained the same. Although relatively few chess games were recorded until the late 18th century, records of early chess games allow meaningful comparisons to be made between the standard of modern chess today and the game as played 300 years ago. This is one of the most exciting aspects of the history of chess. Imagine if football experts had full-colour videos of 19th-century matches, with action-replay facilities, in order to see how the sport's originators played it (and to find out if they were good players). Chess players are fortunate to have this fascinating capability available to them.

Below: In the painting, *Still Life*, by Lubin Baugin (1612/13–1663) the box on the right is a chessboard with the pieces stored inside.

A fashionable game

By the 17th century, chess was firmly established as a fashionable board game throughout Europe, and a small number of leading players engaged in matches for high stakes. One such player was Gioacchino Greco (b.*c*.1600–1634), from Calabria, in Italy. Nicknamed 'the Calabrese' and credited (almost certainly erroneously) with inventing the Greco Counter Gambit, he played matches with rivals in Paris, London and Madrid, becoming famous for his flamboyant style of play. While in England, he sold his chess opening analyses (which purported to be records of his games) to supplement his income. Some of these manuscripts still exist. Much of Greco's chess analysis makes perfect sense today, although some of it consists of tricks that would be unlikely to snare a well-coached modern chess player.

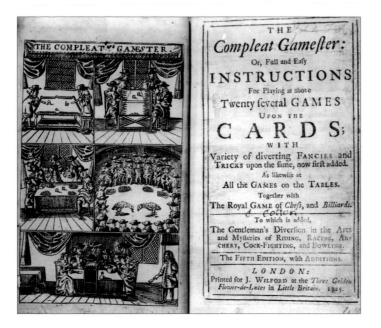

Above: The title page of the fifth edition of *The Compleat Gamester*, attributed to Charles Cotton (1630–1687). This book gave instructions on playing billiards, bowls, card games and chess.

In the 18th century, the proliferation of coffee houses coincided with the growing popularity of chess. As well as normal games between the clientele, these were also the venues for challenge matches between the best players of the era. Coffee houses tended to be upper-class establishments in the 1700s, but were frequented more by the middle classes in the 19th century.

So, how do early generations of players compare? The big difference between chess in the 21st century and in the 19th century (and before) is that we have the benefit of knowing what each successive generation has discovered about the game. Some of the strategies of early chess players seem naive to the modern chess master, particularly when it comes to the opening moves of a game. This part of the game has been studied in enormous detail by chess experts, with many books and computer databases published containing vast arrays of opening move possibilities. Dissemination of information on this scale only became possible relatively recently, although some chess masters of the Victorian era wrote substantial manuals on chess openings, and there were quite a number of chess periodicals and regular columns in newspapers. Some of the games show that chess of quite a high order was being played from the earliest days of the modern rules – the players were certainly accomplished enough to beat all the upper strata of modern competition chess players.

PHILIDOR

François-André Danican Philidor (1726–1795) is generally considered to be the best chess player of his era, and he was also a profound writer on the game. One of the most remarkable people of the 18th century, he was born into a musical family and grew up to become one of the leading French composers of his day. He made his living in the world of music but soon learned and fell in love with chess, which he played at the Café de la Régence, a celebrated chess haunt in Paris. He played with great skill, being one of the first people to master blindfold chess – in which one or both of the competitors plays without sight of the board and pieces (moves being communicated verbally). He could play more than one game at a time in this mode. Philidor spent time in the Netherlands and England, and made money teaching and displaying his chess skills while abroad. Once home in France, he concentrated more on his music and composed comic operas. After the French Revolution he moved to London, where he lived for the rest of his life. From the records of his games, it is evident that he was the greatest chess player of his age, and he far exceeded those before him. He remains as famous a name in the world of music as he is in chess.

Above: This portrait of François-André Danican Philidor was engraved by Augustus de Saint-Aubin in 1772.

CHESS IN THE VICTORIAN ERA

As happened with many other sports and games, the 19th century saw great developments in the organization and codification of chess. It had hitherto been played privately or in various meeting places but many chess clubs and associations sprang up during the 19th century. Chess also became the main attraction at other very notable venues, such as Simpson's Divan, a well-known cafe-restaurant on the Strand in London. Founded in 1820, it became a mecca for all the leading chess players of the Victorian era as well as those who would challenge them, and continued to be a leading chess centre into the early years of the 20th century. It is still a restaurant in the 21st century and retains its connection with chess: some chess relics are on display there.

Growth of chess clubs

Most of the countries of Europe, as well as North America and Australasia, had well-established clubs from about the middle of the 19th century. Most of them began to run formal competitions and club championships, and the concept of team chess was born. Clubs would line up a number of their best players and play the teams from other clubs, with normally one game played between each representative, and the best player of each team meeting that of the other (and so on, in descending order of strength). Although it was some time before a player came along to match Philidor in strength, there was a significant explosion in the strength of the top players from the 1820s. French players were generally

Above: *The Coffee Boiler*, a chalk lithograph made *c.*1840 by August Strixner, depicts the busy but convivial scene of a Viennese coffee house. The chess game in progress is watched with interest by the other customers.

Right: Though men dominated the game in this era, it was by no means a male preserve. Here, two Victorian women enjoy a game of chess.

reckoned to be the best during the early years of the 19th century, although this was often by reputation and hardly put to a rigorous test.

Above: In 1818, T. Leeming painted this portrait of the gentlemen of the Hereford Chess Society. This was an early British club, and it reflected the burgeoning interest in the game.

Technological developments

Progress in technology in the fields of publishing, travel and communication also contributed to the growing popularity of chess. The earliest periodical devoted to chess, *Le Palamède*, was first published in Paris in 1836 and it was quickly followed by chess magazines in Britain, Germany and elsewhere. As well as general articles on chess and reports of club activity, magazines contained game scores (i.e. transcriptions of the moves of games) from recent matches, which meant that players could learn from games played by stronger players and acquire intelligence about future rivals. These magazines proved very popular with club players and some had long runs. One, *British Chess Magazine*, has appeared every month from 1881 to the present day.

The invention of the telegraph made it possible for chess games to be played over vast distances. The first electric telegraph match was between Washington and Baltimore in 1844, linked by the first American telegraph line. In Britain in 1845, two leading players journeyed on the railway from London to Gosport, where they played a game via telegraph with some opponents back at the London terminus. By the end of the century it had become possible to play a transatlantic game via cable, the first successful one being played in 1896 between the British and Manhattan chess clubs.

A CHALLENGE TO THE FRENCH

♛ ♝ ♘ ♚

Alexandre Deschapelles (1780–1847) and Louis de la Bourdonnais (1795–1840) were leading habitués of the Café de la Régence, with the younger man gaining ascendancy over the older from about 1821. A challenge to French supremacy came from across the English Channel, and Bourdonnais played a vast match (consisting of 85 games) against an Ulsterman named Alexander McDonnell (1798–1835) over a period of four months in London in 1834. The Frenchman won the match, but the quality of the games was of a high standard, and the match fostered a taste for chess competition among the general public.

THE EARLY WORLD CHAMPIONS

Chess statisticians treat the 1886 match between the Austrian, US-resident player Wilhelm Steinitz, and the Polish chess master Johannes Zukertort as the first official championship of the world. Indeed, modern world chess champions are often accorded an ordinal number that connects them back to Steinitz, the winner of the match and the first world champion. However, it is appropriate to include some of Steinitz's predecessors in this section since, despite not holding an official title, they were nevertheless acclaimed as the greatest players of their respective eras.

Howard Staunton

After the death of Louis de la Bourdonnais in 1840, the best player in the world was unnofficially considered to be Pierre Saint-Amant (1800–1872). On a trip to London in 1843, Saint-Amant defeated a Shakespearean scholar and chess writer named Howard Staunton (1810–1874) in a short match. However, the defeated Englishman challenged him to a return match that took place over 21 games in front of large audiences at the Café de la Régence. This time Staunton won the match, and with it the unofficial title of the world's best player. To this day, Staunton is the nearest thing Britain has had to a world chess champion. Sadly, his win against Saint-Amant was his high-water mark, and his play thereafter was less impressive.

Staunton also forged a career as a chess writer and journalist, writing the famous *Chess Player's Handbook*, which his fame helped to sell as the main chess instructional manual of its time. In one of the earliest examples of sports sponsorship, he also gave his name as the registered trademark of the standard design of chess pieces, which are still used today.

Paul Morphy

The next major player of the 19th century was an American, Paul Morphy (1837–1884). Born in New Orleans and of Creole descent, Morphy was the first recognized chess prodigy, who became an exceptionally strong chess player as a boy. He took on the best players in New Orleans at the age of eight, and by the time he was 13 he could beat them all.

Below left: Howard Staunton (1810–1874) is still the only British player to have been considered the world's best chess player of his era. As well as a chess player, he was a Shakespearean scholar.

Below centre: Paul Charles Morphy (1837–1884) was considered to be the greatest player in the world in the 1850s. After qualifying as a lawyer, he travelled to Europe, seeking to play and defeat the top European chess masters.

Below right: Wilhelm Steinitz (1836–1900) was born in Prague, later settling in London. In 1888 he became a US citizen. He is regarded as the first official world chess champion, winning the title in a match with Johannes Zukertort in 1886, but he was probably the world's best player from 1866 until 1894, when he lost his title to Emanuel Lasker.

Above: Emanuel Lasker (1868–1941) had a longer reign as world champion (1894–1921) than anyone before or since.

Right: Johannes Zukertort (1842–1888) lost to Wilhelm Steinitz in the first official world championship match, held in the USA in 1886. Born in Poland, he later moved to Berlin and finally settled in London. He excelled at blindfold chess (playing without sight of the board) and was able to play 16 games simultaneously in this fashion.

After completing his studies to become a lawyer, Morphy travelled to Europe to seek out and beat the top European chess masters. In 1858 he met several of them in matches and defeated them all, except that he was thwarted in his attempts to play a match against Staunton. It is almost certain that Morphy would have won had he played Staunton, since the Englishman was past his best by then.

Morphy was now considered the finest player in the world, but chose to concentrate on his legal career thereafter. Following Morphy's return to the USA, one of the players he had beaten in 1858, Adolf Anderssen, was for a time considered to be the best player in the world, but in 1866 he was beaten by Wilhelm Steinitz (1836–1900), originally from Prague but by now resident in London. From that time forward, Steinitz was generally considered to be the world's best player.

World chess champions

The formal title of world chess champion is generally recognized as dating from 1886, when Wilhelm Steinitz was challenged to a match by Johannes Zukertort. Steinitz, by now a US resident, won the match comfortably and is known formally as the first world chess champion. Finally, his proud record of 24 match victories came to an end in 1894 when he was defeated by a young German rival, Emanuel Lasker (1868–1941).

Lasker was a man of many parts, with a doctorate in mathematics and a strong ability in many other games. However, such was his skill at chess that he held the world championship title until 1921, when he lost it to a Cuban, José Raúl Capablanca (1888–1942). Capablanca, like Paul Morphy, was a child prodigy at chess who was seemingly able to play despite very little study or coaching in the strategy of the game.

GREAT 20TH-CENTURY PLAYERS

José Raúl Capablanca was perhaps the first true chess celebrity. A good-looking and well-educated man, he divided his time between acting as a diplomat for his native Cuba and working as a globe-trotting chess player. He lost few games during his time as champion and was widely expected to see off the challenge of Alexander Alekhine (1892–1945), an expatriate Russian player, when they met at a match in Buenos Aires in 1927. But the Russian succeeded in defeating the Cuban in a 34-game match, by six wins to three (with the other games drawn). Capablanca and Alekhine remained rivals throughout the interwar years, but all attempts to organize a rematch were spurned by the new champion, now a French citizen.

Alekhine met a number of other challengers and in 1935 faced a young Dutch schoolmaster named Max Euwe (1901–1981) whom nobody – least of all Alekhine – expected to give him much trouble. However, Euwe narrowly defeated Alekhine and became the world chess champion – the only true amateur player ever to do so. In 1937, Euwe granted Alekhine a return match and was well beaten.

Having regained his title, Alekhine remained world champion throughout World War II, during which chess activity more or less ceased. He died in 1946 just as plans were afoot to organize a match between him and a Soviet Russian challenger, Mikhail Botvinnik (1911–1995). Until this point, the organization of championship matches had been a private matter between champions and potential challengers, but with the hiatus caused by the champion Alekhine's death, the World Chess Federation (known as FIDE, the abbreviated form of its French name) stepped in to organize a match-tournament between the strongest players in the world. In 1948, a five-player tournament was held to fill the world champion title vacancy. Botvinnik triumphed ahead of Vasily Smyslov (USSR), Samuel Reshevsky (USA), Paul Keres (USSR) and Max Euwe (Netherlands).

Below: Mikhail Botvinnik (1911–1995) (seated, centre) was world champion 1948–1957, 1958–1960 and 1961–1963. Botvinnik lost some of his prime chess-playing years to World War II, but still reigned as world champion for 13 years after the war. He was the most influential Soviet chess player of his era, and helped guide the early careers of players such as Karpov and Kasparov. Here he is shown with the top young English players of the early 1980s.

Below: Samuel Reshevsky (1911–1992) was the most celebrated child prodigy in the world after World War I. Born in Poland, his family emigrated to the USA where he toured the country giving simultaneous displays. His fame as a chess player is reflected in this photograph, where he is seen playing with Charlie Chaplin in Hollywood.

World chess championship

From this point forward, FIDE took control of the world chess championship and instituted a regular cycle of qualifying competitions and title matches. The regulations were heavily influenced by the demands of the very powerful Soviet Chess Federation. Under the new regulations, the world champion had to defend his title against an official challenger every three years, retaining the title in the event of a drawn match and with the right to a rematch the following year should he lose his title. Botvinnik was to take full advantage of these clauses. In 1951 he met another Soviet grandmaster, David Bronstein (b. 1924), in the

championship final and the match was drawn. Botvinnik thus retained his title, as he did in 1954 when he drew with Vasily Smyslov (b. 1921). In 1957 Smyslov beat Botvinnik to take the title but lost it back in the regulation return match in 1958. Botvinnik lost the title to a brilliant young Latvian, Mikhail Tal (1936–1992), who became the youngest-ever world champion in 1960. But Botvinnik once again regained the title in 1961. In 1963, Botvinnik played and lost to an Armenian, Tigran Petrosian, but by this time the rematch clause had been rescinded, and Botvinnik decided to retire from championship chess. Despite his variable results as champion, Botvinnik was universally admired for his ability to work out a method to revenge himself on each challenger in turn. He became one of the greatest-ever chess coaches, and played a significant role in the development of future champions Anatoly Karpov and Garry Kasparov.

Tigran Petrosian (1929–1984) was to be champion for six years. He defended his title successfully in 1966 against Boris Spassky (b. 1937) but lost it in another match against the same opponent in 1969.

Left: Alexander Alekhine (1892–1946) was Russian by birth but settled in France in the 1920s. He was world champion from 1927 to 1935 and from 1937 to his death, in 1946. The vacant title was not held again until 1948, when Botvinnik won a five-player match-tournament.

Below: Mikhail Tal (1936–1992) was born in Riga, Latvia. Despite long bouts of very poor health, he was one of the most spectacular and successful chess players in history.

Below left: José Raúl Capablanca (1888–1942) was born in Cuba. A child prodigy, his ability at chess seemed effortless. He won the world championship in 1921.

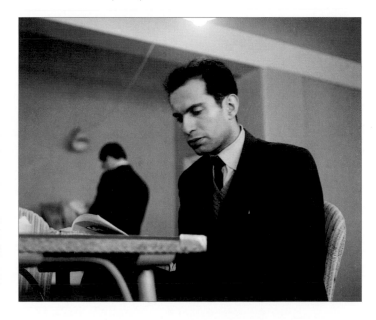

BOBBY FISCHER

Although chess had been popular in the USA since the days of Morphy, and a number of gold medal successes were achieved in team events between the wars, the game had never been high profile, and financial support always remained scanty. This was the chess culture into which Bobby (Robert James) Fischer was born in Chicago on 9 March 1943. Brought up in Brooklyn by his mother, who was a divorcee, he was introduced to chess at the age of six and soon became completely absorbed in the game. However, although Bobby Fischer was very good, it was to be some years before his exceptional ability became fully apparent and he was to meet his rival Boris Spassky, a Russian, in the world championship.

Chess had been popular in Russia since the 19th century, but under the Soviet regime its value as a propaganda tool for demonstrating the country's cultural and intellectual superiority was recognized. Following World War II, the Soviet Chess Federation had virtually become a government department, with a handsome budget and large numbers of chess players receiving stipends as players, coaches and administrators. No other country put anywhere near as many resources or as much professional expertise into the game, and therefore it was hardly surprising that the Soviet Union had achieved total domination of championship-level chess.

Fischer's success

The year 1957 was to be Fischer's *annus mirabilis*. First he won the US Junior Championship, then tied first in the US Open and finally he won the US (closed) Championship ahead of all the country's top grandmasters. Fischer's success in the 1957/8 US Championship qualified him for the World Championship inter-zonal tournament, held in Yugoslavia in August 1958. This was a massive event, where 21 of the world's top players would meet each other over the course of more than a month. Against all expectation, Fischer finished fifth and qualified for the final rung on the world championship qualification ladder. This success not only brought him the title of youngest-ever grandmaster, but also international fame.

Below: Bobby Fischer (right) at the Siegen Chess Olympiad in 1970. He became the most famous chess player in history when he won the right to challenge Boris Spassky for the world championship. In 1972 he was the first Western player to win the title since the 1930s, but he never defended his title and became a recluse.

Above: After becoming world champion in 1972, Bobby Fischer (right) disappeared from the chess scene and played no competitive games for 20 years. However, in 1992, he played another match with his former rival Boris Spassky in Yugoslavia. This was billed by the organizers as 'the world chess championship', but in reality chess had moved on, and the two players would no longer have been serious candidates for the real chess title, by then held by Garry Kasparov.

Left: A large crowd tries to catch a glimpse of Bobby Fischer playing world champion Boris Spassky in the 1970 Siegen Olympiad. Spassky won this game and never lost a game to Fischer until they met in the 1972 world championship match in Reykjavik.

In 1959, Fischer played in an eight-man World Championship Candidates' tournament to decide who would go on to challenge the world champion. Unfortunately, he was still too raw to get the better of a group of top Soviet grandmasters who stood between him and the pinnacle, and he finished fifth. He went on to challenge again in 1962 but once again found himself thwarted by a group of Soviet grandmasters in a Candidates' competition. This time he made accusations that they were colluding among themselves. Many years later, after the collapse of the Soviet Union, some of them admitted that he had actually been right.

Although the championship system was changed to match-play to avoid group collusion, it was not until 1970 that Fischer again competed for the championship. Once again, he had an easy win at the inter-zonal stage, and in 1971 he won three qualifying matches with flying colours. Two opponents,

Taimanov and Larsen, were summarily beaten 6–0 (such whitewashes were practically unprecedented) and then the former world champion Petrosian was also well beaten in a match in Buenos Aires. Fischer reached 20 games unbeaten in this match; this was the longest winning run in the history of chess.

This qualified Fischer to face Spassky in 1972. The match became a symbol of the Cold War between the West and the Soviet bloc, and Fischer's reputation for out-spokenness and prickliness with the press only added to its mystery. The world's press watched closely as Fischer first showed reluctance to journey to the match venue, Reykjavik, and then defaulted the second game after a disaster in the first. The odds were that Fischer would once again withdraw and Spassky would retain his title without a fight. However, Fischer came back, played the third game and won it. This was his first-ever win against Spassky and he soon took the lead and won the match.

ANATOLY KARPOV

Anatoly Karpov was born on 23 May 1951 in Zlatoust in the former Soviet Union and learned to play chess at the age of four. In 1974, this young star of Soviet chess had made such remarkable progress that he won the right to challenge Bobby Fischer for the world crown.

Bobby Fischer's conquest of the world chess championship in 1972 ushered in a new age for chess in the West. The game received a massive boost from his title success, with many Western countries, such as the UK, enjoying a chess boom on the back of increased sponsorship. This later translated into the development of a group of professional grandmasters who were able to play on equal terms against Soviet players. However, Fischer himself never played a single game as world champion. Despite some large offers of sponsorship, he could not be tempted back to the board. In 1975 he was due to meet his first official challenger but he failed to meet the deadline set for agreeing terms to the match, after finding fault with all manner of conditions laid down for it.

Karpov versus Fischer

The World Chess Federation believed that they had no option other than to strip Fischer of the title and award it without a fight to his challenger, Anatoly Karpov. The loss of the world title in 1972 had been a major blow to the prestige of the Soviet chess establishment, but even before Spassky had lost the title, Karpov had emerged as the outstanding candidate to win it back. He had won the World Junior Championship in 1969 and had qualified to meet Fischer in 1974 via a series of tough matches against top players, including the former champion Boris Spassky and the formidable Soviet star Viktor Korchnoi (b. 1931). Chastened by the defeat of their champion in 1972, the Soviet Chess Federation put all its considerable resources behind Karpov to ensure that the title was regained with all speed.

Having won the title without playing Fischer, Karpov was left with the unenviable task of proving himself to a chess world that was at first slightly sceptical of his right to the title. This he did highly

Above: Viktor Korchnoi (b. 1931) is believed by many to be the strongest chess player never to become world champion. After defecting from the Soviet Union in 1976, he played two bitterly hostile title matches with Anatoly Karpov, but lost them both.

Right: Anatoly Karpov (b. 1951) became world champion by default in 1975 when Bobby Fischer failed to defend his title. He held the title until 1985 when he lost it after a match with Garry Kasparov. He later regained the World Chess Federation version of the title in 1993.

Above: Here, Karpov is seen contemplating a move while competing in the 1981 World Chess Championships held in Merano, Italy. Karpov would go on to win the match, easily defeating rival Viktor Korchnoi, 11–7, in what became known as the 'Massacre of Merano.' Three years earlier, the two had also played for the title – a match that Korchnoi had come close to winning.

effectively by playing regularly in major tournaments and winning a long string of first prizes, something that few of his predecessors as world champions had been able to do.

Karpov versus Korchnoi

In 1978 Karpov faced his first challenger for the world title. Once again he faced Viktor Korchnoi, whom he had beaten in the final eliminator in 1974. But since that time, Korchnoi had defected from the Soviet Union and become a highly vocal critic of its regime, which had prevented other members of his family from joining him in the West.

Once again a chess match caught the world's attention, more because of its fraught political background than the chess moves played on the board.

It was a longer match than normal. Most post-war matches had been the best of 24 games, but this one was to be won by the first player to win six games. As many top-level chess games end in draws, this meant that the match was to last somewhat longer. Karpov reached a score of five wins to two, but then visibly tired and lost three out of the next four. However, with both players needing a single win for victory, Korchnoi tried too hard in the next game and lost. Karpov had retained his title.

Karpov continued to win many first prizes in tournaments during the next three years and, in 1981, his challenger was once again to be Viktor Korchnoi. However, Karpov was by now in his prime (aged 30) while his opponent was rather past his, and Karpov won comfortably.

Karpov continued to effectively dominate the chess world throughout the 1980s, but he soon came up against a young and determined challenger, also from the Soviet Union, who would prove to be his nemesis: Garry Kasparov.

GARRY KASPAROV

Garry Kimovich Kasparov (b. 1963 in Baku, Azerbaijan) was from a very different generation and background from Anatoly Karpov. His name at birth was Harry Weinstein, but after his father's death he was given a Russified version of his mother's family name, Kasparian. Like Karpov, he was soon picked out by the highly efficient Soviet talent-spotting network and placed under the wing of former champion Mikhail Botvinnik. In 1978 Kasparov finished eighth in the Soviet Championship, indicating that he was probably as good as Fischer had been at the same age. He officially became a grandmaster in 1980 when he also won the world junior championship.

Kasporov versus Karpov

In 1981 Kasparov won the Soviet Championship and a number of other major tournaments, and it was already apparent that he would soon challenge Karpov. In 1983/4 he qualified as Karpov's official challenger. Once again the match winner would be the first to six wins. However, it was to be the last time that such an open-ended match was tried. The match started in September 1984 and Karpov's experience told as he progressed to four wins to zero by the ninth game. However, Kasparov managed to dig his heels in at this point. A run of 17 draws followed. Karpov then won his fifth game, so needed just one to retain his title. But Kasparov held on, won his first game and, after more draws, won two more games. The score stood at five wins to Karpov and three to Kasparov, after five months' play. At this point, the president of the World Chess Federation controversially decided to declare the match void, proposing another match between the two (but limited by the number of games) for later in the year. Thus, the most protracted match in chess history was left unfinished, with both contestants claiming that the annulment had unfairly favoured their rival.

Karpov duly defended his title against Kasparov in September 1985. By this time Kasparov had become much stronger and he managed to win the

THE TIMES WORLD CHESS CHAMPIONSHIP

KASPAROV **SHORT**

Above: The controversial breakaway chess title match between English grandmaster Nigel Short and Kasparov in 1993.

Left: Garry Kasparov (left), in animated discussion with Peter Leko (b. 1979). Both were child prodigies. Leko qualified as a grandmaster aged 14. He has yet to win the world championship, although he drew a title match with Vladimir Kramnik in 2004.

championship. But this was by no means the end of the Karpov–Kasparov story. Karpov was entitled to a return match, which took place in 1986. Kasparov also won this match, although only by one point.

Karpov won the right to challenge Kasparov yet again in 1987. Karpov needed only a draw from the last game to regain his title, but the younger man then won one of the most exciting chess games in history to clinch a win, and tie the match, thus retaining his title. The fifth and last Karpov–Kasparov match took place in 1990, and Kasparov won again, finally setting the seal on the greatest and closest chess rivalry in history (in 144 championship games, Kasparov won 21 to Karpov's 19).

The breakaway match

In 1993 Kasparov played a title match against the English grandmaster Nigel Short. It caused great acrimony in the chess world because the two players had broken away from the World Chess Federation and held the match under the auspices of a newly formed organization called the Professional Chess Association (PCA). Kasparov won the match quite easily, but he was stripped of his official title. However, such was Kasparov's personal prestige that his breakaway version of the title was generally recognized by the chess world at large.

Like Karpov, Kasparov went on to win many first prizes in major chess tournaments throughout the world, defending his title in 1995 and 2000 in privately sponsored matches. In 2000 he met a young Russian prodigy, Vladimir Kramnik (b. 1975) and, surprisingly, lost a close match. But Kasparov remained the dominant figure in the chess world into the 21st century, heading the world rankings until his retirement in 2005.

CHESS STARS OF THE 21ST CENTURY

Although Kasparov remained at the top of the official rating list until his retirement in April 2005, there are now many more professional chess players, and several players have challenged for Kasparov's mantle as the world number one.

Knock-out championships

Since the late 1990s, the World Chess Federation has run a new format world championship system, with 128 players taking part in a knock-out based on short-duration matches of no more than two games, with 'rapidplay' and 'blitz' games used to decide them in the event of a tie. The speeding up of the game has the effect that the chance element plays a bigger part than it did in the traditional long-distance match format. After Kasparov forfeited the official title in 1993, Anatoly Karpov came back to regain the title and held it until 1999 when a knock-out event in Las Vegas was won by Russian grandmaster Alexander Khalifman. Khalifman was ranked only 45th in the world at the time, when FIDE ratings indicated that the best players in the world were Garry Kasparov, Vladimir Kramnik and the Indian grandmaster Viswanathan Anand.

However, the following year, Anand duly won the world knock-out championship to add a degree of credibility and prestige to the new championship system.

The next world knock-out championship was held in 2002 and featured an all-Ukrainian final between the country's leading player, Vasyl Ivanchuk, and the much younger and more inexperienced Ruslan Ponomariov. However, it was a triumph of youth over experience as the 19-year-old beat his older rival to become the youngest-ever world chess champion. In 2004 the next world knock-out championship was held in Tripoli, Libya, and the final contested by Michael Adams of England and Rustam Kasimdzhanov of Uzbekistan. Although the event was not widely publicized in the general media, by now it had become possible to watch major championship games via the Internet. Consequently, many thousands of chess fans watched a nail-biting finale in which Adams came within a

Right: Viswanathan Anand (b. 1969) challenged Garry Kasparov's world title unsuccessfully in 1995, but won the World Chess Federation version of the title in 2000. Subsequently one of the highest-ranked players ever, he is a top blitz player, earning the nickname 'Lightning Kid'.

Below: World chess champion Vladimir Kramnik (b. 1975) is interviewed by the press after an exhibition game against David Howell (b. 1990) in 2002.

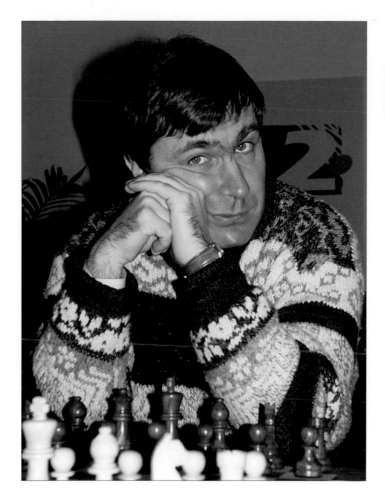

Above: Vasyl Ivanchuk (b. 1969) is one of the world's most talented chess players, with several wins against Garry Kasparov to his credit. He has been less successful in world championship competitions, his best being second place to Ruslan Ponomariov in the 2002 world championship knock-out.

Above: Veselin Topalov (b. 1975) won the official 2005 world championship tournament held in Argentina. In July 2006 he was the top-ranked chess player in the world but lost his world title to Vladimir Kramnik in October of that year.

move or two of becoming the only Englishman to win the world championship. He missed his chance, and the Uzbek player triumphed.

Reunifying the championships

While FIDE continued to hold their new-style knock-out championships, the breakaway Professional Chess Association maintained the tradition of a match-play championship following the Kasparov–Short breakaway in 1993. After defeating Kasparov in 2000, Vladimir Kramnik rebutted invitations to a rematch, instead playing a championship match with Peter Leko of Hungary in 2004. Leko had qualified to meet Kramnik via a Candidates' tournament. Kramnik won the final game of the match to secure a drawn match, thus retaining his title. The World Chess Federation organized a world championship tournament of eight players in Argentina in 2005. The world match-play champion, Vladimir Kramnik, was invited but did not accept the invitation. The tournament went ahead anyway as a replacement for the world knock-out championship. The winner was a Bulgarian grandmaster, Veselin Topalov (b. 1975), who finished comfortably ahead of his rivals. This success, and several others in major tournaments, soon carried him to the top of the world rating list.

Eventually, in 2006, the World Chess Federation managed to broker a reunification match between its official champion, Veselin Topalov, and the holder of the rival match-play title, Vladimir Kramnik. The two players met in Elista, Kalmykia, Russia. Kramnik raced into a 2–0 lead by winning the first two games but controversy soon broke out when unsubstantiated allegations of malpractice were made by the Topalov delegation and not resolved by the match officials to the satisfaction of Kramnik, who defaulted a game in protest. However, despite the handicap of losing a point like this, Kramnik eventually ran out the winner of the match after a tie-break, thereby becoming the first undisputed world chess champion for 13 years.

GREAT WOMEN CHESS PLAYERS

To date, only one woman chess player – Judit Polgar – has reached the top ten in the chess rankings. The fundamental reason for women's inferior competitive results is that far fewer women than men play chess. Although more girls and women are playing the game now than before, things have not changed in terms of the proportions of men and women playing. In April 2006, 50,423 chess players were registered by the World Chess Federation as active in international competitions worldwide, but only 2,956 of them were female. That is less than 6 per cent and equates to 1 in 17 players. It is perhaps to do with the cultural background of chess, with clubs being more male-oriented and the game traditionally being played in male-only schools. More simply, it may be that the game appeals to men more than women.

The first female chess star

Vera Menchik (1906–1944) was the first woman chess player to make a significant impact on the game. Born in Moscow to a Czech father and English mother, she won the first women's world championship in 1927, conceding only one draw in ten games. She won all the women's world championship events held before World War II. Although less successful in mixed events, she enjoyed notable one-off successes in games against

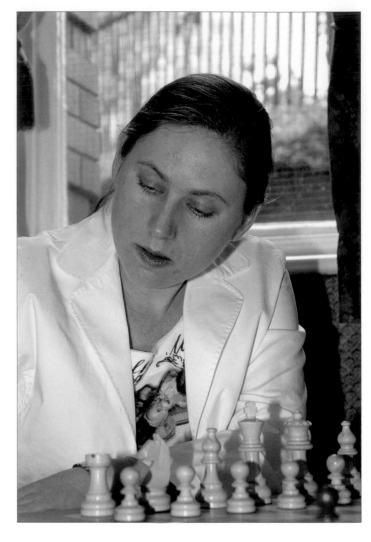

Above: Judit Polgar (b. 1976) is universally regarded as the finest woman chess player of all time. In 2002 she won a rapid chess game against Kasparov. She was for a time the youngest player ever to qualify as a grandmaster (at 15), beating Bobby Fischer's record.

Below: Vera Menchik (1906–1944) was born in Moscow, the daughter of a Czech father and an English mother. Along with her mother and sister, she died in a bombing raid in England. She was easily the best woman player from 1927 to her death.

Right: The world's top female player, Judit Polgar (b. 1976) plays 2000 world champion Viswanathan Anand.

Right: Former women's world champions Zsuzsa (Susan) Polgar and Xie Jun, playing for the USA and China respectively, in the 2004 Chess Olympiad, held in Mallorca.

Above: Xie Jun (b. 1970) was the first Chinese player to win a world individual championship. She won a national title in Chinese chess before taking up the Western form of the game. In 1991 she beat Maia Chiburdanidze to become the women's world champion and held the title until 1996, when she lost to Zsuzsa (Susan) Polgar. In 2000 she regained the title when the championship became a knock-out.

leading players. She beat the future world champion, Max Euwe, twice in the early 1930s. Sadly, she died during an air raid in England in 1944.

Soviet dominance broken by China

After World War II, Soviet women players dominated the women's world championship competitions for many years. The most notable was Nona Gaprindashvili (b. 1941), who won the title in 1962 and held it until 1978, when she was dethroned by Maia Chiburdanidze (b. 1961). Both these players came from the Soviet republic of Georgia, which had developed a particularly rich tradition of women's chess at that time.

The Soviet Union enjoyed an unbroken series of successes in women's chess competitions until the 1980s, when its dominance was broken by China, the world's most populous country. China had only started to take an interest in the Western form of chess in the 1970s, and concentrated on the women's game. The country's first success came in 1991 when Xie Jun (b. 1970), who had played Chinese chess from the age of six, beat Chiburdanidze to take the women's world championship title.

The Polgar sisters

Meanwhile, in Budapest, three young sisters were being brought up to play the game by a chess-playing father. Laszlo Polgar and his wife Klara educated their three daughters at home, and included advanced chess coaching among their academic studies. All three girls became very strong players at an early age. The eldest, Zsuzsa (now Susan) Polgar (b. 1969), became the world under-16 champion aged 12, was the first woman to qualify for the grandmaster title (in 1991) and went on to take the women's world championship title from Xie Jun in 1996. She is now semi-retired from tournament play. The second sister, Sofia Polgar (b. 1974), also competed successfully in mixed chess events, although she was the least strong of the three and has ceased to play in tournaments.

The third sister, Judit Polgar (b. 1976), is universally acclaimed as the strongest woman chess player in history. She has never competed in women-only events, preferring to hone her talents in the company of the world's top players. She achieved the title of grandmaster in 1991, beating the old record held by Bobby Fischer by a matter of days. In recent years she has ranked as high as eighth in the world (men and women) and she played in the eight-player world championship tournament held in 2005. In 2006 she stood at number 14 in the world rankings, and the next woman player – her sister Susan – was down at number 195.

CHESS PRODIGIES

Chess is like music and mathematics in that it can be learned and mastered at a remarkably young age. Among major chess figures, Morphy, Capablanca, Fischer, Karpov and Kasparov were all demonstrating exceptional chess ability before the age of ten. Morphy is reputed to have learned the game simply from watching his father and uncle at the age of eight, and by nine was able to beat the best players in New Orleans. A similar story is told of Capablanca. Fischer also played exceptionally good chess before the age of ten, although the sophisticated opposition he met in New York in the early 1950s was such that eye-catching successes took a little longer to achieve. Karpov and Kasparov reached a similar level (known as 'first category' in the old Soviet ranking system) at the ages of ten and nine respectively.

Below: Samuel Reshevsky, the chess prodigy, at the age of six. Here he is pictured at one of his simultaneous exhibitions, which astounded the chess world.

The first chess prodigy

Samuel Reshevsky (1911–1992) was the first player to receive wide publicity for his exploits as a chess prodigy. Born to a Jewish family in Poland, his prowess soon won him attention and he toured the country giving simultaneous exhibitions at the age of six, during which he would win the majority of his games against 20 or more experienced adult players. He settled with his family in the USA at the age of nine, and then went on two years of similar exhibition tours. From the age of 12 he concentrated on his studies for a number of years before returning to chess. Although he was one of the very best players in the world from 1935 to the late 1960s, he never became world champion, lacking the sort of support that Soviet rivals enjoyed during that period, and perhaps sufficient motivation.

Below: Sergey Karyakin (b. 1990) was the youngest player ever to qualify for the chess grandmaster title – he was 12 years and 7 months when he did so in 2002. Here he is playing at the 2003 annual Hastings International Tournament in the UK.

Nigel Short

In later times, the emergence of child prodigies has coincided with the flowering of chess interest in a given country. The Fischer–Spassky match caused a chess boom around the world, particularly in the United Kingdom, and the most famous chess prodigy there was Nigel Short (b. 1965). He received widespread publicity when, aged only ten, he defeated world title contender Viktor Korchnoi in a simultaneous exhibition. At the age of 12, he competed in the 1977 British Championship, during which he won a game against Jonathan Penrose, who still holds the record for winning the most British Championship titles. Short went on to a stellar career, defeating former world champion Anatoly Karpov in a match on his way to challenging Garry Kasparov for the title in 1993.

Breaking records

Since the 1990s, the age at which a player has qualified for the grandmaster title has become the yardstick by which the achievements of young players have been judged. Fischer became a grandmaster at 15, and his record stood until 1991, when it was broken by the Hungarian player Judit Polgar. Since then, the record has been broken several more times, although it should be born in mind that it has become significantly easier to qualify as a grandmaster since Fischer's day (the rating system employed has a known inflationary effect). Another Hungarian, Peter Leko (b. 1979) became the first 14-year-old to qualify as a grandmaster

Above: Hou Yifan (right) was born in 1994 and is tipped to be one of the greatest players of the 21st century. She reached the last 16 in the 2006 women's world championship and made a big score for the Chinese women's team in the 2006 Women's Olympiad. In July 2006, aged 12 years and 5 months, she was rated eighth best female player in the world.

in 1994, the Chinese player Bu Xiangzhi (b. 1985) became a grandmaster at 13 in 1999, and the Ukrainian player Sergey Karyakin (b. 1990) became the first pre-teen grandmaster, at the age of 12 years and 7 months, in 2002.

There are signs that more girls are now emerging with the ability to achieve a level comparable to anything that boys have attained. Humpy Koneru (b. 1987, India) reached the grandmaster qualification at the age of 15 and in January 2007 was ranked the second-best female player in the world, while a Chinese girl, Hou Yifan (b. 1994), achieved a near-grandmaster score in a major tournament in 2006.

Left: China played its own version of chess for many hundreds of years but is now becoming very interested in 'Western chess'. The girl on the left of the front row is Hou Yifan (b. 1994), one of the greatest players of the 21st century. Pictured here is the entire squad of junior players that the Chinese Chess Federation sent to the World Junior Championships in Halkidiki, Greece, in 2003.

CHESS IN LITERATURE

One of the first-ever books to be printed in English was a book on a chess theme. It was William Caxton's 1474 edition of *Game and Playe of the Chesse*, a translation of a series of morality stories, with a chess allegory written by Jacopo da Cessole, a Dominican monk of the late 13th and early 14th centuries who liked to use chess as the theme of his sermons. It was by no means the first allegory along these lines: a long 14th-century romantic poem titled *Les Échecs Amoureux* (*Chess of Love*) had been translated into English around 1412 and had been much imitated.

William Shakespeare seems to have had some fondness for the game of chess and used it in the context of a cosy flirtation in *The Tempest*. Two lovers are shown on stage playing chess, with Miranda making the teasing accusation that Ferdinand was 'playing [her] false'.

Chess is prominent in *Tales from the Arabian Nights* and Lewis Carroll's *Through the Looking Glass*. In the latter the chess pieces come to life when Alice goes through the mirror (the author, however, displays his ignorance of the game by referring to rooks as 'castles').

Chess as a novel theme

One of the first works of literature with a major chess theme was Vladimir Nabokov's 1929 novel *The Defence*. It tells the story of a brilliant but troubled chess professional called Luzhin and his obsession with the game at the expense of real life. The novel was made into a film titled *The Luzhin Defence* in 2000 in the USA; it starred John Turturro as the chess genius, and depicted tournament chess (as played in the 1920s) in a vivid and compelling way. Nabokov himself was a keen chess player, with a particular interest in composing chess problems.

Another novel with a story woven around chess was Stefan Zweig's *The Royal Game*, which he wrote in 1942. In it, the world chess champion (improbably, an idiot-savant) plays chess games with fellow passengers on a boat voyage from Europe to South America, and with one particular passenger who survived solitary confinement by the Nazis by playing chess matches entirely in his head. As in *The Luzhin Defence*, chess is seen as a very alienating preoccupation, a view that is not very popular in the chess-playing world.

Left: 'The Chess Players', one of the classic Sir John Tenniel illustrations for *Through the Looking Glass* by Lewis Carroll (1832–1898). This particular illustration shows a king and queen conversing while a bishop sits on a boulder reading a newspaper. Behind them stands a pawn, arms akimbo, and a pair of marching rooks, presumably on sentry duty. To the rear, a group of knights and bishops socialize.

Above: This 19th-century painting by Lucy Madox Brown depicts the chess game that takes place in *The Tempest*. Chess was a popular pastime in Shakespeare's day. Indeed, Queen Elizabeth I was said to enjoy playing it.

Intrigue, suspense and poetry

Mystery writers have been fond of weaving chess into their plots. Although these are often contrived and bear little relation to real-life competitive chess, they can be very entertaining. One notable example is *The Flanders Panel* by Arturo Perez Reverte, where the meaning of a hidden inscription on a 500-year-old artwork turns out to be a chess puzzle that contains the clue to a murder. Ian Fleming also incorporated a scene depicting championship chess into his 1957 James Bond book *From Russia With Love*, which appeared in the movie of the same name.

Chess also appears in poetry, from *The Rubaiyat of Omar Khayyam* to the poems of Ezra Pound and more modern poets. The second part of T.S. Eliot's 1922 work *The Waste Land* is headed 'A Game of Chess', although anyone expecting significant chess content is to be disappointed. There is none, as the line mentioning it was supposedly removed, at the request of Eliot's wife. It is also possible that Eliot is alluding to a satirical play of the same name by the Jacobean playwright Thomas Middleton, which used chess and chess pieces in an allegory on Anglo-Spanish politics in the 1620s.

Above: Sean Connery in the film version of Ian Fleming's book, *From Russia With Love*. The game played in the film replicates a Spassky–Bronstein game that took place in Leningrad in 1960.

CAÏSSA

Chess enjoys its very own muse or goddess, named Caïssa (pronounced *Ky-eéssa*). She originated as a nymph in a 1763 poem by Sir William Jones (1746–1794), who is famous as the founder of comparative linguistics. In the poem, Mars persuades the god of sport to invent chess as a way of softening the heart of the nymph towards him. Although the original poem is not widely known in the chess world, Caïssa's name is familiar to all keen players, some of whom occasionally attribute their success to 'Caïssa smiling on them'.

CHESS IN FILM

Film-makers have found many creative ways to exploit chess in films and on the small screen. Although chess has rarely been the central theme of a major film, the game lends itself to being used in depicting various themes, both positive and negative. The earliest film with a significant chess content was *Chess Fever* (1925), a delightful short Soviet comedy about a young man obsessed with the game to the detriment of his relationship with his fiancée. This silent movie contained real footage of a major chess tournament taking place at the time in Moscow. In fact, the then world chess champion at the time, José Raúl Capablanca, played a short scene in the film and was given star billing in order to popularize it. The film is much beloved of chess buffs as it contains the only extant moving images of some early chess legends, including Capablanca and the long-time US champion Frank Marshall.

Chess-playing film stars

One big-screen icon, Humphrey Bogart, was himself a very good chess player and was instrumental in seeing that his favourite game be used to good effect in his films. Bogart's most famous film was *Casablanca* (1942), in which his character is first seen sitting alone at a chessboard. The basis of this scene was actually Bogart's own suggestion to the director, Michael Curtiz, and his meticulous care in getting the scene right is demonstrated by the position on the board in the scene, which was one of Bogart's favourite starting positions in his own games. This was not the only time in Bogart's film career that his character was introduced as he played chess – the same device was used in *Knock on Any Door* (1949).

Many other movie stars and directors have been chess players. John Wayne was a keen player and often played Marlene Dietrich during breaks in shooting. Charlie Chaplin was keen on chess, and a photo from the 1920s showed him playing against the then child prodigy Sammy Reshevsky when the future grandmaster was in California.

Chess is probably most often exploited as a metaphor for scheming and conflict, but it has also been used in the context of seduction. Probably the most famous example was in *The Thomas Crown Affair*

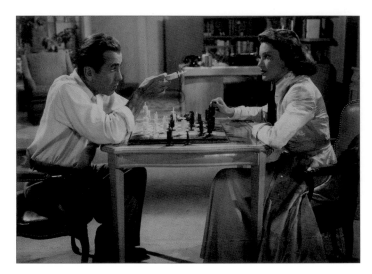

Top: As suggested by Bogart himself, Peter Lorre and Humphrey Bogart play a game of chess in a scene from *Casablanca* (1942).

Above: Humphrey Bogart and Susan Perry play chess in a scene from the 1949 film *Knock on Any Door*.

Right: Humphrey Bogart's position in *Casablanca*, which also happened to be one of the actor's own favourite starting positions.

(1968), in which Steve McQueen's millionaire-turned-bank-robber character plays chess with an attractive insurance investigator played by Faye Dunaway. There are three games in one: boy woos girl, cop chases robber, and the chess game itself, which ends when McQueen (in a lost position) says to Dunaway: 'Let's play something else.' The chess moves in the game were based on a real game played in Vienna in 1898. The scene has been rated highly in various polls to decide the most memorable moments in films, including fourth place in a poll of the 'sexiest sexless movie scene'.

Real-life connections

Perhaps the best-known film of recent years with chess content was *Searching for Bobby Fischer* (1993), also known as *Innocent Moves*. This was based on the book of the same name by Fred Waitzkin, which documented his real-life son Josh's early career as a young American chess prodigy, the family pressures it involved and the rivalry between child chess players and their equally competitive parents. Bobby Fischer appears in documentary footage shown over the opening credits. The 'search' is purely metaphorical and refers to the pinnacle of chess achievement to which every ambitious player aspires.

Chess plays a key part in the film *Harry Potter and the Philosopher's Stone*. Harry Potter and his schoolfriend Ron Weasley enjoy playing what they call Wizard Chess. The rules of the game are as in real-life chess except that the pieces on the board are animated and enact battles when captures are made. Ron's chess prowess proves to be a key element in the film's climax.

Left: A celebrated moment from *The Thomas Crown Affair* (1968), in which Steve McQueen plays a match against Faye Dunaway.

Below: A scene from *Searching for Bobby Fischer* (titled *Innocent Moves* in the UK): the boy who wants to emulate Bobby Fischer plays against a chess hustler in the local park.

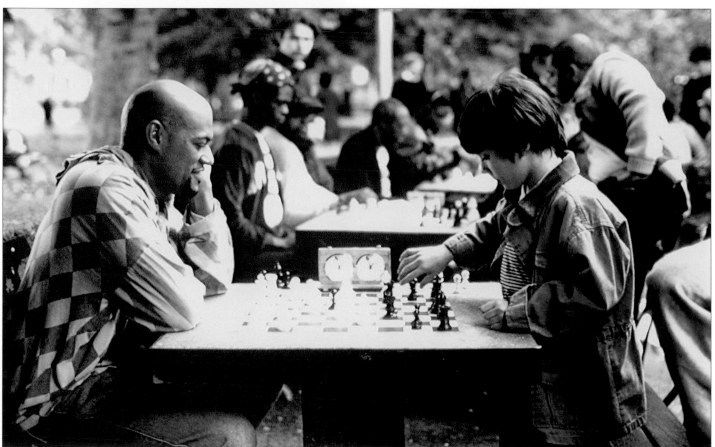

CHESS IN ART

Since medieval times, chess has always been a popular subject for the visual arts. Paintings of a man and a woman playing chess have been used to symbolize courtship, while the pieces themselves also make suitable subjects for inclusion in still-life depictions. Among great artists who have used chess as a theme in their work are Delacroix, Magritte, Matisse, Sargent and Ernst.

Early medieval art
Chess and chess playing has also been depicted in mosaics, tapestries and murals from the early medieval period, and seems to have been a favourite subject from the time when secular subjects became acceptable.

One example is a frieze in the Cappella Palatina in Palermo, Sicily, which shows two people playing chess. The chapel forms part of a Norman palace built by Roger II, the Norman king of Sicily, in the middle part of the 12th century. Much of the painting is believed to have been done by Islamic artists, and the chess scene shows two turbaned figures engaged in playing on a standard 8 x 8 chessboard.

Another beautiful chess representation is *The Chess Players* by the Italian Renaissance painter Liberale da Verona (*c.*1445–1530). It is a painted panel from a

Below: *Arabs Playing Chess* (*c.*1847–1849) by the artist Eugene Delacroix (1798–1863) is one of his classic paintings.

Above: *The Chess Game*, a 15th-century painting by the Italian female painter, Sofonisba Anguissola. An idealized landscape provides the backdrop to two sisters playing chess, watched by their younger sister. The game was one of the few considered sufficiently refined for young women.

Above: This image entitled "Playing Chess in a Castle Garden", is taken from the *c.*1400 manuscript *Li Livres du Graunt Caam* (*Travels of Marco Polo*). The miniature is by the artist Johannes and his school.

larger work and is now housed in the Metropolitan Museum of Art, New York. It shows a group of young men watching a young couple playing chess. Another good example of such a scene is Lukas van Leyden's 1508 work *A Game of Chess*. Once again, a crowd of spectators are watching the game as a young woman makes her move (on a chessboard with rather more than eight files, for some reason). Such scenes were also very popular with much later artists, a good example being John Singer Sargent's *The Chess Game* (1907).

Modern art

Many modern artists have also been attracted to chess as a subject. Matisse's 1928 work *Femme à côté d'un échiquier* shows a woman lying asleep on a couch with a chessboard beside her. Chessboard patterns have particularly attracted abstract painters. One example is Paul Klee's *Super Chess* (1937), which shows a patchwork chessboard with figurative chess pieces, rather like diagram representations in chess books.

Probably the most famous artist to take chess as a regular subject was the French surrealist painter and sculptor Marcel Duchamp (1887–1968). As well as being a famous artist, Duchamp was a chess master

who played well enough to be selected to represent France in international competitions in the 1920s and 1930s. So obsessed was he with the game that his wife grew frustrated and one night glued all his chess pieces to his board while he slept. They were divorced soon after.

Duchamp's Cubist work *The Chess Players* (1910) is one example of the overlap between his two passions, as is his design for a pocket chess set (1943), which was practical as well as artistic. His evident love for playing chess was also turned into photographic art, including the famous 1963 Julian Wasser photograph showing Duchamp engrossed in a game of chess and apparently oblivious to the charms of the nude female player on the other side of the board. The photograph was taken at the Pasadena Museum of Art and shows artistic works by Duchamp in the background.

A number of major art exhibitions have been devoted to chess themes. One such was *The Art of Chess* exhibition that ran at the Gilbert Gallery in London, in 2003. The exhibition concentrated on artistic interpretation of the chess pieces and board, with striking chess set designs by modern artists including Damien Hirst, Jake and Dinos Chapman, and Paul McCarthy placed beside designs by 20th-century artists such as Duchamp, Man Ray, Max Ernst, Alexander Calder and Yoko Ono.

CHESS SET DESIGNS

Chess set designs have varied enormously over the centuries. They can be broadly divided into two types: pieces designed to be used for practical play, and pieces that are primarily for show. As far as the first group is concerned, the pieces are primarily game tokens, with key design factors being that the different pieces should be easily distinguishable and comfortable to handle as well as stable and sturdy. Aesthetic design is a secondary factor, particularly when it comes to organized competitive chess, but clarity and elegance can still be an important adjunct to the enjoyment of the game. These factors can also be important when it comes to ornamental chess pieces, but usually it is the visual impression of the pieces that forms the primary consideration.

The Lewis chessmen

Probably the best-known ancient chessmen in existence are the Lewis chessmen, 67 of which were acquired by the British Museum in London and another 11 by the National Museum of Antiquities in Edinburgh, Scotland. Made of walrus ivory, their exact age is not known and has not so far been scientifically verified. They are of a 12th-century Viking design, but this does not preclude the possibility that they were made several centuries later. In 1831 they were found hidden in an underground structure on the Isle of Lewis in the Outer Hebrides, Scotland. The chessmen differ from conventional modern chess piece designs in that they are human representations, with facial expressions, weapons, helmets and crowns, except for the pawns, which have been said to resemble gravestones. All the six different chess pieces are represented among the 78 pieces and it is most likely that they came from at least seven different chess sets originally.

Arab influence

The fame and appeal of the Lewis pieces lies in their striking appearance, their completeness and the fact that they are unquestionably chessmen. There are other artefacts, surviving in smaller numbers, which pre-date them and which may also be chess pieces. In 1972 archaeologists in Uzbekistan discovered two small animal figures dating back to the 2nd century AD that are thought to be chess pieces. A better-attested chessman is a carved ivory Arab king that dates to the 8th or 9th century AD. Many other early medieval chess pieces show Arab influence in their design, with walrus ivory, whalebone and, later, rock crystal being favoured materials for their construction.

Right: Chess had travelled to northern Europe by the 11th century. These are nine ivory chess pieces that form part of the Lewis Chessmen (dating from around c.1150–1200) from a collection of 78 found at Uig on the Isle of Lewis in the Outer Hebrides, Scotland.

Below: For a time in the 7th century, chess was banned for Muslims, and the abstract shape of these pieces reflects Islamic concern over the carving of images.

Left: One of Napoleon's chess sets, which he used while in exile on St Helena. The chessmen were prized by the Emperor and have been much copied since. Contemporaries of the emperor reported that he was an enthusiastic but, ultimately, weak chess player.

Below: There are many variants of chess across the world, including Indian, Chinese and Thai chess. In this, Thai chess, not only are all the pieces different (except for the knight) but the squares are all the same colour, rather than chequered.

Change in style

Prior to the 16th century, chess set designs tended towards the ornate and representational, but towards the end of that century, designs gravitated towards the simpler, symbolic designs that have been familiar for the past 100 years.

Chess set design has often reflected the architectural style of the times, and chess pieces once again became richly ornate in the 17th and 18th centuries. Indian and Chinese sets were made and imported into Europe, with ivory becoming a favourite material for their construction, often beautifully carved into the most delicate designs. It became fashionable to style the white and black pieces as rival armies. Chinese-made sets showed the Chinese army facing the Mongols, Indian sets showed opposing armies from the time of the Indian Mutiny, while European manufacturers chose Napoleonic War themes. Chess sets were even made in ceramic pottery by the famous English Wedgwood factory.

For all the exotic and elaborate designs of chess sets through many centuries, pieces used for practical play tended to be less ornate and less representational. Even so, there was no hint of true standardization in design until the 19th century, when the advent of chess salons and clubs meant that cheaper sets were needed in large quantities.

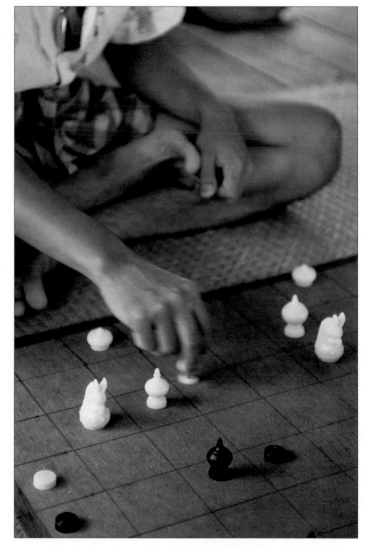

MODERN CHESS SET DESIGNS

As chess became more popular and widespread as an organized competitive game in the 19th century, there came a need for more functional chess sets with a standard design. For the first half of the century, the favoured design in the UK was the so-called Saint George chess set, which was broadly based on the type of designs on ivory Indian chess sets, but in wood. They were relatively easy to turn on a lathe, hence cheaper. In comparison with chess sets used today, they tended to be slimmer where the main body of the piece connected to the base, and featured two or three rings, similar to ruffs, between upper parts and base. In some designs, bishops were slightly similar to pawns and even queens.

In France the favoured design was the Régence chess set, named after the famous chess venue, the Café de la Régence, in Paris. A number of other designs (for example the so-called English Barleycorn and the central European Selenus) existed side by side with the Saint George and the Régence, but the pieces of all of these designs were perhaps too tall and unstable for their intended purpose, and players sometimes had difficulty in recognizing the pieces when using an unfamiliar set.

The Staunton pattern

Clearly, what was required for practical play was a standardized design, so that players from all parts of the world would be readily able to recognize the pieces and not be handicapped by unfamiliarity with the style of chessmen with which they were required to play. In the 1840s, the game-making company John Jaques of London came up with a new design based on existing styles but flavoured with the neo-classicist fashion that influenced the architecture and culture of the times. Responsibility for the design is often attributed to Nathaniel Cook, who registered it in 1849, but it may actually have been his brother-in-law, John Jaques, the owner of the company, who drew up the new designs. Much thought had gone into the redesign. The rings above the base had been pruned back to one and replaced (in the case of the bishop, queen and king) with some smaller, neater rings below the mitre, coronet and crown. The bases had been made more sturdy, and weighted down with a small slug of lead. The knights were particularly beautiful, having been modelled on the horse's head sculpture from the Elgin marbles (the collection of Parthenon friezes in the

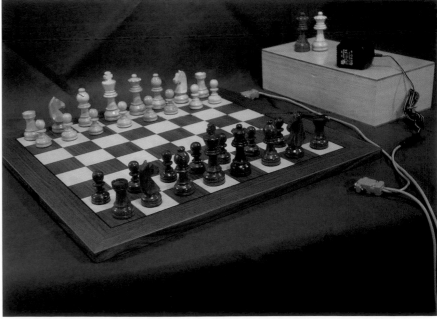

Above: An elegantly designed modern chess set, in gold and walnut, based on the Staunton pattern. Though the design has become the only officially accepted standard, the board and pieces can be made of various materials. Wooden pieces are typically used in competitive play.

Above: This board and set are made to a standard wooden Staunton design but equipped with electronic sensors that detect moves played and transmit them (via cables or wireless) to a computer. The moves can be redirected on to the internet, allowing top-level chess games to be watched by thousands.

British Museum). The last touch of genius on the part of the manufacturers of the redesigned pieces was to get the best-known chess player in the world, Howard Staunton, to lend his name to the new pattern. As a reward, he was paid a percentage for every set sold. This sort of sports-celebrity endorsement is routine today when it comes to the marketing of golf or tennis equipment, but was quite revolutionary for its time.

The Staunton pattern (as it came to be known) was immediately successful and has passed the test of time. Today it is the official – and only recognized – pattern for chess sets used in chess competitions played under the auspices of the World Chess Federation. It allows for some flexibility of design. In eastern Europe, some of the minor decorative elements of the pieces can vary, but there is rarely any difficulty in adapting the eye to such slight readjustments. No restrictions concerning materials to be used are included in the Staunton pattern, but the best-quality sets tend to be made from boxwood and ebony. In modern chess competitions, where the large amount of equipment required makes storage and transportation a major issue, the pieces are often made from plastic and are less heavy than the traditional design.

Above: A modern de luxe wooden Staunton-pattern chess set. The board is made of tiger ebony and maple wood. The black pieces are also made of ebony and heavily weighted with lead inserts in the bases to give them a substantial feel.

Below: In the Staunton set, the design of the knight is based on a horse's head on the Parthenon frieze, which forms part of the Elgin Marbles. The work of the Athenian sculptor Phidias, the marbles were taken to the UK in 1806 by Thomas Bruce, 7th Lord of Elgin.

CHAPTER TWO:

HOW TO PLAY: THE BASICS

This chapter explains the basic rules of chess, right from the beginning. It assumes that you have absolutely no prior knowledge of the game. It covers the layout of the chessboard, the moves of the pieces, chess notation, basic terminology, and also a few basic principles of strategy to help you get started. Once you have read this chapter, you will have some insight into chess and will know enough to enjoy your first few games. It is essential to follow the chapter in the given order, as it is important to make sure that you understand each element that is introduced before moving on to the next one. The first rule of chess is that it requires two people to play, so while you are reading this chapter you ought to consider who your first opponent is going to be. It is a good idea to find someone who can help show you the ropes, which makes learning the game even more enjoyable.

Right: The pawn is the least powerful piece on the chessboard — but the appreciation of its merits is the hallmark of a strong chess player.

THE CHESSBOARD

Chess is played on a square board marked out with 64 smaller squares in an 8 x 8 grid in alternating light and dark colours, and is identical to the board used for English draughts (or American checkers). The light-coloured squares are most often cream or white, and the dark squares can be black, brown or green, but chess players always refer to them as white squares and black squares, regardless of their physical colour.

Which way up?

It is important to set the board up the right way around at the start of the game. The two players sit opposite each other and both players should see a white square in the corner of the board nearest their right hand. If you are an English speaker, it is easy to remember the rule, as it rhymes – white on the right.

Finding your way around

There are three important ways of referring to squares on a chessboard. A column of eight squares running across the board between where the two players sit is called a file, shown vertically in the diagram. There are eight files. Ranks are the eight horizontal equivalents, rather like the ranks of soldiers in a battle – very apt, because chess is a war game.

Chess players also talk about diagonals. These straight lines of squares of the same colour, touching corner to corner, are of varying lengths. For instance,

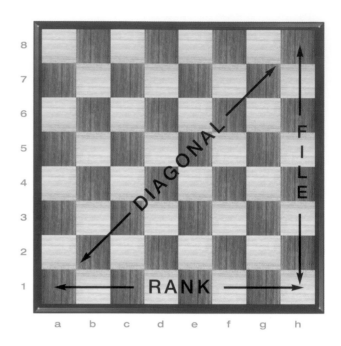

Above: The horizontal squares running across the board are called ranks; the squares going up and down are called files. A diagonal is a straight line of same-coloured squares running obliquely across the board, which can be of varying lengths.

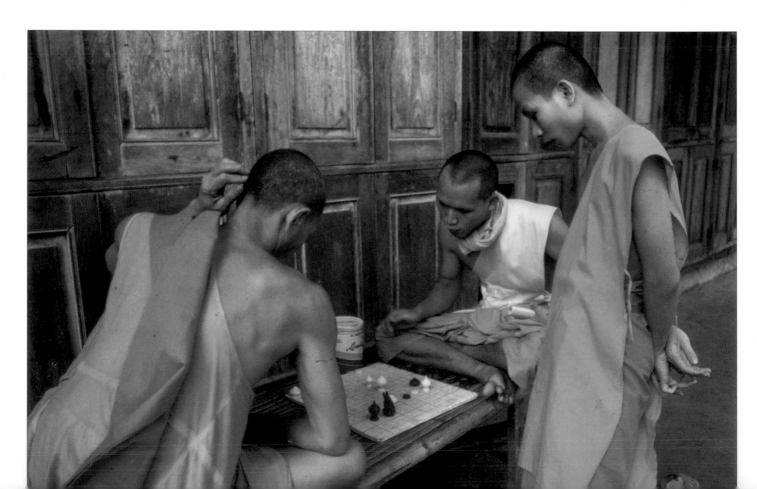

the line of eight squares between a1 and h8 is a diagonal, as is the line of two squares from h7 to g8. If you look at the diagram opposite, you will see how this works.

The diagram below shows the chessboard with the chessmen (more commonly referred to as pieces) on it, in their starting positions. There are two players in a game of chess, one having what are called the white pieces, and the other having the black pieces. As you can see in the diagram below, both players start with 16 pieces. As with the squares, the physical colour of the pieces is not relevant: chess players are effectively colour blind, and the player with the white pieces is simply referred to as White, and his or her opponent as Black.

The two-dimensional diagram shown below represents the board and chess pieces as set up at the beginning of the game, as if we were looking down upon it vertically. You can probably see that each player starts with pieces of six different types in various quantities: on the next page you will learn what each piece is called, but for now the important thing is to make sure you have the board the right way around.

Below: A chessboard with pieces ready to play. Each square has a unique name, which is defined by its file and rank (1-8 and a-h). These co-ordinates are shown around the edges of the diagram. Square h1 is always a white square when the board is set up.

CHECKING THE BOARD

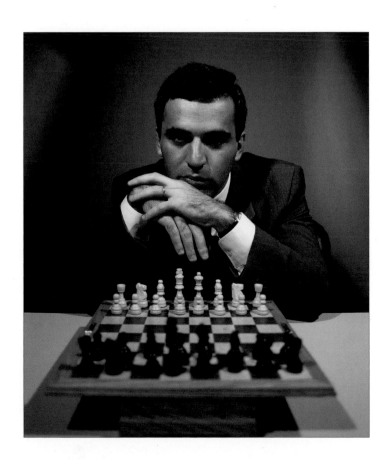

Above: A board with the pieces positioned incorrectly.

Next time you are watching a film or TV programme in which the characters are shown playing chess, look carefully to see if they have the chessboard the right way round (remember – *white on the right* as you sit facing the board). If you think about it, you have a one in two chance of getting it right (or wrong) if you put the board down without regard to its orientation. But you'll be amazed at how often they get it wrong in films and on TV – around eight times out of ten!

Left: Chess is played by millions of people all around the world. It is as much a game as a part of refined culture, a symbol of intellect, logic and raw skill. It can be enjoyed by people of all ages and played at different levels of skill, competence and experience.

Right: World Champion grandmaster Garry Kasparov with the chess pieces in position at the start of a game. Kasparov announced that he would be retiring from serious competitive chess in March 2005, but would continue to play events for fun.

THE CHESS PIECES

There are six different types of pieces (or chessmen) used in a game of chess – pawn, rook, knight, bishop, queen and king. It is important to recognize what each piece looks like, both in real life on a three-dimensional chessboard, and on the printed page (such as in this book).

It is noticeable from the illustration below that the pieces vary in size. The king is usually the biggest piece, and the pawn invariably the smallest. This corresponds to their relative values in the game, but this is not true of all the pieces. We will discover later that the rook – which is physically shorter than a bishop or knight – is actually a more valuable piece than either of them.

| King | Queen | Bishop | Knight | Rook | Pawn |

The king

The diagram shows the two kings (white and black) on their starting positions in a game of chess. The king is usually the tallest piece in the set, by a small margin relative to the queen, but readily distinguishable by the small cross on top of the crown. The king is the most important piece on the chessboard, and translates as king in virtually all languages (for example, *könig* in German and *roi* in French). Most importantly, the result of a game of chess is decided by the fate of the king. When a king has been trapped, or in chess terms 'checkmated', by the opposition pieces and cannot escape, the game is lost and ends immediately.

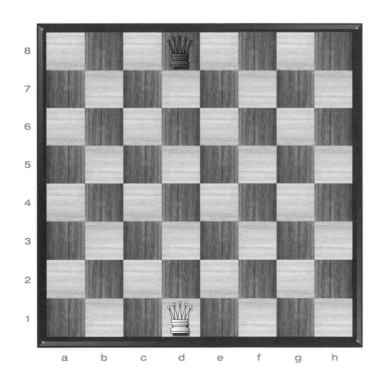

The queen

The diagram shows the two queens on their starting squares, beside their respective kings. The queen is distinguishable from the king by the five prongs of the coronet (and absence of a cross); it is slightly shorter, but taller than all the other pieces. The queen is the most powerful piece on the chessboard in modern chess, but this was not always the case: at one time it was the most limited. That fact is reflected by a less august title by which it is known in many languages (e.g. *dame* in French, or *dama* in Spanish, although it is *regina* in Italian). It is important to remember that the two queens stand on squares of their own colour at the beginning of the game.

The bishop

There are four bishops on the board at the start of the game, split between the two players. They are placed on the c-file and f-file, flanking the squares occupied by the king and queen. They are called 'bishops' in the English-speaking world because the upper part of the piece is thought to resemble a bishop's mitre, but English is alone in making this association. In some cultures, the piece is thought to resemble a jester's cap – for example, in French, it is referred to as *le fou* – 'the jester', and in German it is called *läufe*, meaning 'courier'. Bishops in chess sets from eastern Europe can be a little disconcerting: the small round globe on top of the mitre is often the opposite colour to the colour of the piece – a black bishop will have a white globe at the top and vice versa.

Below: The pieces are lined up at the start of a game, ready to do battle. The knights are placed on squares b1, g1, b8 and g8.

The knight

Each player has two knights at the start of the game. The name is not entirely apt: as you can see, they look rather more like horses than riders. Competition chess players sometimes jocularly refer to the knight as 'horse', and in many languages this piece is indeed called a horse (for example, *caballo* in Spanish). The Germans, however, call it a *springer* which, as you might expect, means 'jumper' or 'leaper'. This name has more to do with the way the chess piece is moved (it does not move along straight lines as do the other pieces). The standard design of the knight is modelled on a horse as it appears in the frieze of the Parthenon.

The rook

Each player has two rooks in the starting position, and they are placed in the four corners of the board. Chess-playing beginners are often tempted to call this piece 'a castle' because it looks rather like the tower and battlements of a medieval castle, and perhaps also because they have heard the chess word castling. But experienced chess players never call it a castle, even in jest. In English it is always called a rook. This has nothing to do with the crow-like bird of the same name: it comes originally from Sanskrit *ratha* and a Persian/Arabic word *rukh*, both meaning 'chariot'. Other languages, however, make the connection with its appearance and call it a 'tower' (French *tour*, Spanish *torre*, German *turm*).

The pawn

Each player starts the game with eight pawns, placed as shown in the diagram on the rank in front of the rest of the pieces. The name derives from the Latin for 'foot' and an old French word for 'foot soldier', which gives a true indication of the pawn's status as the lowest ranking chessman in a player's army. The pawn is also the smallest piece on the chessboard, so it is usually easy to distinguish it from the other pieces by reference to its size, though in some designs it can look rather like the bishop. Despite its limitations, the rules relating to the pawn are slightly more complicated than those of the other pieces – so we will be considering how it moves after introducing the rules relating to the moves of the other pieces.

THE BISHOP

On a single turn or move, the bishop can be moved any number of vacant squares along the diagonal on which it stands. It can capture enemy pieces that stand in its way. The nearer it is to the centre of the board, the greater will be its scope in different directions.

The bishop in the above diagram can be played to any of the 13 squares marked with a black dot. You should note that all of these squares are white: because they only move diagonally, bishops are restricted to squares of one colour. The white bishop in the diagram can be referred to as a white-squared bishop because it is only capable of visiting one of the 32 white squares on the chessboard.

The players start the game with two bishops each, one of which stands on a white square and the other on a black square. Thus, one of the bishops can visit the white squares, and the other the black squares. Between the two of them, if placed in the middle of the board, they can control 26 squares.

Bishops cannot jump over other pieces of either colour. If there is a piece of the same colour (i.e. a piece belonging to the same player) along the diagonal, it can go no further.

In the diagram above, the bishop can go to any one of the five squares marked by black dots, but cannot jump over or displace any of its own pieces.

Generally speaking, it is a good idea to give the pieces plenty of scope for action. The more squares a piece has access to, the more useful it will be in the game. Bishops are particularly susceptible to becoming blocked in by their own side's pawns.

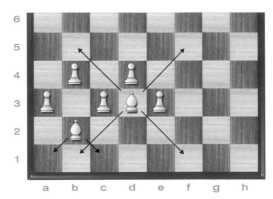

Above: The bishop on b2 is 'bad', whereas its partner on d3 is 'good'.

The part diagram, above, shows examples of a well-placed and a poorly placed bishop. The white bishop on the b2 shown here has only two moves in this position and, even if it moves to the c1 square, its further scope will remain limited by the white pawn on e3. Chess players would refer to this as a 'bad' bishop. However, the bishop on d3 is much better placed: it is unrestricted by the pawns, with plenty of scope for forward movement, and is therefore a 'good' bishop.

Capturing other pieces

A bishop cannot jump over an enemy piece either, but (with the exception of the king) it can capture (or take) it. When a piece is captured, it plays no further part in the game: it is removed from the board and replaced by the piece that effects the capture.

In the diagram above, with White's turn to move, as well as playing to any one of the five marked squares, the white bishop can capture on the squares marked with crosses: the black pawn on the b7 square or the black knight on the f7 square. The bishop in the diagram thus has seven legal moves: five ordinary moves and two captures. If White takes the black knight with the bishop, the position after the capture would be as follows:

One curiosity: because bishops only move on squares of one colour, it means that white-squared bishops and black-squared bishops never cross each other's path.

In the diagram above, the white bishop can only move to black squares and the black bishop only to white squares. These references to white and black in different contexts can cause confusion, hence chess players tend to refer to the white bishop on e5 as a 'dark-squared bishop' and the black bishop on d3 as a 'light-squared bishop'. Note that neither of these can ever capture the other.

The above diagram shows enemy bishops of the same (square) colour. If it is White to play, White can take the bishop on d4 with the bishop on b2. Similarly, if it is Black to play, Black can take the b2 bishop with the bishop on d4.

THE ROOK

On a single move, the rook can be moved any number of squares along the file or rank on which it stands. As we will see, this gives it great strength, especially when it is supported by a second rook that stands either on the same rank or the same file.

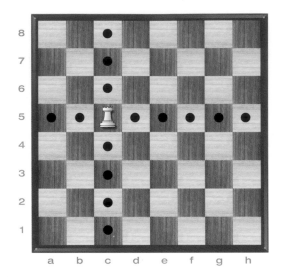

The rook in the above diagram can be played to any of the 14 squares marked with a black dot. Note that, unlike the bishop, the rook is not restricted to squares of one colour. Hence, it has the potential to visit all 64 squares on the chessboard and, if there are no other pieces in the way, it can reach any square in a maximum of two moves. For this reason, it is a particularly powerful and valuable piece.

The players start the game with two rooks each, which stand in the four corner squares of the board. Like bishops, rooks need to be given plenty of scope in order to exploit their power, and they are also susceptible to being hemmed in by their own army. This is noticeable right from the beginning of the game, when they are restricted by the line of pawns ahead of them, particularly the one immediately ahead of it on the file. This problem often takes time to

resolve itself, and rooks tend to enter the main battle rather later than the other pieces.

Rooks often benefit from a reduction in the overall forces, particularly when some of the pawns have disappeared from the board. An open file is one on which there are no pawns, and they make particularly good paths for rooks to travel in order to attack or infiltrate the enemy camp. They are much less happy on closed files, where their scope is restricted.

Above: The rook is on a closed file and restricted by the white pawn.

Above: The rook is on an open file and can advance into enemy territory.

Above: Start position: the rook on a1 has no moves.

Capturing other pieces

The rook can capture enemy pieces along both files and ranks.

Above: If White is to play, White can capture the rook on d7. If Black is to play, Black can take the rook on d2.

In the diagram above, the rooks attack each other. If it is White's turn, White can play rook on d2 to d7, removing the black rook from that square. Conversely, if it is Black's move, Black can take the white rook on d2 with the rook on d7. Notice that, if it is White's move and White captures the rook on d7, Black can then take the white rook with the bishop on f5. This move is referred to as a 'recapture'.

Below: In this position, the white rook on d4 is able to move along the open rank and capture the bishop on h4.

ATTACKING AND DEFENDING

Here is another example of chess terminology: in the diagram to the left, it would be said that the black bishop is 'defending' the black rook. In other words, it would have the option to recapture any piece that captured the black rook. Incidentally, chess players also talk in terms of 'attacking' or 'defending' specific squares. Usually it is defending when referring to squares adjacent to its main forces and attacking for squares in or near the enemy camp, but the meaning is the same. For example, in the diagram, the black bishop attacks the empty square at c2. If White moves a piece there, it is liable to capture.

Recapture

Generally speaking, it is a good idea to capture enemy pieces, as it depletes the opponent's forces, and bigger armies tend to prevail. Captures are often answered by a recapture. This is slightly misleading terminology, as a piece never reappears on the board after being captured. It simply refers to the immediate capture of a piece that has just taken another man. Where equivalent pieces are captured on consecutive moves, it is called an 'exchange' or 'swap'.

THE QUEEN

On a single move, the queen can be moved any number of squares along the file, rank or diagonal on which it stands. This makes her very versatile and thus the focus of many winning attacks, though, as we shall see, this very strength brings certain drawbacks.

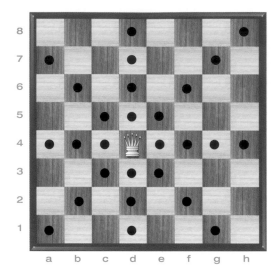

Located in the middle of the board (above), the queen can reach no fewer than 27 squares (represented here by the black dots). Thus, it combines the functions of the bishop and the rook, and is considerably more powerful than either of those pieces. In fact, it is potentially the strongest piece on the chessboard, with fast access to any square on the board.

At the beginning of the game, the two players have one queen each. Queens cannot jump over their own (or the opponent's) pieces any more than bishops and rooks can, but such is their manoeuvrability that it is less common for them to be hemmed in.

Above: Despite some restriction, the white queen still has some scope for action.

Capturing other pieces

The queen captures exactly as it moves – along a file, rank or diagonal.

In the diagram above, Black attacks (i.e. threatens to capture) both the white rook and the white bishop. Note that neither of the white pieces is attacking the black queen – the bishop is as powerless along the file as the rook is along the diagonal. This double attack by a single piece against two or more enemy pieces is called a 'fork'. Double attacks are often hard to defend against – often it is a case of defending or moving away the most valuable of the two pieces and leaving the other to its fate. Here, White could move the rook away from attack by playing it to the g7 square, which simultaneously defends the bishop. An alternative is to play the bishop to h3 to defend the attacked rook. In either case, this would almost certainly discourage Black from capturing, since the more valuable queen would be lost in exchange for a rook or bishop. This is known as an 'unfavourable exchange'.

Paradoxically, the queen's superiority in value can be its Achilles' heel. It is less expendable than its colleagues. As we have seen above, it is often possible to defend a piece from capture (i.e. threaten recapture), but it is rarely appropriate to defend a queen in this way (except from capture by another queen). Usually the queen is simply too valuable to be defended from capture by inferior pieces and its owner will have to move it away from the attack.

In the diagram above, the queen and rook are attacking each other, with both being defended by a bishop. If it is Black's move, Black would capture the queen in exchange for the rook. This is known as a 'favourable exchange'. However, if it is White's move, it would be highly unlikely to take the rook and lose the queen. In this instance, the best idea would be to move the queen to a safe square.

USING THE QUEEN WITH CARE

Beginners are often infatuated by the power of the queen and tend to move it repeatedly from a very early stage in the game. However, strong chess players usually prefer to deploy (or 'develop') their less valuable pieces first and rarely embark on solo escapades with the queen. It is true that the queen can often get behind enemy lines quicker than other pieces, but it can equally easily become trapped there. Like other pieces, the queen works best in co-ordination with the other pieces. Also, beginners often get discouraged or depressed if queens are exchanged (i.e. both players' queens have been captured) at an early stage in the game. There is no need to worry in this situation, since it is the same for both players and it is still perfectly possible to win a game without queens.

THE KNIGHT

The knight can be moved to one of the nearest squares to that on which it stands, but not on the same rank, file or diagonal. Its move may sound somewhat complicated when expressed in words, but it becomes more clear when shown graphically.

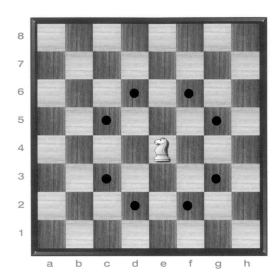

The knight in the diagram above can be played to any one of the squares with the black dots. This move is perhaps less intuitive than those of other chess pieces that move along visible lines of squares on the board, and thus can be slightly trickier to remember. For the purpose of visualization, some players prefer to think of the move as an 'L'-shape: the knight moves two squares along a rank or file and then one square at a right angle.

Another key difference between the knight and other pieces is that it can jump over other pieces (of either colour). In the diagram above, the white knight can be played to any of the eight marked squares, just as if the

surrounding pieces were not there. However, it is possible for the knight to be blocked in by its own side's pieces if they are placed on one of these target squares.

Capturing other pieces

Knights use the same move to make captures.

In the diagram above, the white knight cannot play a backwards move (since its target squares are occupied by pawns), but it has two moves (to empty squares

---

PRACTISE THE KNIGHT MOVE

Look again at the diagram showing knight paths across the board. There are several possible paths other than those shown that would get the knights to their destinations in the same number of moves, but none would get them there any quicker. Because the knight move is counter-intuitive, it is a good idea to practise moving it around the board. First, try to find alternative ways to get the knight from a1 to h8 in six moves. Try some other paths: for instance, it might surprise you to find that it takes four moves to get a knight from a1 to b2 – the adjacent square on the diagonal.

with black dots) as well as two possible captures (of the black rook or black bishop).

The knight is the only piece with a move that the queen cannot emulate. This makes it especially useful in playing deadly forks.

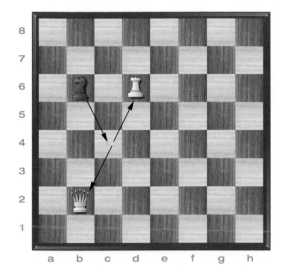

In the diagram above, the black knight is under attack from the white queen and the white rook. However, it can turn the tables on the attacking pieces by moving to c4, where it will attack both queen and rook at the same time. In all likelihood, the queen would then have to move away, leaving the rook to be captured by the knight.

Despite its unique powers, the knight is generally reckoned to be less valuable than the bishop and considerably less powerful than the rook or queen. Compared to a queen, rook or bishop, it lacks manoeuvrability and takes too many moves to cross the board. It also lacks options when situated on the edge (or in the corner) of the board.

In the diagram above, the white knight shown on h1 has only two possible moves: to f2 or g3. As for the white knight on a1, it would take no fewer than six moves to reach h8, the square at the end of the diagonal. And should the black knight on a8 need to reach the c6 square (which is only two squares away on the diagonal) it would take four knight moves to get there. However, unlike the bishop, the knight has the potential to visit every square on the board.

Below: The knight knows no barriers. Unlike other chess pieces, it can jump over any piece, of either colour. Here, with White to play, the white knight on d4 can capture the black queen on e6.

THE PAWN

The pawn is the most limited piece on the chessboard in terms of its power and value, but the way it makes moves and captures is a little more complex than the other pieces. It is worth spending time mastering the way the pawn moves as good pawn play is often a key factor in success at chess.

The diagram above shows the basic move of the pawn: one square forward to the square immediately in front of it, so long as that square is unoccupied. White (to play) can play the pawn from e4 to e5. If it is Black to move, the pawn can be played from h6 to h5. The pawn is different from all the other moves in that it never moves backwards. For this reason the decision to move a pawn is highly committal.

Players start the game with eight pawns each, arrayed along the rank immediately in front of their other pieces. On its first turn, a pawn may move either one square or two squares forward (provided both of those squares are unoccupied). Thus, in the diagram above,

the pawn on e2 may move either to e3 or to e4 (as indicated by the arrow) and if it is Black's move, the pawn on c7 may move forward to c6 or c5.

A pawn's forward trajectory can quickly become blocked, often by an opposing pawn. A common example, as shown below, occurs right at the beginning of the game.

The position above frequently appears on the chessboard after the players have made just one move each. White starts the game by moving a pawn from e2 to e4, and Black replies by moving a pawn from e7 to e5. These two pawns effectively immobilize each other, and neither pawn can make any further moves until such time as the situation changes around them. Often one or both of them will be attacked and captured and play no further part in the game. Immobility leads to vulnerability, and is one of the key limiting factors that makes the pawn the least-powerful chess piece.

However, it is easy to overlook one of the cardinal virtues of the humble pawn – its value (in conjunction with its colleagues) as a strong protective barrier against attack. The line of eight pawns across the board provides a front line of defence for the more valuable pieces that stand behind it. But sometimes a pawn barrier can be a disadvantage, restricting the scope of a player who wants files, ranks or diagonals to be open so that the opponent can be attacked with queens,

Above: Pawns usually lead the way at the start of a chess game, helping to contest the centre. Here the black pawn on e4 can capture on d5 or push forward to e5.

rooks and bishops. Advanced chess players always take care over the arrangement of their pawns – what is known as the pawn structure – having both defence and attack in mind.

Capturing other pieces

Unlike other pieces, a pawn moves differently when it captures compared to when it makes a move to an unoccupied square – a pawn may capture a piece that is one square ahead of it diagonally on an adjacent file.

In the diagram above, the white pawn on c4 may capture either the pawn on b5 or the rook on d5. If it is Black's turn, the pawn on h6 may capture the white knight on g5, or the black pawn on b5 may take the white pawn on c4. Note that, if it is White's turn, White may not play the pawn on c4 one square forward because the path is blocked by the pawn on c5.

A stout defender

We have already seen how the mighty queen often has to run away quickly when it is attacked. The pawn, however, has no such problems. So long as it is defended, it can usually just stand its ground. This is just as well, because it cannot run as fast or as far away as the other pieces.

In the above diagram, the white pawn on d4 appears to be under a withering attack from all three of Black's pieces. However, White need not be concerned. The d4 pawn is defended by the pawn on c3. Should Black capture the d4 pawn with knight, bishop or rook, the capturing piece would be captured by the pawn on c3. This is an unfavourable exchange, even though Black could capture the second pawn on the following turn. Two pawns are usually worth less than one knight, bishop or rook.

THE PAWN: SPECIAL MOVES

Though it may seem a very ordinary piece, it is true to say that the humble pawn has some surprises up its sleeve. First, unlike any other piece, it has the potential to upgrade itself to a queen, rook, bishop or knight. Second, in a special circumstance it has a unique way of capturing opposing pawns.

Promotion

We now know that the pawn is the least-valuable piece on the board, but this condition is not necessarily permanent. Should a pawn succeed in advancing all the way to the other side of the board, something magical happens – it is 'promoted'. This means that it changes from being a pawn to a queen, rook, bishop or knight of the same colour. The player chooses which of these four pieces it becomes. As the queen is the most powerful piece on the board, normally the player chooses to exchange the pawn for a queen.

Here's how it happens:

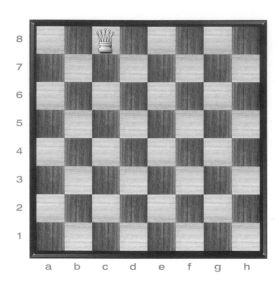

In the diagram above, White plays the pawn from c7 to c8. Now the player must choose whether to promote the pawn to a queen, rook, bishop or knight. Let us say that White chooses to promote to a queen (the most usual). The white pawn on c8 is then replaced with a white queen.

What had previously been one of the weakest pieces on the board has become one of the most powerful, with the potential to help win the game. Lowly it may be, but the further it advances up the board, provided it is defended against capture, the more of a threat each pawn becomes, especially in the later stages of a game.

White now has a queen on c8 and that completes the turn to move. This new white queen has all the powers of White's original queen. It is perfectly permissible for White to have two queens on the board – or even nine, in the unlikely event that all eight pawns are promoted to queens, and the original queen is still on the board. This is extremely unusual in practice, but two queens of the same colour are occasionally seen, or more rarely, an extra rook, bishop or knight.

NOT ENOUGH PIECES!

Pawn promotion sometimes brings about a small practical problem: most chess sets only contain those pieces that are used to start the game, so it is sometimes necessary to find another small object that can be used to betoken a second queen or a third rook, bishop or knight. Often, a captured rook is used and turned upside down to show it is being used as a second queen. The important thing is to agree with your opponent what you are doing and ensure that you both know what the substitute token is.

En passant

We have already seen how pawns can make captures, but there is one special capturing move that pawns can make in specific circumstances. The pawn can capture an opposing pawn *en passant* if it attacks a square crossed by the opposing pawn which has crossed that square in one move from its original square. This capture can only be made on the move immediately following the opposing pawn's advance.

The *en passant* rule is, understandably, one which beginners find quite hard to remember. Let us see how it works in practice.

In the first partial diagram, the white pawn stands on its original square, a2, while the black pawn stands on b4. It is White's turn to move, and the white pawn is moved two squares forward to a4 as it is entitled to do on the first move of any pawn. The second partial diagram shows the position after White's move. Black can capture this pawn *en passant* because it has crossed a square (a3) that is attacked by the black pawn. So, on the next move, Black takes the white pawn off the board and puts his own pawn on a3, producing the position in the third partial diagram. If Black were to make any other move instead, he would forfeit the right to make this *en passant* capture on a subsequent move.

Effectively, the pawn captures its opposite number as if it had moved only one square forward. Note that this is the only situation in chess in which a capturing piece is placed on a square other than the one on which the captured piece stood previously.

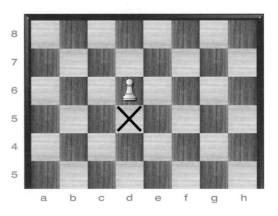

Above is another example. Black has just played the pawn from d7 to d5. On the next move only, White has the right to capture this pawn *en passant,* using the pawn standing on c5, as if the black pawn had only travelled as far as d6. White plays his pawn diagonally to d6 and simultaneously removes the black pawn on d5 from the board (marked with a cross in the partial diagram).

THE KING

Although it is able to move in any direction along the file, rank or diagonal on which it stands, the king can only move one square at a time. This limited mobility makes it a particularly vulnerable piece, especially when either the opposing queen or the opposing rooks are still on the board.

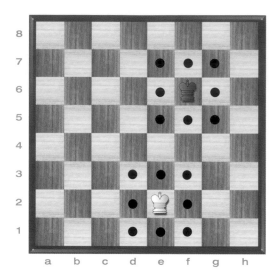

The diagram above shows the possible squares to which the white and black king can move. Hence, the king moves rather like a queen, but its range is more restricted.

Capturing other pieces

The king can capture enemy pieces that stand within its moving range.

However, the king cannot be captured like other chess pieces, nor can it be placed or left on a square which is attacked by an opposing piece. It is the most important piece on the board – the fate of the king decides the game.

Checking the king

There are pieces, other than the king, that are liable to capture by the opposing force. Although it is usual to try to stop the opponent capturing valuable pieces, it is permissible under the rules to leave pieces where they can be captured or even to move a piece to a square where it can be taken immediately. However, it is against the rules of chess to play a move that allows a king to be captured on the next turn. An attacked king is said to be 'in check'.

A king can be attacked (or checked) by any opposing piece except for the opposing king. Kings are not permitted to stand on adjacent squares.

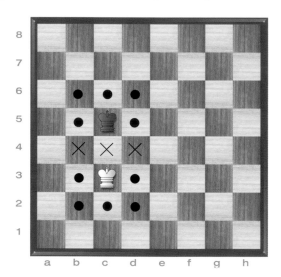

In the diagram above, neither king can move to any of the squares marked with a cross. Thus, kings can never attack each other, although they can restrict each other's scope for movement considerably.

A player whose king is in check (attacked by an opposing piece) must make a move on the next turn which escapes the check. There are three possible ways to escape check: capture the checking piece; move the king away from check; interpose a piece between your king and the checking piece.

If there is no legal move that achieves any of these options, the game ends and the player unable to escape check is said to be 'checkmated' (or 'in checkmate'). The first option is to capture the checking piece.

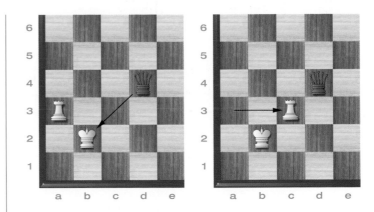

In the above diagram, the black rook attacks the white king, which is in check. On the next turn, White must move to escape the check. The best move would be to capture the rook with the white bishop. This escapes the check and gains valuable material for White.

A second way to escape a check is simply to move the king away from the attack. This could be achieved in the above diagram by moving the king to an adjacent file, as it is being attacked along the file by the rook. Here is another example.

The final way to escape check, as long as the attacking piece is not a knight, is to block the check. This is where the player places a piece between the king and the attacking piece to block the check.

In the first partial diagram above, Black has played the queen to d4 to check White's king. White can reply, as shown in the second partial diagram above, by playing the rook on a3 to c3, thereby blocking the queen's attack on the king.

No legal move

Positions where the king has no legal moves are not necessarily a cause for alarm. Take, for example, the situation shown in the diagram below.

The white king on f3 is in check from the black knight on e5. White cannot capture the knight because the knight is not attacked by any white pieces. So White must move the king away from check. There are eight squares around the king but three of them are controlled by black pieces. The king can move to any of the five squares marked with a dot, but not to one of the three squares marked with a cross. The g4 square is also attacked by the knight, while the f4 and g3 squares are both attacked by the black bishop.

With White to play, the king has no legal moves. It cannot displace one of its own pieces and cannot go to any of the squares along the g-file because they are attacked by the black rook. However, the king is not directly attacked and White can proceed with a move of the bishop. Had the piece on h4 been, say, a protected black pawn rather than one of White's own pieces, the situation would then, as we will see later, have been very different.

SPECIAL FORMS OF CHECK

Checking the king can be a very useful weapon in a game of chess as it forces the opponent to defend the attack on the king immediately rather than indulging in some offensive action of his own. Some forms of check are more useful than others, having a potentially lethal impact.

Discovered check

One particular type of check that can often be devastating in its effect is the 'discovered' check. This is a move that uncovers an attack by another piece on the opponent's king.

In the diagram above, Black's king is not attacked. The rook is on the same file, but it is blocked by its own bishop on a3. However, if, for example, White plays his bishop to c1, it will reveal (or 'discover') a check by the rook against the king on a1.

Discovered attacks often can be truly devastating, as shown below.

In the first partial diagram above, Black's king is not attacked by the bishop because its scope along the diagonal is blocked by the rook. However, when White plays the rook to a2 (see the second partial diagram),

it discovers check by the bishop against the black king. Black must escape the check on the next turn. The bishop cannot be captured (notice how the rook blocks the queen's attack on the bishop). There is no way to block the check, so Black will be obliged to move the king. On the following move, White will be free to capture the black queen with the rook.

Double check

Another form of check that can be very strong is the 'double check'. This is an extension of the discovered check except that the moved piece as well as the unblocked piece gives check to the king, shown below.

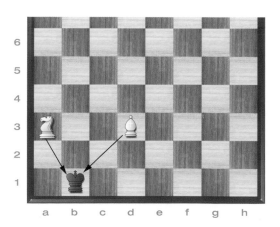

From the first partial diagram above, White plays the knight to the a3 square. From there, the knight checks the king on b1 and also reveals an attack on the king from the bishop on d3.

It is sometimes possible, as shown below, to escape from a double check by capturing (if the king stands on an adjacent square to one of the two checking pieces), but it is never possible to block a double check.

White could play the bishop to b2, which would be double check from the rook (along the file) and the bishop (along the diagonal). But it would not be very clever, because Black could simply capture the bishop with the king, simultaneously capturing one checking piece and moving away from the attack of the other. However, a better-executed double check can offer immunity from capture or blocking attempts to the attacking side. The double-attacked king is usually reduced to moving away from the attack, often at the expense of a lot of damage elsewhere on the board.

One key difference between the above example and the following one is that the two pieces involved in delivering the double check that follows are at some distance from the enemy king. This means that neither piece can be captured, since the king remains in check from the piece that remains.

On the face of things in the diagram above, White is not doing particularly well, with fewer pieces and both rook and bishop under threat. But there is the option of moving the rook to d5, which is a double check.

The rook checks the king along the rank while the bishop checks the king along the diagonal. Black must make a move to escape both checks, and cannot capture the rook (although it is attacked by both queen and pawn), or block by playing the pawn to e5, because neither move would do anything to escape the bishop check. Similarly, Black cannot capture the bishop (also attacked twice, by queen and knight) or block (by playing the knight to d3) because the king would still be under attack from the rook. Black's only option is a king move (to f6, f4 or g4). Whatever Black does, on the following move, White could capture the queen with the rook and gain a major advantage.

CHECKMATE

A player whose king is in check must escape the check on the next turn. He can do this either by capturing a checking piece, blocking the check or by moving the king to a square where it is not attacked. If the player is unable to achieve any of those three things and the king has no escape, the game ends immediately. It is checkmate, and the player whose king is thus trapped has lost.

The diagram below shows an example of a queen giving checkmate.

The white queen has just moved to e7 and attacks the black king. Black cannot capture the queen because the e7 square is adjacent to the white king on f6, so the white king effectively defends the queen. There is no blocking possibility, and the four contiguous squares to which the king could otherwise move are also attacked by the white queen. Black's king is attacked and there is no escape. It is checkmate and the game ends immediately in favour of White.

It is worth noting that a piece cannot give checkmate to a king without some help from other pieces – of either colour. In the diagram on the left, the queen is supported by its own king. If the king were further away from the action, it could not defend the queen, and Black could capture the queen with the king, thus preventing checkmate.

There are also occasions when a player's own pieces contribute to their own defeat. The position below demonstrates that a player's own pieces can sometimes prove to be a liability.

White, to move, plays the white rook to the a8 square. This gives check along the rank to the king on g8.

Below: In this scenario, White will play the rook to a8 and checkmate the black king on a4.

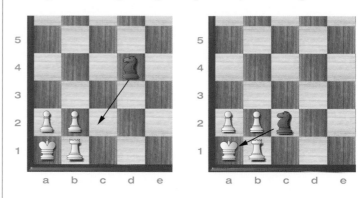

The diagrams below show another less common example of a king being hampered by its own pieces.

Black is obliged to escape check. The white rook cannot be captured, and the king cannot move away from the rank on which it is situated because it is impeded by the row of three pawns in front of it. The only option to continue the game is to block the check by playing the black rook to d8, as shown above.

Back-rank mate

White simply takes the rook on d8 with its own rook. Now Black has the same problem with the king. It has no good move, still being imprisoned by its own pawns. The black rook has disappeared from the board. There is no longer any escape: it is checkmate, and White wins the game. This particular example is called a 'back-rank mate' because the king is trapped on its own back (starting) rank. The sequence of moves in this example might be referred to as 'mate in two', meaning that White plays two moves to achieve checkmate. To avoid the calamity of a back-rank check, it is often prudent to move the pawns one square forward so that the king can escape a back-rank check.

Black, to move, plays the knight to the c2 square, attacking the white king on a1. White cannot capture the knight, nor can the check be blocked (attacks from knights can never be blocked because they have the power to jump over intervening pieces). The king cannot be moved because it is entirely surrounded by pieces of the same colour. It cannot escape, so is mated. Game over!

The pawn is the humblest of pieces, but on occasion it can deliver mate as effectively as any of its more powerful colleagues, as shown below.

White, to play, moves the pawn from e4 to e5. Pawns give check diagonally, just as they capture, so this move attacks the black king on f6. The pawn cannot be captured by the black king because it is defended by the white king. In addition to this, Black's king cannot retreat because all the retreat squares are occupied by its own pieces. It cannot go to f5 or g5 because they are next to the white king, and it cannot go to g6 because that square is threatened by the pawn on h5. It has no moves and thus has been mated by the pawn on e5.

MORE CHECKMATES

We have seen two examples of checkmate being achieved via surprise ambushes from lone pieces (pages 68–69), but these are exceptional and require negligence from the opponent in deploying their forces. In normal circumstances, a player's pieces must work together to force checkmate and end the game.

All the pieces on the chessboard, except for the king, are liable to capture, and it is possible for all the pieces on the board to disappear, leaving only kings on the board. A king on its own cannot checkmate another, so the game ends immediately as a draw.

If one side has a single queen or rook left, checkmate can be achieved with some help from the king. Below are typical examples of a queen giving checkmate.

In both of the above diagrams, it can be seen that the white queen gives checkmate but with significant support from the white king. In the first diagram, the white king defends the queen from capture and in the second, it prevents the black king from moving away from the file on which it is attacked. A rook can effect a similar checkmate to the second queen.

As shown below, the rook attacks the king along the file and the white king prevents the black king from escaping the attack via the squares b1, b2 or b3.

A lone bishop or knight cannot force checkmate against a lone king, even if the defender played the worst moves possible. So a position with bishop and king against king, or knight and king against king, is a draw. A lone pawn, however, can win against a lone king if it can be promoted to a queen or rook.

In the above example, White is left with just a pawn to accompany the king. But there is nothing to stop the pawn racing through to promote to a queen. This can be accomplished in five moves (count the arrows – the pawn can move forward two squares on its first move). Black's king is too far away from the action to stop it. In five moves it can only get as far as the c-file, so White will promote the pawn to a queen and, with just a modicum of skill thereafter, win the game.

Combining forces

Two pieces in tandem can work very well together, particularly a queen and rook. Two rooks are equally effective, being able in just a few moves to checkmate the opponent's king without any support of their own. The process is illustrated below and, as you can see, is relatively simple.

White starts by moving a rook from g8 to e8, checking the black king on e1. The king's only option is to move to a square on the d-file as all the squares on the e-file and f-file are attacked by the rooks.

White now moves his other rook to d7, bringing about much the same situation, except that Black can now only move to a square on the c-file. But White can continue alternating moves with the rooks to push the black king to the edge of the board.

Black plays the king to c3 and the white rook goes to c8. The black king must go to the b-file and the white rook on d7 goes to b7, now forcing Black to the a-file. White now plays the c8 rook to a8 and it is checkmate.

This series of five moves by White is designed to push Black to the edge of the board. It is common for a king to meet its end at the side of the board because it is thus deprived of three escape squares which it would otherwise have access to.

In some positions it is possible for the king to get close to the rooks so that they cannot checkmate quite so easily, but the technique then is to move the rooks to a distance, but at the same time keeping the king boxed-in, nearest the edge of the board.

STALEMATE

We have already seen that – when neither side has sufficient material to deliver checkmate – not all chess games end in a decisive result. Another draw possibility in chess is stalemate. Stalemate occurs when a player has no legal move, but the king is not attacked. The game ends immediately as a draw.

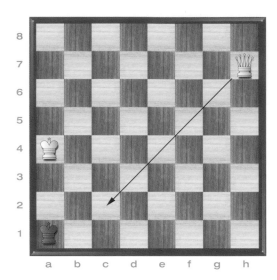

In the above position, White might be tempted to play the queen to c2 in order to prepare checkmate in a couple of moves. The snag is that this deprives the king of any moves at all, although the king is not directly attacked. So it is stalemate, and a rather lucky draw for Black. Instead of moving the queen to c2, it would be a similar mistake for White to move the king to a3 or b3, as this would also deprive Black of any legal moves and create a stalemate position.

It is always worth making sure that the opponent has a legal move or two at their disposal when rounding up a king. Below is an amusing trick that allows White to escape with a draw.

White's position (below left) looks miserable, but there is a way out of his problems. The white king cannot move, but it is not stalemate because there is still a rook on the board which can (and indeed must) be moved. The rook can move to g4 and give check to the black king on h4. The rook is undefended and the black king can simply capture – but if it does, White no longer has a legal move and the game ends in stalemate.

Perpetual check

If Black avoids the capture and instead plays the king to h5, White carries on with the plan and plays the rook to g5, giving check again. It is the same situation as before: if the white rook is captured, the game ends immediately in stalemate. Black can continue to move the king up and down the h-file and White will follow with a rook check in the hope that Black will capture.

In fact, this process will continue ad infinitum and there is no way for Black to break the sequence. This is known as 'perpetual check' and, when Black gets fed up trying to win, the game will be agreed a draw. In a formal competitive game, where the players keep a record of the moves, a player can claim a draw when the same position on the board has occurred (or is about to occur) three times.

The fact that stalemate constitutes a draw in circumstances where one player has such a large material advantage might seem rather unfair but it is a fact of chess. It is perhaps seen to be fairer in situations where the difference in material is much smaller.

In the position above right, White can play the king into the corner and sit tight. If Black advances the pawn to a2, it is stalemate because the white king has no legal move. In fact, it makes no difference whatever Black does in reply to the king moving to the a1 square. White can simply move the king backwards and forwards from b1 to a1. Black cannot force the white king out of the corner and will eventually have to give up and agree a draw.

Right: Vladimir Kramnik (left) waits for reigning world champion Garry Kasparov to make his move at the World Chess Championship at Hammersmith, London, UK, on 31 October 2000.

Offering a draw

In tournament chess, chess players often agree draws when there are still several pieces on the board. The protocol is to make a move and ask: 'Would you like a draw?'

The player offered a draw may decide at their leisure whether to accept the draw (usually by proffering a handshake) or by continuing the game (by making a move and, optionally, replying verbally). Once a further move has been made, the draw offer is deemed to have lapsed.

CASTLING

The only time in a game of chess when a player is allowed to move two pieces on the same turn is called castling. This is a special move involving the king and a rook of the same colour. The mechanics of the move are very simple. However there are a number of provisos that need to be understood first.

A player is only allowed to castle when both king and rook are on their original squares and have not moved previously in the game. There must be no pieces of either colour between the king and rook. And the king must not be attacked on its original square, its target square or any intervening squares between the two.

Above, the king and rook are on their original squares. Castling is effected by first moving the king two squares to the right (to g1 in the case of White) and the rook two squares to the left (to f1 in the case of White). After the moves are completed, the board looks like this:

This is called 'kingside' castling, because it involves the rook that stands on the king's side of the board at the beginning of the game (the files lettered from e to h). A player can also castle with the rook that stands on the queen's side of the board (the files lettered from a to d). Below is an example of queenside castling.

First, the king is moved two squares to the left (to c1, in the case of the white king) and then the rook is moved three squares to the right (to d1 in the case of the white rook), as seen below:

When castling is not allowed

Castling is only allowed if the pieces involved have not yet been moved in the game (even if they have returned to their original squares after moving). Here are some examples where a player may not castle:

Above, White may not castle because the king is in check from the knight on d3. Should the knight subsequently move to a square from where it did not attack the d1 square, castling would be possible.

In the above position, White may not castle because the king would land on a square attacked by the black bishop. If the black bishop moves away and leaves g1 unattacked, castling would become permissible.

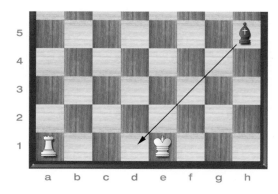

Above, White may not castle – it would mean the king passing over a square attacked by the black bishop. Note that an attack on a rook or a square over which a rook passes is not a bar to castling.

Below left, the rook on a1 is attacked by the bishop, but it is permissible for White to castle, by moving the king to c1 and the rook to d1.

In the above example, assuming that White has not previously moved the king or either rook, White can legally castle on either side of the board. So White castles kingside (as shown by the arrows).

Above is the position after White has castled. Can Black now castle? Answer: no, because there is a bishop in the way on the queenside, while on the kingside the white rook is attacking the square f8, over which the black king would need to pass.

Note that, when castling, the king should always be moved before the rook. In formal competitive chess, a player touching the rook first would not be allowed to castle but must make a move with the touched rook.

MORE RULES AND CONVENTIONS

As well as the basic rules of the pieces, chess has several conventions that are traditionally respected. If you're playing informally with a friend you may well choose to ignore these, but anyone wishing to take part in serious matches must learn them until their observance becomes second nature.

Touch-piece-move rule

You now know the rules for moving the chess pieces. If a player whose turn it is to move touches one or more of his own pieces, then he is obliged to move the first piece touched that can be moved. If the piece or pieces touched belong to the opponent, then he must capture the first piece touched that can be captured. Having moved a piece to a square, the actual move is not complete until the player releases the piece. If he still has a hand on the piece, he is committed to moving the piece (because it has been touched), but can move it somewhere else.

In practice, it is not a good idea to make moves tentatively. Some inexperienced players make a move and leave a finger on the piece while they perform a last-minute check to see if the move is alright. Strong players never do this. Leaving your hand on a piece (or hovering over the piece with your hand) can partially obscure the opponent's view of the board (and is arguably poor manners); and visible indecision encourages the opponent psychologically. Good chess players make their moves with precision and panache, giving an impression of brisk efficiency and confidence. Another rule with which many chess players are unfamiliar: the laws of the game stipulate that a move may be made with one hand only.

In informal chess games between friends, strict application of what is called the 'touch-piece-move' rule is often relaxed, with players requesting and being allowed 'take-backs' when they realize that they have done something silly. However, a take-back is never allowed in a chess competition and, if it is done too often in informal play, it can lead to a sloppy or lazy approach to the game. It is good practice to adhere to the touch-piece-move rule even in informal games.

Below: It is customary to centralize all the pieces on their squares before starting play. World champion Vladimir Kramnik adjusts his pieces before a big game against Grandmaster Peter Leko at a tournament in Germany.

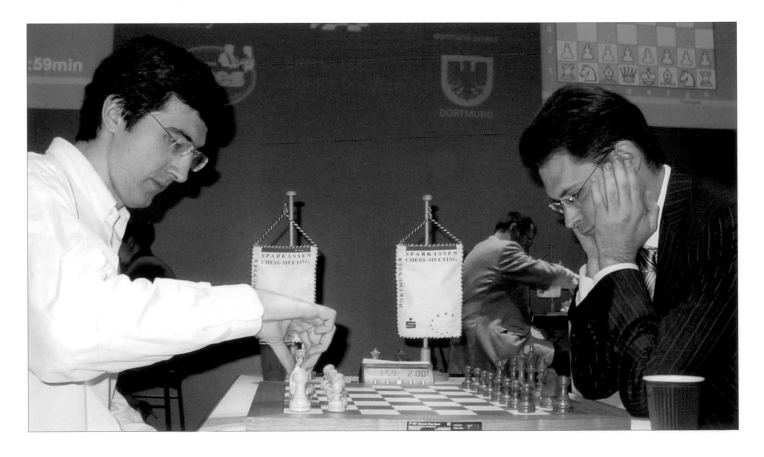

No-talking rule

In formal competitions, chess players rarely talk at the board. One exception to this is to offer a draw. This should be done verbally, immediately after making a move. If you offer a draw without making a move, the opponent can ask to see a move before they decide whether to accept or not. After you have moved, they may choose to accept, politely refuse or simply continue play without saying anything. It is conventional to accept a draw by offering a handshake. Having made a draw offer and had it refused, it is bad form to make further draw offers unless the position on the board changes markedly.

Another exception to the no-talking convention is that you may decide that your position is so bad that it is time to give up. You are permitted to resign the game in these circumstances, either by saying: 'I resign', toppling over your king or perhaps by offering a handshake. It is usually clear from the context of the game whether the handshake denotes a resignation or a draw acceptance – but there have occasionally been misunderstandings. Having said that chess players do not talk during play, it is perfectly normal to exchange small talk or offer to buy refreshments, provided it does not disturb the opponent or neighbouring players.

Right: Leading Dutch player Tea Bosboom-Lanchava moves her queen in a tournament in London.

Below: White's bare king is up against a large army of black pieces, so White decides to resign – signified by toppling over the white king.

THE 50-MOVE RULE

One obscure rule that is rarely invoked is the 50-move rule. If 50 consecutive moves are played by each player without a single pawn move or any capture, either player can claim a draw. In practice, the players would need to be keeping score of the moves in order to make such a claim, so it does not arise in informal play.

RELATIVE VALUES OF THE PIECES

We now know, in general terms, that the queen is more valuable than the other chessmen, and that the pawn is the least valuable piece on the board. We also know that the point of the game is to checkmate the opponent's king. But in order to bring about a checkmate it is generally true that the side with the most valuable force of pieces will have an advantage in achieving the goal of checkmate.

The most valuable force is not the same as the largest force. In the position above, White has only two pieces to Black's five. But White has a very powerful queen and Black only has four pawns that are a long way from promotion. On the first move, the white queen can capture the black pawn on e7, and it will then be threatening to capture the pawns on b7 and g7, and the remaining pawn will also disappear in a further move or two. White will then soon be in a position to checkmate the lone black king using the queen supported by the white king.

Above: Although the least powerful piece, the pawn is unique in that it is capable of promotion. When promoted, it can be exchanged for a queen, rook, bishop or knight.

Thus it can be seen that the white queen's relative value is much greater than that of the four black pawns. This is a simple example, but things can become more complicated if there is a greater variety of pieces in different configurations on either side.

Above, White and Black have the same number of pieces, but everything depends on their relative value – and whose turn it is to move. White has a bishop and knight and one pawn, which is more valuable than three pawns. However, with Black to play, everything changes. Black can advance the pawn on e2 to e1 and promote it to a queen, as shown below.

9   5   3   3   1

Above: Each of the pieces is assigned a points value but this is only a general rule of thumb. The true value varies in accordance with the specific position on the board.

The points system

Now Black has a queen and two pawns to White's bishop, knight and one pawn. It is not so easy to quantify the value of the two forces, but chess players have devised a handy rule of thumb that can be used to estimate the difference in relative value of a position. Each chess piece is assigned a relative value in points, these being:

Queen	=	9
Rook	=	5
Bishop	=	3
Knight	=	3
Pawn	=	1

The king is not assigned a points value because its value is effectively infinite, and because there is always one king of each colour on the board, so their values cancel each other out. Similarly, there is no need to tot up the values of those pieces that both players have in common (so in the previous diagram we may discount White's pawn and one of Black's pawns as being of equal value). We are only concerned with the differences between the two opposing forces. Therefore, the differences between the two sides are White's bishop and knight (if you add it up that's 3 + 3 = 6 points) compared with Black's queen and pawn (that's 9 + 1 = 10 points). This equates to a difference in relative value of four points in favour of Black.

Above: Try adding up the points value of the pieces of each side. It should come to 11 points for White and 10 points for Black. So White stands a better chance because he has a material advantage of one point.

As far as beginner play goes, a difference of one point may not be terribly significant, but a difference of three or four points is starting to get dangerous for the player with the lower point count. This suggests that the position illustrated opposite is very good for Black. A number of other factors, such as the advanced white pawn on a6, swings the pendulum back slightly towards White. But the overall assessment would still favour Black.

THE STARTING POSITION

We have explored how individual pieces work in isolation, or in situations where there are much-reduced forces on the board, but these situations occur well into the game, after some pieces have been captured. Now it is time to learn how a chess game begins, with both sides having their full set of pieces on their starting squares.

This is the starting position for a game.

In two-dimensional diagrams of chess positions in books and magazines, it is usual to show the board from White's point of view, with the white pieces at the bottom of the diagram (with the pawns moving up the page) and the black pieces at the top of the diagram (with the pawns moving down the page). When looking at a diagram (or indeed a chessboard), it is particularly important to be clear which way the pawns can move, since they can only move in one direction – forwards. Chess players sit behind their forces (as do modern army commanders) and move their pawns towards the enemy.

The positions of the pieces have to be memorized, with particular attention to the king and queen. Remember that, as players look at the board, they should see a white square in the right-hand corner ('white on the right') and that both queens stand on their own colour square (i.e. white queen on a white square, black queen on a black square). It is usually easy enough to distinguish the pieces in a chess set. The king and queen might appear a little similar, but the king in a conventionally designed Staunton pattern set has a small cross on the top, compared to a coronet on the queen. Chess players use the terms kingside and queenside in reference to the two halves of the board on which the king and queen sit in the starting position. The dividing line in the adjacent diagram does not actually appear on a real chessboard – it is to show the conceptual division of the board.

Below: The two armies face each other across the board, ready to do battle. Each king stands on its opposite colour square, with the corner square to its right being white.

Above: Play usually starts with a pawn move (though knight moves are possible). Here White (who always starts) plays a pawn from e2 to e4. This is probably the commonest first move.

Making the first moves

The game starts with White making a move. White always moves first. This confers a small advantage, rather like the advantage of serving first in tennis, but it is not significant at the beginner or elementary level of the game. When playing a series of informal games, chess players normally turn the board round after each game and take turns to have White. In competition chess, the same applies: as far as possible, players are given White and Black in alternate rounds in order to even up the chances. In every other respect, the two sides are level.

White has to make a move. This is mandatory: it is not possible to 'pass' as in some other games. How many options are there? The king, queen, rooks and bishops are currently hemmed in by the rank of pawns ahead of them and cannot move. The knights however are able to hop over other pieces. The two knights have two possible moves each. The eight pawns also have two possible moves each: either one or two squares forward. So, in total, White has 20 possible moves to start the game. The adjacent diagram shows White's 20 first move options.

After White has moved, it is Black's turn, with exactly the same possible options with the black pieces. This means that the possible number of positions after White and Black have made just one move each is 20 x 20 = 400 positions: a very big number, considering that the game has only just begun. This should give you an inkling of the number of chess positions that becomes possible after a few more moves, or after the 30 to 50 moves played in most games of chess. It is, quite simply, colossal and goes a long way to explaining why every possible chess move has yet to be resolved by human or computer.

STANDARD NOTATION

The diagram on the previous page showing all 20 of White's first-move options was rather cluttered, but there is a much simpler way to record and communicate chess games than using a diagram for every move played. This is called chess notation. This book uses standard notation, also commonly known as algebraic notation because of the cross-reference system used to identify the squares.

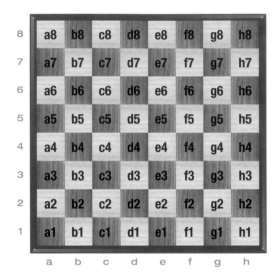

Each file is lettered, from a to h, while the ranks are numbered 1 to 8. Consequently, each square on the chessboard has a unique grid reference, from a1 to h8. Note that the letters denoting files always appear in *lower* case.

Each piece is assigned a capital letter. In English, this is as follows:

K	KING
Q	QUEEN
R	ROOK
B	BISHOP
N	KNIGHT (K is already used for the king)

No letter is assigned to the pawn – if no capital letter appears in the move code, then it can be assumed that the move is made by a pawn.

Recording chess moves

In standard notation, a chess move is recorded by giving the capital letter denoting the piece used (except in the case of a pawn) and the coordinate of the square to which it is moved. Hence, 'Qe4' signifies 'the queen moves to the e4 square', 'Rc7' that 'the rook goes to the

c7 square', 'c7' that 'the pawn goes to the c7 square', etc. Note that there is no need to record whether it is a white or black piece being moved. White and Black make alternate moves, so this can be deduced from the sequence of the moves, and usually from the layout on the page. Let's see a simple example, from the starting position, numbering the moves in pairs as we go.

1   e4   ...

LEARN AS YOU PLAY

♛ ♝ ♞ ♚

Don't worry too much about the notation just yet, or try to memorize where all the squares are on the grid. You'll most certainly pick it up as you go along, and you can always come back to this section of the book for reference if you are unsure. Many people learn chess from other people, rather than from a book, and enjoy playing chess all their lives without even knowing that such a thing as chess notation exists. However, it is undoubtedly an advantage to be 'chess literate', so that you can consult written sources of chess information in order to improve your game.

This means that White starts the game by moving a pawn that can go to the e4 square. Only one pawn can do this – the one sitting on e2. So that pawn moves from e2 to e4.

1   **...**   **Nf6**

Now it is Black's turn, as shown above. Notice that the move is indented to the right after three dots to show that we are talking about Black's move. The code Nf6 means 'knight to the f6 square'. Only one of Black's two knights has the possibility of making this move – the one on g8. So it means 'knight on g8 moves to f6'.

2   **e5**   **Nd5**
3   **Nf3**   **d6**

We have noted two more pairs of moves now. White's moves are those shown in the left-hand column and Black's are in the right. After making these moves, the position of both players pieces will be as in the following diagram.

As you can probably see, White is about to capture the pawn on d6 with the white pawn on e5. This is signified by an 'x' in the notation below. Additionally, for clarity in the case of a pawn capture, an extra small letter signifies the original file in addition to the destination file. Thus:

4   **exd6**   **...**

White moved the pawn on e5 (hence 'e'), made a capture ('x') and put the pawn down on d6.

continues on the next page ➔

Black then captures the pawn on d6 with the queen.

4   ...   Qxd6

5   Bb5+   ...

White plays the bishop to the b5 square. This move gives check to the black king, signified by the '+' character after the move notation.

5   ...   Kd8

Black moves the king to the d8 square. Now White decides to castle.

6   0-0   ...

Notice the special notation used for castling: 0-0. For castling queenside, the notation would be 0-0-0. Let's move the game on a couple of moves.

6   ...   Nd7
7   d4   ...

EQUIPMENT

♕ ♗ ♘ ♔

Although the rest of the book will contain plenty of diagrams for guidance, there will not be diagrams to show every position as games and sequences of moves are explained. It is therefore a good idea to play through the moves on a chessboard as you read the book. If you don't already own one, now is the time to acquire a full-sized chess set. It is best to use a wooden or plastic set that is as close as possible to the design of the pieces shown on this page. It does not have to be expensive – a plastic set with a board is generally very inexpensive. Two more important factors in choosing a set are: it should be easy to distinguish one type of piece from another, and the pieces should be in proportion to the board. Big pieces on a tiny board are as bad as small pieces on a big board. Look for a set with a king height of about 9cm (3½in) and a board with squares of about 5cm x 5cm (2in x 2in).

Now the board looks like this.

On the next move, Black intends to move the knight on d7 to f6. But notice that both black knights can go to that square in this position, so it is necessary to distinguish between them. It is no good referring to the file on which they are standing because they are both on the d-file. But one is on rank 7 and the other on rank 5 (normally we would say 'the seventh rank and the fifth rank'). So we distinguish by referring to the rank, thus:

7   ...   N7f6

Simple and unambiguous. This means that the knight on the seventh rank goes to f6. Had Black moved the other knight to this position the notation would instead be N5f6.

Now, White wants to reply by moving the knight that is currently on b1 to d2. Again, there is an ambiguity, so it is no good just putting 'Nd2'. One way to solve the problem would be to make a reference to the rank, as with Black's 7th move, i.e. 8 N1d2. In fact, standard notation prefers to make a reference to a file rather than a rank, where both are possible. So the correct notation is:

8   Nbd2   ...

This means 'White's knight currently on the b-file is moved to the d2 square'. To reiterate, where two identical pieces could move to the same square, indicate the file from which the correct piece is to be moved. If both are on the same file, indicate the rank instead. The following diagram, top right, shows how the board looks after the pair of knight moves made above.

That is as far as we are going with this game (which, incidentally, contains some rather poor moves). It contains nearly all the standard notation that you will need to read and understand chess moves, both in this book and in most other chess literature.

Other codes and symbols

Here is a summary of the various codes and symbols used as part of standard notation, including some not yet discussed:

0-0	CASTLES KINGSIDE
0-0-0	CASTLES QUEENSIDE
+	CHECK
#	CHECKMATE
x	(CAPTURES)
1-0	WHITE WINS (OR BLACK RESIGNS)
0-1	BLACK WINS (OR WHITE RESIGNS)
½-½	GAME DRAWN
!	GOOD MOVE
!!	BRILLIANT MOVE
?	BAD MOVE
??	AWFUL MOVE (chess players often use the word 'blunder')

STRATEGY 1: THE PIN

We already know that the king cannot expose itself to an attack by an enemy piece. The same rule applies to any piece that is currently blocking an attack on its own side's king. It is not permitted to move away and, in doing so, expose the king to attack. This position is known as a 'pin'.

In the diagram above, with White to play, the rook is not allowed to move away because that would put the white king in check to the bishop on d4. White would have to play either Kb1 or Ka2, i.e. move the king to the b1 or a2 squares. The white rook is said to be 'pinned' to the king.

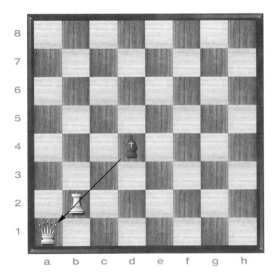

The above diagram shows another example of a pin. Here, the bishop is pinning the rook against the queen. That does not mean that the rook is forbidden to move in this case. It can be moved if White wants to, but it means that a more valuable piece (the queen) might be captured by the bishop, which is usually a very bad idea.

Above, it is White to play. The white bishop is pinned against the king by the black rook on d8. But White doesn't care because he can play Qh7 mate. The white queen moves to the h7 square next to the black king, where it is protected by the white bishop on d3 and cannot be captured by Black – checkmate: White wins. 'Not so fast,' protests Black. 'The bishop on d3 is pinned, so it doesn't really defend the queen!' Good try – but in fact it really is checkmate. Black cannot take the queen with the king because it would mean exposing the king to attack by the bishop. Although the bishop has no legal move, it still prevents the king from moving to any of the squares which it controls. A pin can be very useful in negating the power of a defending piece.

Only bishops, rooks and queens can effect pins. Kings and pawns only move one square at a time, while knights can jump over intervening pieces. In terms of vulnerability, all pieces other than the king can be pinned. One dangerous pin to look out for is where the queen moves one square diagonally from its starting square to the square in front of the king on its original square (i.e. Qe2 for White or Qe7 for Black). Beginners' queens often fall victim to an enemy rook pin played to the open e-file.

White can play Qa3 mate, i.e. queen to the a3 square, checkmate. Black has no king move, or blocking move, available. At first sight it looks like Black could reply Bxa3 (bishop takes the queen on a3), but in fact, the black bishop is pinned against the king by the white bishop on d4, so that move is illegal. The white bishop prevents the black bishop from performing this vital defensive function.

Countering a pin

If one of your pieces is pinned, it can often be a good idea to break the pin.

In the above position, White's queen is pinned against the king. Of course, queens can move along diagonals as well as bishops, so White has the option of capturing the bishop on d4. However, the bishop is stoutly defended by a pawn on c5, so it would be a bad exchange for White – the loss of the queen (9 points) for the bishop (3 points), making a deficit of 6 points. But there is another simple way to break the pin.

White can play c3 – i.e. move a pawn from c2 to c3 – and suddenly it is the black bishop that must take evasive action.

Another way to counter a pin is to play a cross-pin.

Here, with White to play, White's queen is pinned by the black bishop (which is defended by the black knight). However, White can reply Be3! (white bishop to the e3 square, a good move) and now the black bishop cannot take the queen because it is pinned against the black king. Black can play Bxe3 (capturing the e3 bishop), but then White plays dxe3 (pawn on d2 takes the bishop on e3), which is a level exchange. White's problems are solved.

Above: The rook pins the queen against the king on a1. The black queen cannot move away from the first rank.

STRATEGY 2: THE FORK

Where a piece threatens more than one enemy piece at the same time, it is called a fork. All chess pieces are capable of doing this. The knight is particularly deadly at performing forks because its move is unique and higher value pieces such as queens and rooks cannot return fire when attacked by a knight.

Here, the knight is attacked by both queen and rook, but, with White to move, it hits back with tremendous force (Nc2+!!) that is, knight to c2, giving check to the king on b4. This is a very good move.

Pawns are also capable of forking pieces. Below, White can play c3, forking queen and rook.

It is a scene of devastation: the king is in check, and the queen and rook are also attacked by the knight. All three pieces are said to be forked. Black would have to deal with the check and the only solution would be to move the king. Next move, White would be free to play Nxe1 – i.e. knight captures the piece on the e1 square, which is the queen. Here, a lower-value piece proves more powerful and the notion of the relative value of pieces is turned on its head.

The queen can take the forking pawn but it is defended by another pawn on d2 and it would cost Black the queen. Black could also take the pawn on d2 – 1...Qxd2 – but then the game would proceed 2 cxb4 (the pawn on c3 takes the rook on b4) Qxb4 (the queen takes the pawn on b4). The body count after this little skirmish would show White to have lost two pawns (1 + 1 = 2 points) while Black would have lost a rook (5 points). White would therefore be three points better off in material terms – the equivalent of capturing a bishop or knight: a highly successful operation.

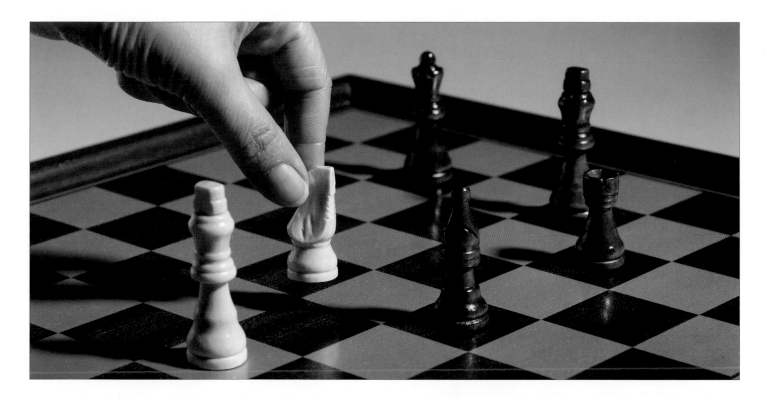

Above: The knight will move to d5, where it will fork four of Black's pieces. The black king is in check and will have to move. Then White will have the choice of three pieces to capture.

Chess players usually only refer to a simultaneous attack as a fork when the move leads to some sort of advantage for the player making the move.

In this position, White can play 1 Nc3+, which attacks the king, queen and knight simultaneously. But there is no particular virtue in the move because Black can play 1...Nxc3 – the black knight captures the knight on c3 – and the attack has been rebuffed. After White recaptures with 2 dxc3 (pawn takes the black knight on c3), all that has happened is that White and Black have exchanged knights. Therefore, no advantage accrues to either side.

Countering a fork

Having your pieces forked need not be the end of the world. In the following position, Black has two satisfactory ways to counter a fork.

White has played 1 Qc2 and is simultaneously attacking the rook on b3 and the knight on c4. Both black pieces are undefended so Black has to do something about the safety of both pieces in only one move. There are three common ways to meet an attack on a piece – move it somewhere safe, block the attack or defend it with another piece. Black cannot block here but can run away with one piece and defend the other in one go. Black can either play 1...Na5 (knight to a5, which defends the rook on b3) or 1...Rb4 (rook to b4, where it defends the knight on c4).

STRATEGY 3: THE SKEWER

A 'skewer' is a lot like a pin, as both can only be achieved by pieces that can move more than one square along lines (files, ranks and diagonals). The difference with a skewer is that the more valuable piece is the one caught in the direct line of fire, with the lesser value one behind it usually being the ultimate casualty.

White plays Bf3+ – bishop to f3, check. Black has to move the king out of check, and on the following move White plays Bxa8 – bishop takes the queen on the a8 square. The move Bf3+ is called a skewer.

Skewers can only be achieved by pieces that move more than one square at a time along files, ranks and diagonals. Here is an example of a rook skewer:

White is in check from the black queen. 1 Kg1?? – king to g1 – would be a dreadful mistake. Black would reply 1...Qh1# – queen to h1, checkmate. The queen is defended by the rook on h8 and the white king has no escape squares. However, White can play a blocking move instead.

1 Rh3!! (rook to h3) is an excellent move. It skewers the rook on h8. The rook on h3 directly menaces the queen. The queen cannot sensibly play 1...Qxh3+ – capturing the rook on h3 with the queen – because the rook is defended by the pawn on g2. But it is equally disastrous if the queen is moved away from the h-file with, for example, the move 1...Qf6. White would play 2 Rxh8+ – the white rook captures the undefended rook on h8 – giving check to the black king as shown below.

If we make a small adjustment to this example – relocating the black pawn that was on g7 to the f6 square, it makes a big difference to the outcome.

White again plays 1 Rh3 to block the check (and avoid checkmate), but this time it is not really a skewer. Black can safely play 1...Qg7 – queen to the g7 square – to accomplish the two-fold purpose of getting the queen away from the rook's attack and providing a defender for the rook on h8. White plays 2 Rxh8+ – rook takes rook on h8 with check – but Black can then play 2...Qxh8+ – queen recaptures the rook on h8. The outcome is a simple exchange of rooks.

A pin, a fork and a skewer – in one

Occasionally you may get the chance to play a move that is a pin, fork and skewer at the same time:

Let's do a quick point count of this position. First, discount all pieces that the two players have in common, or where the piece values are identical (i.e. bishops and knights, which are both worth 3 points): two pawns, one pair of knights and one knight for bishop. That leaves White with a bishop/knight and two pawns (3 + 1 + 1 = 5 points) for Black's two rooks

Above: The bishop skewers the queen. If the queen moves, the bishop will be able to capture the black rook further down the diagonal.

(5 x 2 = 10 points). So Black is way ahead of the game. However, White can play the move 1 Bxe5!! – bishop takes the pawn on e5. It is an excellent move.

The bishop on e5 pins the knight against the king on h8, forks the two rooks on c3 and d6 and skewers the knight on b8. Black must try and capture as much material for one of the rooks as possible. In this position, the best move is 1...Rcxd3 – rook on c3 takes the pawn on d3 (note that it is necessary to include the original file identifier here, because both rooks can legally capture on d3). White plays 2 exd3. If we tot up the points, we find that White has bishop/knight and two pawns (3 + 1 + 1 = 5 points) against Black's rook (5 points). In theory this indicates a level position, but White still has the pin and skewer in place and is much better placed to win.

STRATEGY 4: PASSED PAWNS

If there is one thing that distinguishes a good chess player from a poor one, it is a deep respect for the pawn. While weaker players know that the pawn is the lowest rank in the chess army, they often fail to appreciate how useful and powerful it can be in many chessboard situations.

It is true that, at the beginning of the game, the pawn is the least valuable piece, but its value can grow as its path to the promotion square begins to clear. One pawn with more potential than most is a passed pawn. This is how a pawn is known when it faces no enemy pawn on the same file, or adjacent files, ahead of it. Its journey to promotion can only be stopped by higher-value enemy pieces. If a pawn becomes passed while there are still many pieces on the board, it is unlikely to be too dangerous, but as pieces disappear from the board and the endgame begins, a passed pawn can become much more dangerous.

Above: All the pawns shown here have a clear run to the eighth rank. In the context of a game they are said to have be 'passed' pawns.

2 Bf1 and next move can advance the a-pawn to a6. After that Black would probably have to give up the bishop to stop the pawn from 'queening' (i.e. reaching the a8 square where it would become a queen).

The two highlighted pawns in this position are both passed pawns. Note that the white pawn on f4 and the black pawn on g6 are not passed pawns because they are on adjacent squares; each can therefore potentially capture the other should it advance up the board.

A check on the relative values of the pieces possessed by both sides reveals that the position is equal as regards material. In reality, the situation is more complex. White's passed pawn on a5 is rather more menacing than Black's pawn on h5. True, both are blockaded by pieces (the black bishop and the white king), so neither can advance as yet. However, White has an advantage of being able to force Black to give ground. For example, 1 Bg2, and now if Black moves the bishop, e.g. 1...Bc8, then White can play

The position is equal as regards material, but in a game between good chess players White would almost certainly go on to win because of the advantage conferred by the powerful passed pawn on a5. By contrast, Black's passed pawn on h5 is being kept securely at bay by White's king and the pawn on f4.

Two connected passed pawns, well advanced up the board, can be as powerful as a queen.

Black has two connected passed pawns on a3 and b4. If it is White's turn to play here, it would be an easy win with 1 Rxb4 – rook takes the pawn on b4 – when 1...a2 – pawn to a2 – loses after 2 Ra4, and White will gobble up the pawn, or the queen on the next move if Black plays 2...a1Q+ (note that, when a pawn is promoted, the capital letter denoting the piece it becomes is appended to the notation).

However, it is a very different story if it is Black's turn to move in the above position. Black plays 1...a2, threatening to queen next move. White has to stop that with 2 Ra8, but then Black plays 2...b3, defending the a2 pawn.

White has a large material advantage (rook = 5, two pawns = 2), but the horrible truth is that White should now lose with best play. If White tries 3 Ra3 to attack the b3 pawn, Black simply plays 3...b2!

Right: No black pawn can block the progress of White's pawn on b4. As such it poses a serious threat to Black, the black king being tied to obstructing its progress.

White cannot stop one of the pawns from becoming a queen. If White plays 4 Rxa2?, Black replies with 4...b1Q+, making a new queen and forking the king and the rook on a2.

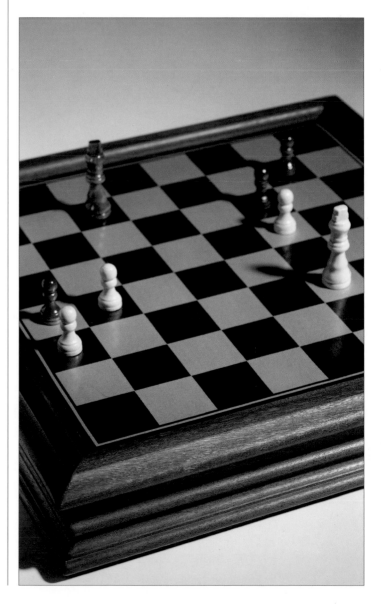

SIMPLE OPENING STRATEGY

The opening moves of a game of chess have a strategy all of their own. The basic idea is to make a general advance in the direction of the enemy forces but in a controlled manner. Below are a number of general principles that will help you to select the right piece to move and the right place to move it to.

We have already had a look at the start position in chess, and seen that White has 20 possible moves from the starting position.

Of those 20 moves, four are highly regarded and regularly played by professional chess players, another three or four are also reasonable (but not played so often), and the rest are regarded as unorthodox and unproductive. However, none of them actually loses outright.

Occupying the centre

We are not going to deal with any specific opening moves in this section, but will instead concentrate on a few general principles to get things started. First, the initial 10 or 15 moves of a chess game are referred to as 'the opening'. There are a very large number of openings that have been worked out by chess players over the centuries. Very few of them, even the most ancient, have been totally disproved (or refuted), although some have better reputations than others. The selection of an opening is often a matter of taste, based on whether a player prefers an attacking or a more restrained game.

One general principle is that players should try to occupy the centre. By the centre, chess players mean the four squares in the middle of the board that tend to be the focus of the battle in its early stages.

One way for White to do this in the initial position is to advance either the e-pawn or d-pawn. For example, 1 e4:

The pawn on e4 effectively occupies one of the central squares. Note that it is usually just as useful to control the centre as it is to occupy it – in other words, to put pieces on squares from which they can capture enemy pieces that land on a central square.

Top right: Following the general principle of mobilizing pieces during the opening, White here develops the knight on b1 to d2, from where it exerts pressure on the centre.

Far right: Black here pushes his pawn from c7 to c6, defending the pawn on d5 which, in turn, occupies and contests the centre.

Mobilizing pieces

Another general principle is that it is a good idea to mobilize the pieces. This is often referred to as 'development'. The idea is that you should try to 'develop' pieces to squares where they have more scope, or can exert pressure against the enemy pieces. Notice that the initial move 1 e4 helps to achieve this objective. It frees the bishop on f1, and the queen on d1, to develop via the f1–a6 and d1–h5 diagonals.

Another general principle is that you should, as far as possible, make the minimum moves by each piece in the opening. Try to make one move only with each piece during the development stage. This should not be treated as a hard-and-fast principle – there are plenty of exceptions – but it is important not to waste time in mobilizing the pieces.

It is usually prudent to mobilize lower-value pieces in preference to higher values in the early stages. It is usually better to move knights and bishops into the fray before queens and rooks. It is also a little easier for knights and bishops to find space to move while the two armies are at full strength. It can be quite hard to find good vantage points to exploit the full power of queens and rooks while there are still eight well-defended pawns strung across the board. Rooks, in

particular, benefit from exchanges of pawns, which can result in open files on which to operate.

Never advance up the board with your king in the early stages of a game. The king is too valuable to be risked in this way. It is better for the king to stay on its home rank, and usually a good idea to make use of the special castling move, tucking the king away in a safe corner, preferably with a row of three or four unmoved pawns in front of it.

One simple, general principle is: after every move of the opponent, ask yourself: 'Is there a threat?'

HOW TO AVOID EARLY DISASTERS

The well-known chess saying 'all the mistakes are there, waiting to be made' does not just apply to beginners – grandmasters also make mistakes. All beginners can expect to make quite a few errors during their first games. Below are a few pitfalls to avoid. More positively, it is also possible to make use of this knowledge to snare an unwary opponent. A game of chess will usually last from 30 to 50 moves, but it can also be over in no time. Just two moves apiece is all it takes in the following extreme case. This is often referred to as Fool's Mate.

1   f3?

White starts the game by moving a pawn from f2 to f3. The question mark after the notation indicates that it is regarded as a bad move. On f3, the pawn blocks the entry into the game of the knight at g1. More significantly, in view of what follows, it also exposes the king to a potential attack on the diagonal from e1 to h4.

1   ...   e5

Black replies by moving a pawn from e7 to e5. The move provides scope for Black's queen and bishop (on f8) to make an early entry into the game.

2   g4??

The two question marks signify that this is a big mistake.

2   ...   Qh4 mate

The queen on h4 gives check to the king along the e1–h4 diagonal. One way to get out of check is to capture the checking piece, but that is not possible here. Another way of escaping check is to move the king out of the way but the only available square (f2) is also attacked by the queen. The third way to get out of check is to block with another piece but none of White's pieces can go to f2 or g3. So in fact it is checkmate. That is a drastic example of how quickly a chess game can finish. Next, we follow a game that was played in a junior match in the 1970s.

1   e4

This was a much better first move for White. The pawn has some control of the central squares and has opened the way for bishop and queen to enter the fray.

1   ...   Nh6?

This was not a very good first move by Black. This knight has no impact on the central squares and will not control many squares from the edge of the board.

2   d4

Since Black has made no attempt to contest the centre, White decides to occupy another important square with a pawn, and also give scope for his dark-squared bishop (on c1) to join the fray.

2   ...   f6??

3   Bxh6!

White cleverly made a mental connection with Fool's mate. It is not exactly the same scenario, since the move 3 Qh5+ does not lead to checkmate - Black could reply by blocking the check with 3...g6 and survive. However, White has a simple combination which makes a quick finish possible.

3   ...   gxh6?

Black could avoid checkmate by playing another move (rather than recapturing the bishop) but the loss of the knight would probably be fatal anyway.

4   Qh5 mate

The checking piece cannot be captured, the king has no move and no piece can block the check. It is important to note the similarity with the checkmate produced in Fool's mate. One of the important aspects in learning chess is the ability to recognize patterns and learn from previous experience.

ANOTHER EARLY DISASTER

The next example of a disastrous chess move is often referred to as 'Scholar's mate'. This is not intended as a complimentary name. An early 17th-century chess author dubbed it this because of its rather childish lack of subtlety. Perhaps it would be better to name it 'Schoolkid's mate'.

1   e4   e5

2   Qh5

This early sally by the queen is regarded as an inferior move. Though it is not positively disastrous, it is certainly not recommended. In the long run, other moves will yield better results.

2   ...   Nc6

A sensible move, defending the e5 pawn from capture by the white queen. The famous world chess champion Garry Kasparov once played this move so it comes with the highest recommendation. He was playing an exhibition game against the equally famous German tennis star, Boris Becker, at the time.

3   Bc4

Here Boris Becker opted for 3 Qf3. A surprisingly timid move for such a great serve and volley tennis player, and one that violated the opening principle of not moving the same piece twice without good reason. Of course he soon lost. The move Bc4 contains a powerful if crude threat. It is important to study the position for a moment to make sure you can see what is coming. Thousands of rookie players have failed to do so and as a result have suffered the humiliation of early defeat.

3   ...   d6??

Disaster.

4   Qxf7 mate

The queen is defended by the bishop on c4 so the queen cannot be captured. The black king cannot move or block the check, so it is checkmate. In the starting position of a game of chess, the f7 square is one of the weakest points in Black's structure – as the f2 square is in White's – and it is usually a good idea to keep a special eye open for summary attacks in this area. Such vulnerability tends to arise after 1 e4 e5 where White plays either Bc4 or Qh5, or Black plays Bc5 or Qh4. Examine the danger to your f7 (or f2) square to make sure you have enough defence from a summary attack.

Let's look at the diagram position again after 3 Bc4.

Suppose that Black played instead ...

3   ...   g6

A very sensible move which blocks the threat of checkmate and also attacks White's queen. White must retreat this piece.

4   Qf3

Now, having beaten off the threat of checkmate, Black seeks to harass White's retreating queen further ...

OPENING TRAPS

It can be tempting to play for traps in the opening but this is a bad habit to get into and the long-term effect on your chess will not be good. It is much better to play conservatively in the opening stages of the game and only seek to play tactically when most of your pieces are in open play. You should not assume that your opponent is a poor player. Your choice of moves should be as objective as possible, based on the assumption that your opponent will find the best reply. So the best advice is: develop your pieces first, and only then play for checkmate if the chance arises.

---

4   ...   Nd4??

Black decides to pursue his plan of harassing the white queen. A better move is 4...Nf6, which gets another piece into play as well as blocking the threat along the f-file.

5   Qxf7 mate

Black hadn't noticed that White's move Qf3 had renewed the threat of checkmate. One reason for the popularity of this little trap among beginners is that you get two checkmate tricks for the price of one. If your opponent avoids the first one, he might fall for the second.

In real life, no one but the most unwary or inexperienced chess player would fall for a well-known trap of this sort. Though there are many other opening traps, in practice few games end in such short order. But these early disasters serve to illustrate just how quickly a chess position can become critical. Almost from the start of the game, it is good practice to have a quick look in the vicinity of both kings – to see if danger threatens, or perhaps if a sudden knock-out can be administered to the opposition king.

OPENING 1: THE GIUOCO PIANO

Most regularly used chess openings have names, and some are centuries old. One such is the Giuoco Piano, which means 'quiet game' in Italian. Also sometimes called 'the Italian Opening', it suits players who prefer a restrained game. It also conforms to most of the principles referred to in the previous section.

The Giuoco Piano has several different variations, or different ways to proceed after a few moves have been played. We will look at a variation (or line) that is known as the Giuoco Pianissimo ('very quiet game').

	White	**Black**
1	**e4**	**e5**

White has moved a pawn to e4 and Black has replied symmetrically. Both moves seek to occupy a central square and control an adjacent central square.

2	**Nf3**	**...**

This move develops a piece, exerting some pressure on central squares (d4 and e5) and posing a direct threat: to play Nxe5 and capture Black's pawn on e5.

2	**...**	**Nc6**

Black noticed that White was threatening to capture the e5 pawn. So the first priority was to address the threat, which Black has done by defending the e5 pawn with the knight. It is also a useful developing move in its own right, increasing Black's control over what happens on the central square at d4.

3	**Bc4**	**...**

White develops the bishop to a useful square. From c4, the bishop adds to White's control over the d5 square and looks farther along the diagonal at the pawn on f7. It does not threaten to take it because the pawn is adequately defended by the king on e8, but note that this threat could come in handy later.

3 ... Bc5

Black's move is similar to White's last move. It develops the bishop, on a strong post along the a7–g1 diagonal.

4 d3 d6

White and Black both make moves to d3 and d6 respectively. The moves were made to free the bishops on the marked diagonals.

5 Nc3 Nf6

One more knight move from each side has brought about a totally symmetrical set-up. Now White, deciding it is time to tuck the white king away somewhere safe, castles kingside.

6 0-0 ...

The king goes from e1 to g1, and the rook comes round from h1 to f1.

6 ... Bg4

Black decides to break the symmetry and play the bishop to g4, where it pins the f3 knight against the queen on d1. Black could have played 6...0-0, or perhaps a move such as 6...h6 (to prevent a pin by a bishop on g5, as Black has just played). The choice of moves here is largely a matter of taste.

Both sides have now completed more than half their development. There now remains the more complicated matter of how to get the queens and the rooks into the fray. The opening phase is coming to an end and the players are about to embark on the 'middlegame'.

OPENING 2: QUEEN'S GAMBIT

The word 'gambit' is used in everyday conversation to mean an attempt to do something with an element of trickery involved. In chess it means an opening in which a pawn sacrifice is offered in order to gain an advantage. The opening called the Queen's Gambit is so named, not because it involves sacrificing a queen but because a queenside pawn is offered to Black in order to speed up White's development.

Here are the opening moves of the Queen's Gambit, which is another well-respected opening.

1   d4   d5

Here, White has opened with the d2 pawn – often called **t**he queen's pawn because it stands on the same file as the queen. Many other openings, collectively referred to as queen's pawn openings, also start with the move d4. The e2 pawn is called the king's pawn and the family of chess openings that begin with 1 e4 are called king's pawn openings. As in the Giuoco Piano, Black mimics White's opening and plays the queen's pawn two squares forward.

2   c4   ...

The diagram below shows the move that gives the Queen's Gambit opening its name. It offers the c4 pawn (which is one of White's queenside pawns) as a small sacrifice, mainly to undermine the control of the centre enjoyed by Black's d5 pawn if it makes the capture on c4. Here, Black has to decide whether to capture the c4 pawn or not – or, to use the correct chess term, whether to accept or decline the gambit. Both options are perfectly respectable but we are going to look at what might happen if Black decides to accept the gambit.

2   ...   dxc4

The Queen's Gambit Accepted

Black takes the pawn, which White cannot immediately recapture. This variation is called the Queen's Gambit Accepted. If White were desperate to restore the material balance, 3 Qa4+ could be played, forking the king on e8 and the pawn on c4, and White could make sure of winning back the white pawn. But White is in no great hurry to recapture the pawn since Black will find it hard to defend in the long run. So White develops a knight, and Black does the same. White and Black play to control some central squares with their next pair of moves. White has a little more control over the centre, because the white d4 pawn still stands there.

3   Nf3   Nf6

4   e3   e6

Once again there is similarity between the two players' pawn moves. Both are played to give the f1 and f8 bishops some scope in order to castle kingside, but note that the moves restrict the scope of the other bishops.

5   Bxc4   ...

After a few simple developing moves, White has managed to recoup the sacrificed pawn. The material is now even, but White might feel that the prominent d4 pawn gives slightly better control in the centre. The game proceeds.

5   ...   c5

The last move challenges White's control of the centre. White has no need to panic as the d4 pawn is adequately defended.

6   0-0   cxd4
7   exd4   Nc6
8   Nc3   Be7

Both players have concentrated on their development. Two pawns have been exchanged and this has resulted in some files opening up for later exploitation by rooks. The position is roughly equal.

OPENING 3: THE COLLE OPENING

The Colle Opening (or Colle System) is named after a 20th-century Belgian chess expert. Many openings are named after famous players, or after countries where the particular opening was first played. This is another tried and trusted system for beginning a chess game. Like the Queen's Gambit, it is a queen's pawn opening.

| 1 | d4 | d5 | 3 | e3 | e6 |
| 2 | Nf3 | Nf6 | | | |

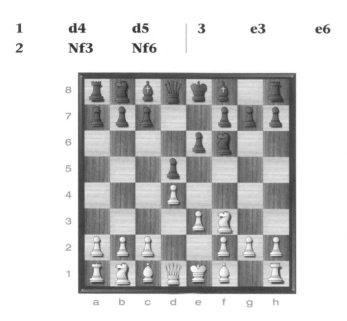

White diverged from the Queen's Gambit on move two, preferring the development of the knight to f3 to the pawn move c4. So far, Black has followed White's lead. Play in the Colle Opening is based on solidity, emphasizing the strength of the pawn structure.

| 4 | Bd3 | c5 |

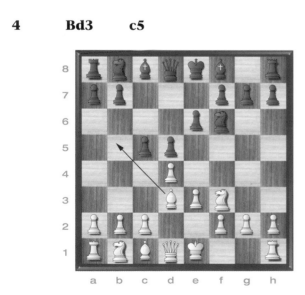

White might now be tempted to play a check with 5 Bb5+. It is not exactly a mistake, but is not very useful. Black can easily parry by interposing a knight or bishop on d7 or c6. It offends against a general principle of the opening – keeping the number of moves with the same piece to a minimum.

The bishop has already moved once and achieves nothing of value by moving a second time here.

| 5 | c3 | ... |

White aims to reinforce the pawn on d4. Rather than taking the initiative, the strategy in the Colle Opening is more circumspect and reactive.

| 5 | ... | Nc6 | 6 | Nbd2 | ... |

White moves the knight that is on b1 to d2 (the other knight could have gone there as well – hence the extra file identifier in the notation). White continues with development, but the knight move to d2 actually blocks the c1 bishop's entry into the game. One snag is that it leaves White in a rather cramped position.

6 ... Bd6 | 7 0-0 0-0

Here, White could keep the position closed, but let's see what happens if some pawns are exchanged.

8 dxc5 Bxc5 | 9 e4 ...

A second move of this pawn, but it is useful in creating scope for the c1 bishop.

9 ... Qc7

The black queen wants to prevent the advance of the e4 pawn to e5, and also has in mind some exploitation of the b8–h2 diagonal.

10 Qe2 Bd6 | 11 Re1 Ng4

Black hopes to play something like 12...Bxh2+ 13 Nxh2?? (bad move) Qxh2+ 14 Kf1 Qh1# – checkmate!

The above position shows Black's idea.

12 h3 ...

If 12...Bh2+? 13 Kh1! and White is quite safe. The Colle Opening is a playable opening for a beginner.

Winning Material

Although the main goal in chess is to checkmate the opponent, stampeding all your pieces in the direction of the opponent's king is rarely successful as a winning strategy. Attacking the king can be effective (as we shall soon see), but many more games of chess are settled by one player gaining a material advantage, after which the process of winning the game becomes relatively straightforward.

In elementary chess, it happens quite often that players gain material simply because the opponent overlooks a threat to take a piece, or actually puts one on a square which is attacked.

This position is complicated. White has one pawn fewer than his opponent. He can capture the f7 pawn with the knight on g5 (which will be defended by the bishop on c4), or capture the pawn on e5. White also has to consider Black's threat to play Nxc2 – knight takes the pawn on c2 – which forks the queen on e3 and the rook on a1. Instead, White becomes confused and tries to pin the knight on d4 against the queen on d7.

1   Rad1??   ...

White plays the rook on a1 to d1, but has overlooked the fact that Black's bishop on g4 attacks the d1 square. Chess players call this putting a piece *en prise* (a French expression: literally 'in take'). The bishop is worth less than the rook, so the exchange is favourable to Black. Winning a rook in exchange for a bishop or knight is often referred to as 'winning the exchange'. After winning a rook for such a piece, players refer to themselves as being 'the exchange up'.

1   ...   Bxd1
2   Nxd1   ...

Counting the difference in material, Black has a rook and pawn (5 + 1 = 6) compared to White's bishop (3 points). Black is, in the language of chess, 'the exchange and a pawn up'. This in itself should be good enough to win in the long run, although with plenty of pieces still left on the board, White can play on in hope.

There are still opportunities for counter-play, which may just possibly enable White to recoup some of the lost material, perhaps winning the exchange in turn later in the game. If Black is a strong player though, this is less likely.

Setting a trap

Rather than simply waiting for the opponent to overlook a threat, a player can set a trap. It is often useful to bait the trap with a pawn.

In this position, it is Black to move. Black notices that the pawn on d4 is only defended once, by the knight on f3. However, Black also notices that the pawn is being attacked twice, with the knight on c6 and the queen on b6. That means that Black can play 1...Nxd4 – knight takes the pawn on d4 – White replies 2 Nxd4 – knight on f3 captures the knight on d4 – and then Black plays 2...Qxd4 – the black queen captures the knight on d4. After those three moves, the players will have exchanged knights but Black will have gained a pawn. However, there is a snag...

It is now White's turn to move. White can play the move 3 Bb5+!! – an excellent move of the bishop to b5, giving check to the king on e8. Black has only calculated the sequence of moves up to and including the recapture of the knight on d4 but has failed to spot what follows.

Now Black has to deal with the threat to the king, but the bishop move has also uncovered an attack on the queen on d4 from White's queen on d1. After Black has countered the check, White will capture the queen – Qxd4 – and, in material terms, White will be a whole queen up. That is pretty much game over. Going back to the original position, we can see that Black fell into a big trap when he played 1...Nxd4.

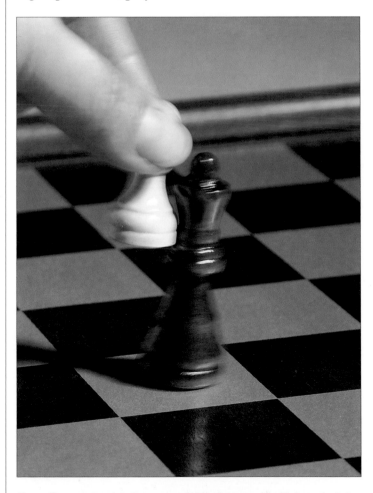

Above: The pawn here is in the process of taking the queen. Humble it may be, but a pawn, like any other piece, can win material, in this case capturing Black's queen.

SIMPLE MIDDLEGAME STRATEGY

The phase of the game after each player has moved most of their pieces (not including the pawns) at least once, and the two armies are at close quarters with each other, is called the middlegame. This is the part of the game where players can deploy all their tactical tricks – pins, forks, attacks on the king, etc – while most of the pieces are on the board. It is a fascinating part of the overall game, and vital to master.

The aim in this phase of the game is to outplay the opponent and gain a material advantage or to attack and give checkmate directly. Not all games reach an endgame, which is the phase of the game when there are somewhat fewer pieces (other than pawns) on the board and the strategy changes.

Scope and mobility

One fundamental of middlegame strategy is to find scope and mobility for pieces that move along lines. This often means open files for rooks and queens, and long diagonals for bishops and queens.

The above diagram is of a typical middlegame position. Most of the pieces have made one developing move, except for the rooks.

No immediate tactical tricks suggest themselves and it is time to consider longer-term strategy. The rooks are not well placed at the moment, still boxed in by their own pawns. White wants to find open lines for the two white rooks. One possibility is 1 Rac1, putting pressure on the semi-open file. The c-file is semi-open because there is only an enemy pawn on it.

By playing 1 Rac1, White threatens to capture the c7 pawn by 2 Qxc7. Black could then capture the queen with 2...Qxc7 and White would then take the black queen with 3 Rxc7 and be a pawn up.

After 1 Rac1, Black might have to think about defending the c7 pawn with a rook, or could try 1...Rfb8 – rook on f8 moves to b8, which is a semi-open file from Black's point of view. If White captures the c7 pawn now, Black exchanges queens as before and then captures on b2 with the black rook. That position would be even.

Another possibility on the first move is 1 Rfe1. The e-file is an open file (as is the d-file): there are no pawns on it. You might not think that the e-file looks very open, because there is a queen and a bishop of each colour standing on it at the moment. The description

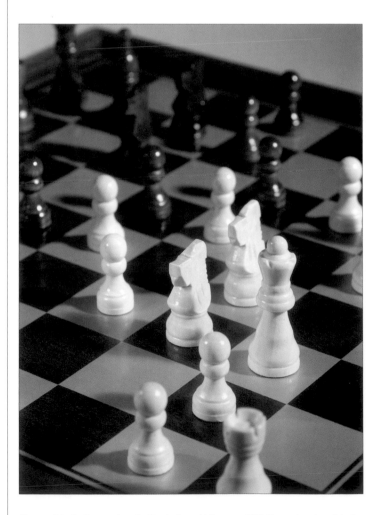

Above: A typically complex situation in the middle game. With the centre closed, both players jostle for position, each looking for some move or tactical combination that will help them seize the initiative.

is more to do with its potential than the actuality. After 1 Rfe1, White has a beady eye on the black queen that stands on the same file. If Black is unwary, things can soon happen on the open file. For example...

1	Rfe1	Rab8?
2	Bc4	...

The situation is beginning to favour White. Notice that White has uncovered a pin along the e-file. The bishop on e6 cannot move because it would expose the queen to capture by the rook on e1. Black now tries to solve these problems by playing a pin in reply.

2	...	Qc5??

Black now pins the white bishop with the white queen. If, for instance, White were to play 3 Bxe6??, Black could triumphantly capture the undefended queen on c2 with the black queen. However, Black has overlooked a vicious tactical blow (or combination), one that turns the position on its head and renders the

pin superfluous. White's combination is not immediately apparent. In two moves, White can win a bishop or even capture the black queen.

3	Rxe6!!	...

White unexpectedly captures the bishop on e6 with the rook, although it is apparently well defended by the pawn on f7.

3	...	fxe6
4	Bxe6+	...

The point of White's combination (the player's series of tactical moves) is revealed. The bishop has captured the pawn on e6 with check, simultaneously uncovering an attack on the black queen by the white queen on c2. Black will have to move the black king, after which the black queen will be lost.

MORE ABOUT THE MIDDLEGAME

Just as rooks thrive on open files, bishops can be lethal on long diagonals, since it is in these positions that they command the maximum squares. Knights, by contrast, are at their most dangerous when placed deep in enemy territory on a square where it is hard for your opponent to dislodge them.

The diagram above shows that bishops which have moved from their original squares (c1 and c8 respectively) are now positioned on long diagonals. However, they can easily become blocked, as seen below, particularly by enemy and friendly pawns.

The two bishops above have limited scope. The white bishop is stuck behind its own pawns and is not playing much part in the game. The black bishop is attacking the pawn on f3, but it is solidly defended by a fellow pawn on g2. Unfortunately, while the pawns stay put, the bishops will not have much influence on the game. Should White push the pawn on g2 forward, however, the situation for Black's bishop would be very different.

In this position, the material is level, but White's bishop has complete control of the a1–h8 diagonal, compared with its rather restricted opposite number. If it is White to move, White plays 1 Qc3! – and Black is suddenly in a desperate situation.

The threat is to play Qg7 or Qh8, both of which are checkmate. If Black tries to run away with 1...Kf8, White plays 2 Qg7+ Ke7 3 Bf6+ Ke6 4 Rae1+ Kd6 5 Rd1+, skewering the queen on d7. Black could try 1...f6, but after 2 Qxf6, White will soon drive the black king out into the open where it will be gunned down by the white rooks: and all the trouble stems from the powerful bishop on b2. Even with Black to move in the above position, Black will be hard put to mount a defence to the threats along the long diagonal.

Outposts

Knights are not interested in open lines and diagonals, but they often become more powerful when located on 'outposts'. An outpost in chess is a square in or near the enemy camp (the opponent's side), where a piece is well defended and hard to dislodge. In particular, it usually refers to a square that cannot be attacked by an enemy pawn. With this, much depends on the pawn structure. If this is still fluid (i.e. able and likely to change), then any outpost will almost certainly be temporary. If they are fixed, however, it's a different matter.

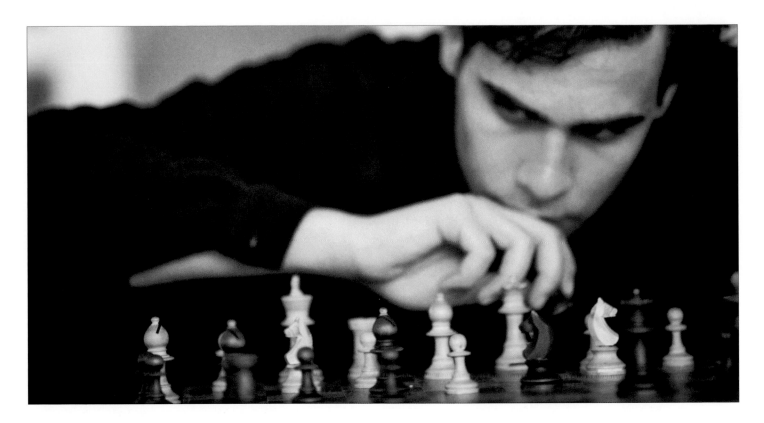

Above: If you find yourself without an obvious plan in the middlegame, start by thinking about which is your worst-placed piece and then see if there is a way that you can improve its position or scope. This might involve moving a different piece to give it more room for manoeuvre.

The diagram above shows a situation where the pawns have become locked. The two b-pawns can still move, but, if they advance, they would be captured immediately. For example if White plays 1 b3, the pawn can be captured either by 1...axb3 or 1...cxb3. If the b-pawn advances two squares – i.e. 1 b4 – exactly the same capture could be made because of the *en passant* rule – 1...axb3 – when the black pawn on a4 goes to b3, capturing the white pawn on b4 as if it had only moved to b3. 1...cxb3 *en passant* would also be possible if White played 1 b4.

So the pawns are locked. However, the pawn structure creates a possible outpost for Black on b3. Were Black to locate a knight there, it would be strongly defended and hard to drive away. The b4 square would similarly be an outpost for White, except that it is one rank further away from the enemy side of the board and likely to be less threatening to Black.

In the position (above), which is level on material, the white knight can occupy the outpost on e6. From there it can never be evicted by an enemy pawn, or anything else of equal or lower value, since Black's bishop only moves on dark squares. It is also well supported by a pawn on d5. So the move 1 Ne6 is a very good choice here, giving White much the better game. Although the black bishop is also well dug in on c5, White would have the future option of exchanging it with his knight should the bishop prove dangerous.

ATTACKING THE KING

So far in this book, we have seen how to improve the position gradually and learned a 'materialistic' approach to winning a chess game. In this context, the term 'materialistic' means trying to accumulate a material advantage with a view to converting it into a long-term checkmate. However, in some positions, it can be appropriate to dispense with this cautious policy and mount a direct attack on the king.

Mounting a direct attack on the king requires fine judgement and precise calculation. Before embarking on such an approach, you must (a) have calculated that the coming series of moves (or combination) leads to a certain checkmate; or (b) that the enemy king will be so exposed to immediate attack from a sufficient number of your pieces that it cannot hope to escape checkmate (or surrendering too much material to escape it).

In such positions, it becomes possible to disregard the relative values of the pieces. Here are some factors to look for when assessing the chances of a direct mating attack. Is the opposing king exposed? If it is not protected by a row of pawns, or is situated towards the middle of the board, it may be vulnerable to a mating attack. Are there fewer defending pieces in the vicinity of the opposing king compared to your attacking army? Sometimes, when an important enemy piece is left stranded too far away from the action (chess players sometimes borrow football parlance and refer to such a piece as 'offside'), it can be a good reason to take direct action against the king.

The Greek gift sacrifice

Sometimes a king can be forced out into the open via a sacrifice (that is, deliberately surrendering a piece for one of lesser value or even for no material at all, with a view to gaining more material in the long term, establishing a winning attack or securing a swift checkmate). One such sacrifice is so common that it has a name: the Greek gift (the name derives from the Greek legend of the wooden horse that contained an invading army, unwittingly taken into the city of Troy by its inhabitants). In chess, a Greek gift is the sacrifice of a bishop on h7 (if played by White) in front of a castled king.

In this position, the material is level, but White has better scope for the pieces. Black's king looks secure

Left: White plays Bxh7, the Greek gift sacrifice, surrendering his bishop to drive Black's king out into the open.

from the point of view of the row of pawns in front of it, but otherwise it is quite hard to cover a possible attack. White, to play, could try 1 Ng5 to create a double attack on the vulnerable h7 pawn. This is quite good, but Black can perhaps defend with 1...g6, which blocks the scope of the bishop on d3. However, White spots a chance to unleash the Greek gift sacrifice and plays 1 Bxh7+!

Black now has two options: to accept the sacrifice with 1...Kxh7, or to decline it with 1...Kh8. If Black declines the sacrifice, playing 1...Kh8, White will follow up with 2 Ng5 and then, after Black's next move, 3 Qh5 will threaten mate on h7. Black could try something like 2...f6 and, following 3 Qh5, play 3...fxg5, but after 4 Bg6+ there is no escape for Black's king. If Black plays 1...Kxh7, White will follow up with 2 Ng5+.

If Black retreats with 2...Kg8, White plays 3 Qh5, threatening checkmate with Qh7 on the next move. In fact this is virtually the end, as Black has to surrender the queen for the knight on g5 to avoid checkmate – with a

queen for bishop and knight (that's 9 points for 3 + 3 = 6), White will be winning. If Black plays 2...Kg6, it is not so straightforward, but after 3 Qd3+, the black king is exposed to a withering attack from the white pieces.

Here is an example line: 3...f5 (blocking the attack) 4 exf6+ (the e5 pawn takes the f5 pawn *en passant*) Kxf6 5 Qf3+ Ke7 (Black tries to defend the rook on f8, which would otherwise be skewered) 6 Re1+ Kd6 7 Qxf8+.

The game has turned into a rout. White is now material up and still attacking the king. If Black plays 7...Kc7, White wins material with 8 Rxe8 Qf6 9 Bf4+ d6 10 Ne6+ Kd7 11 Qg8 when Black has lost a rook and a pawn, while if 7...Kxd5, White plays 8 Nc3+ Kc6 9 Rxe8 and Black's exposed king will not last long. The Greek gift sacrifice is a lovely way to finish a game.

DEFENDING THE KING

A good strategy when it comes to defending the king in the opening or middlegame is to castle. The idea of castling is to relocate the king to a position where it will not get embroiled in the hand-to-hand fighting in the middlegame. Indeed, the middlegame is usually the province of the major pieces (queens and rooks), minor pieces (bishops and knights) and the pawns.

In practice, it is not usually wise to castle to a side of the board where the pawn cover has disappeared or where the enemy forces have built up in a menacing fashion. The king prefers a quiet sector where it can ride out the storm, perhaps joining the fray later when the forces on the board have reduced down to a pair of minor pieces and some pawns on each side.

As well as pawns, the king may need defensive help from at least one piece.

The position in the above diagram is identical to the first one on the previous page used to demonstrate a direct attack on the king, but with two differences – the white pawn on e5 and the black pawn on d7 have been removed. This makes a big difference to the black king's defensive possibilities.

If White were now to attempt a direct attack on the black king with 1 Bxh7+, the chances of success would be slim. Black captures 1...Kxh7 and after 2 Ng5+, retreats with 2...Kg8. If now 3 Qh5, Black can now play 3...Nf6!, attacking the queen and, more importantly, defending against the threat of Qh7 mate.

Black has solved all his problems, and has a material advantage of bishop for one pawn. Looking again at the position at the top of the page, we can see that the row of pawns in front of the king is still an important defensive barrier, but that the potential of the knight on e8 to come to f6 to bolster the defence of the black king makes all the difference in resisting the Greek gift sacrifice.

The diagram above shows a typical castled king set up, with a knight on f3 providing a double defence to the h2 pawn. It is often a good idea to consider the king's safety before making a move, and perhaps count the defenders to the pawn barrier in front of the king. In the diagram below left, we can see that the f2 pawn is defended by rook and king, and h2 by knight and king. The g2 pawn is the weakest point in this particular set-up, because it is only defended by the king. An attack could come down the g-file in the shape of a rook or queen, and could be supported by (for example) a knight on f4.

The diagram (right) shows a very similar configuration, except that the g-pawn has advanced to g3. The f2 and h2 pawns are defended exactly as they were in the previous example, but now White is better defended against an attack down the g-file because the g3 pawn is doubly defended by the pawns on the adjoining flanks. However, there are also potential disadvantages to this set-up. Black could locate a piece on h3, for example a queen or a bishop. If Black could also generate a threat along the a8–h1 diagonal, the undefended knight could be driven away from f3 and black could threaten a checkmate on g2.

Both the above examples show castled kings that are likely to be reasonably safe in many positions – and both are certainly better than having a totally exposed

king – but the truth is that no king can ever be totally impregnable, no matter how defensive the set-up. It depends entirely on the specific position on the board. When playing against an unwary defender, creative attacking players can always unlock the key to the defence.

Below: The king needs plenty of defenders around it to ensure its safety in the middlegame. In the endgame, when the two armies are much reduced, it can be a good time to bring the king out of hiding and use it to attack.

PAWN WEAKNESS

Although it is true to say that all pawns start the game having an equal value to each other, individual pawns can become weaker than others if they become separated from their colleagues, stuck in front of each other (as the result of a capture), or become blocked on a square where they cannot be supported by a fellow pawn.

Above, these three pawns are undefended, but if attacked from the front they can at least move into a defended position. For example, if a rook further up the b-file were to attack the pawn on b2, it could advance to b3 where it would be adequately defended by its colleagues on a2 and c2. Similarly, if the a2 pawn were to be attacked by a rook along the a-file, it could advance to a3 and be defended by the pawn on b2.

The above situation is more problematic for the pawns. If an enemy rook reaches the second rank (or the seventh rank from its original rank), it can be highly effective in threatening to capture a line of pawns on their original squares. If the c2 pawn moves out of the

way, Black can capture the b2 pawn that stands beyond it. For this reason, a rook on the seventh (as it is known) can be a potent attacking weapon in chess.

Doubled pawns

After captures, it is possible for pawns to become 'doubled', i.e. two pawns of the same colour on the same file.

In this position, Black (to play) can capture the knight on c3, and White can recapture with the b2 pawn, thus: 1...Nxc3 2 bxc3.

The pawns on c2 and c3 are called doubled pawns. Note that the pawn on c3 impedes the progress of the pawn on c2. Note also that they are now incapable of defending each other from capture. In fact, all three pawns shown in the diagram above are now incapable of defending each other (unless, for example, one of them has a later opportunity to effect a capture and thus move to the b-file). For this reason, double pawns are usually considered a weakness. The only incidental advantage that could accrue from pawns being doubled is that it can open a file to allow major pieces to advance upon the enemy or attack an important square on the other side of the board.

In this diagram, with White to play, a quick count shows that the material situation is exactly equal. However, Black has a pair of doubled pawns on c7 and c6. It may later be possible to effect an exchange so that they can be undoubled but it is not easy to achieve. Meanwhile, on the other side of the board, four white pawns face three black pawns. There is a serious danger that, after three pawns have been exchanged, White may be left with one passed pawn that could even promote to a queen one day. This is all very long-term strategy, but gives some idea of the problems that can accrue from doubled pawns.

Backward pawns

In the next diagram, the pawn on b2 is what's known as a 'backward' pawn. It is called this because it lags behind the adjacent pawns and cannot easily advance. If it goes to b3, either black pawn can capture – and if it goes straight to b4, they can still capture it, *en passant* (on the first move after the move b4 is played), so it does not have a rosy future. Another aspect to this position is that the two black pawns are effectively tying up three of their adversaries. If the material were

equal – and let's suppose the third black pawn were somewhere on the kingside, Black could be considered to be virtually a pawn up. As things stand, the pawn on b2 would hardly count for the usual one point attributed to a pawn.

WEAK PAWNS DROP OFF

Chess players are fond of saying that 'weak pawns drop off' – and few pawns are as weak as backward pawns. In the diagram below, the pawn on b2 is a backward pawn. It is performing a small service (defending the a3 pawn) but otherwise is particularly vulnerable because it cannot move without falling victim to a capture (*en passant* or otherwise) on b3. The bishop on d4 menaces it and there is nothing to be done. Once it falls, the blockaded a3 pawn will soon follow.

PAWN STRENGTHS

We have already seen that the strongest pawn is what we call a passed pawn – and that the one thing better than a passed pawn is two passed pawns, preferably connected. Now we consider what we need to do to transform an ordinary pawn (or pawns) into the extra-special passed variety.

In the above position, it is clear that White has an extra pawn, so the basic strategy here might be to exchange two pairs of pawns so that White's one remaining pawn will become a passed pawn and eventually advance to the queening square. The extra pawn seems to be the a-pawn, so there may be a temptation to advance it one square towards promotion – 1 a5.

However, this is an error here if the objective is to create a single passed pawn. After 1 a5, White cannot advance either the a-pawn or b-pawn without loss. The correct move to start with would be 1 b5, offering a pawn exchange. Were Black to play anything other than an exchange of pawns (let's assume the presence of kings somewhere remote from this action), White could play 2 bxc6, forcing 2...bxc6, at which point the a-pawn is a passed pawn with nothing between it and the queening square.

Above: After 1 b5 and 2 bxc6 bxc6, White's a-pawn is unimpeded.

If Black replies to 1 b5 with 1...cxb5 2 axb5, we reach this position:

Now White can create a passed pawn next move with 3 c6 and, after the exchange of pawns, White will have a passed pawn on c6.

Creating unstoppable passed pawns

Exceptionally, it can be possible to create an unstoppable passed pawn, even though equal numbers of pawns confront each other.

In the above diagram, White is to play. On the face of it, things look equal, with level material and three pawns apiece apparently blocking each others' path to their respective queening squares. However, there are two points to note about this position: (a) White's pawns are much nearer to their queening squares; and (b) if White can create a passed pawn quickly, Black's king will be too far away from the action to stop the passed pawn. White can now force a black pawn through to become a queen at the price of giving up (or sacrificing) the other two (a very small price to pay for a new queen). White plays 1 b6!.

The b-pawn can be captured by either the a-pawn or the c-pawn. Black has to capture because otherwise the white b-pawn will itself capture one of the two pawns and promote on the next move. Let's say Black plays 1...cxb6. White replies 2 a6!.

Black, who now has doubled b-pawns, is again confronted with two possible captures. If Black takes the c5 pawn with 2...bxc5, it is easy to see that White will reply 3 axb7 and promote to a queen on the next move. In order to slow White's progress Black tries 2...bxa6. White plays 3 c6!.

Something extraordinary has now happened. White has sacrificed two pawns in order to gain one passed pawn on c6. This pawn can no longer be stopped from queening in two more moves. Black cannot get across to stop it with the king, and Black's own pawns are still five moves from queening. The new queen will mop up the three pawns very quickly and win the game.

Note that it makes no difference if, on move one, Black decides to capture the b6 pawn with his a-pawn. Thus, 1 b6 axb6, and now White plays the same trick, this time with the c-pawn: 2 c6!.

This is a mirror image of the problems that Black had in the other line of play. If Black plays 2...bxc6, then White plays 3 a6! – and once again wins easily. In both cases there is absolutely nothing Black can do to prevent the creation of a passed pawn and, in consequence, certain defeat. Take time to learn the techniques shown here; they will serve you well.

PIECES WORKING TOGETHER

We have seen various middlegame stratagems in isolation, but here is an opportunity to see how they all fit together in a real competition chess game played between strong amateur players. We are only going to look at the middle part of the game, concentrating on a remarkable combination found by Black.

A combination is a planned tactical sequence of moves. In this example, Black sees about seven moves ahead, by which we mean pairs of moves, one each by White and Black. Non-chess players are sometimes interested in the number of moves that chess players can see ahead. The answer is that it varies, depending on the complexity of the position. Sometimes it is possible to see as many as ten moves ahead, or even more; at other times, two moves ahead is difficult to evaluate. Black is to move. The material is level, with two pairs of pawns

having been exchanged. A couple of captures are possible (1...Bxa4 and 1...Nxd3) but only lead to level exchanges. Note how well defended the pieces and pawns are. The only undefended pawn on the board is Black's pawn on d6, but it is not currently vulnerable to capture.

In this position, Black conceives an idea that starts with a sacrifice that opens up a file, involves an exchange of knight for bishop to open up a long diagonal, a skewer leading to another exchange, and finally a decisive exploitation of a possible pin along the a7–g1 diagonal. This is quite a lot to see ahead. It may seem totally beyond you at first, but don't despair: it's not as hard as it sounds. The key thing is to keep in mind the tactical manoeuvres mentioned above and look for ways you can engineer them. Try to understand the logical sequence of the following combination.

| 1 | ... | Nxd5! |

Black sacrifices a knight for a pawn. It takes a while before the reason for this becomes clear, but the general idea is to open the e-file (after White plays 2 exd5) and also give the bishop on g7 some scope along the a1–h8 long diagonal.

| 2 | exd5 | Nxd3 |
| 3 | Qxd3 | Bb5 |

Strictly speaking, this is not a skewer (because it simply leads to the exchange of the b5 bishop for the e2 knight), but the ultimate effect is equally devastating. It should already be becoming clearer that Black's pieces (the two bishops and the e8 rook) have open lines of attack, while White's pieces are slightly 'offside'. In particular, the knight on a4 is poorly posted. Although it is defended by the rook on a1, it has no squares to go to from a4. Knights on the edge of the board are usually less effective than when they are placed somewhere nearer the middle of the board. White now has to move the white queen away from the attack of the black bishop.

4   Qd2   Bxe2 | 5   Qxe2   ...

This is the position that Black foresaw when 1...Nxd5 was played. Black spotted the very powerful pin on the bishop on e3 against the queen on e2. This made the bishop very vulnerable. In fact, Black could have exploited this immediately by playing 5...Bd4,

---

ANOTHER EXAMPLE

♛ ♝ ♞ ♜

Here, we can see how four pieces can work together effectively to defend each other.

---

which would win the bishop on e3 – but Black found something more powerful still.

5   ...   Rxe3!

Black captures the bishop, which means that the material balance has swung in favour of Black, who is now a pawn up. White, who by this point is struggling to survive, should probably have run away now with the queen, but dared instead to capture the undefended rook.

6   Qxe3   Bd4!

Black pins the queen against the king. White captured the bishop with the white queen, which was immediately taken off by the pawn on c5. This left Black with queen and pawn (9 + 1 = 10) for rook and knight (5 + 3 = 8) – two points down on material, and with a lost position. Though the result is not a foregone conclusion in a game between beginners, Black was soon able to convert the extra material into a win.

THE ENDGAME: SUFFICIENT MATERIAL

The term 'endgame' refers to the final phase of a game after many of the pieces have disappeared from the board. It is worth noting that not all chess games reach a true endgame: many conclude with a checkmate in the middlegame when there are still many pieces on the board.

Sometimes there are so few pieces on the board that checkmate cannot be achieved. Such a game can be abandoned as a draw. In competition chess, the arbiter would declare the game a draw. The most obvious is bare king versus bare king.

As it is not possible for one king to checkmate another, the game is a draw.

The same applies if one player has only one bishop or one knight left with the king. On their own they cannot effect a mate, so the game is drawn.

Above, Black has to move out of check, but White cannot force checkmate whatever Black plays. As for knights, a player cannot even force checkmate with two knights and king versus a king.

Despite Black's apparent entrapment in the corner, White cannot force checkmate. 1 Nc7+ Kb8 2 Na6+ Ka8 and now any move of the knight on d6 would result in stalemate. It is possible for Black to be checkmated but only by incompetent defence.

A single rook or queen with a king is sufficient material to force checkmate, and it is also possible to checkmate with two bishops, or with one bishop and one knight. A single pawn with a king is sufficient material to win, but only if it is possible to promote the pawn to a queen or rook. Positions tend to be drawn if the king of the player with the extra pawn is behind the pawn, and the defending king is able to stop the king supporting the pawn from in front. A typical example appears below. It shows optimum play by both players.

1   Kd4   Kd6!

White's first move aims to outflank the black king, get to d5 and then shepherd the pawn through. Black must confront the white king with his own king.

2   e5+   Ke6   3   Ke4   Kd7

Black has to give ground but it is not critical at this stage.

4   Kd5   Ke7!

Black must stop the white king from getting in front of the white pawn, so Black has to play the king to e7.

5   e6   ...

Black must play his king back to e8 to get the draw.

5	**...**	**Ke8!**	**7**	**e7+**	**Ke8**
6	**Kd6**	**Kd8**			

Now, if White plays 8 Ke6 it is stalemate and if he plays anything else, Black takes the e7 pawn. So it is a draw. However, going back to the previous diagram, if Black plays 5...Kd8??, this is what happens.

5   ...   Kd8??
6   Kd6   Ke8
7   e7   ...

We have reached the same position as above but with a different player to move. Now it is Black's turn. He must play 7...Kf7, allowing 8 Kd7 and White promotes the pawn on the following move. So this time Black loses.

SIMPLE ENDGAME STRATEGY

One very important thing about endgame strategy is that the king becomes a fighting piece. After keeping out of the battle for much of the middlegame, the king emerges to play an important role in the game once the two armies have become depleted. This is particularly true in endgames with pawns and no other pieces (or king and pawn endgames). The king should head towards the centre of the action, getting involved in the creation of passed pawns or standing in the way of enemy pawns as they advance towards the queening square.

In the case of king and pawn versus king: if the attacking king can get in front of a single pawn, then it can often steer it home to promotion.

Here the move 1 e5? would be a bad move, allowing Black to draw with best play. Instead, White can win by getting the black king in front of the pawn. Let's first consider the *wrong* way to proceed.

1   Kd5?   Kd7!

Now White cannot make progress. If the king moves to one side, Black can move his king in the same direction, which means he will be once again confronting the king. White cannot gain ground.

From the original diagram, White should play thus:

1   Ke5!   ...

The kings oppose each other along the same file, but Black is obliged to move. In chess parlance, White is said to 'have the opposition', meaning that the player to move has to give ground with the king. Whichever way the king goes, White can gain ground with his own king.

| **1** | **...** | **Kd7** | **3** | **e5** | **Kf8** |
| **2** | **Kf6!** | **Ke8** | | | |

After White moves the pawn, Black has to give more ground.

4	e6!	Ke8
5	e7	...

Black now has to move away from the pawn's queening square.

5	...	Kd7
6	Kf7	Kd6
7	e8Q	...

White has duly queened the pawn and now has to win a queen and king versus king endgame. The strategy is fairly straightforward. The king needs to be corralled towards the edge of the board with the queen, using the king as necessary. Once there, it can be checkmated quite easily.

7	...	Kd5

Black tries to make things a bit more difficult by getting as near to the centre of the board as possible. This is the best defensive tactic when left with a bare king in the endgame.

8	Qa4	...

Queen and pawn endgames can be like sheepdog trials! The queen ('dog') boxes off the king's escape routes, pushing it in the direction of its own king ('shepherd').

8	...	Ke5	10	Qb5	...
9	Qc4	Kd6			

To avoid stalemate, make sure that the opposition king always has at least one legal move available.

10	...	Kc7	12	Kd6	Kd8
11	Ke7	Kc8			

White has a choice of checkmates: 13 Qd7# or 13 Qb8#.

MORE ENDGAME STRATEGY

Checkmating with the rook and the king against the opponent's king is similar to the checkmating technique using the queen and the king but it takes just a little bit longer to effect. Using the same example as previously, but this time promoting the pawn to a rook, we reach this position.

Once again the defensive technique for Black will be to stay as close to the centre of the board for as long as possible.

1	...	Kd5		4	Rd8+	Ke4
2	Rc8	Kd6		5	Rd6	...
3	Kf6	Kd5				

It is still not entirely clear where White's strategy is leading, but White is gradually limiting the black king's scope.

5	...	Kf4		7	Kf5	Ke3
6	Rd4+	Kf3				

The defending king in a rook endgame as compared with a queen endgame has the advantage that it can approach the rook on a diagonal and harass it to some extent. However, the rook can keep it cut off just as easily as a queen along ranks and files.

8	Rd6	Kf3		9	Rd3+	...

The white rook and attacking white king work together to herd the black king towards the edge of the board.

9	...	Ke2		12	Kf4	Kf2
10	Ke4	Kf2		13	Re4	...
11	Re3	Kg2				

Using the 'opposition' concept, White plays a move with the rook so that Black has to cede ground.

| 13 | ... | Kg2 | 14 | Re2+ | ... |

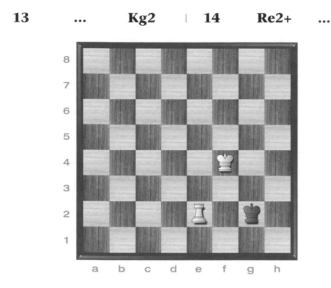

If Black now plays 14...Kh3, White can play a 'pass' move with the white rook, e.g. 15 Rd2, and Black has to play 15...Kh4, allowing 16 Rh2# – checkmate. Black can last two moves longer as follows.

14	...	Kf1	17	Kg3	Kg1
15	Kf3	Kg1	18	Ra1#	
16	Ra2	Kh1			

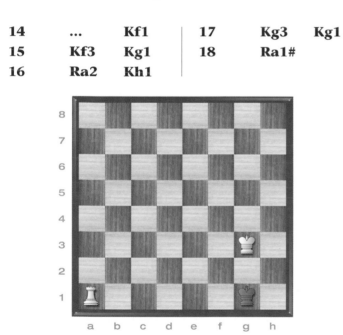

King and Rook Pawn Endings

In king and pawn endgames, we have seen how it can often be possible to force through a pawn to promotion when the attacking king gets in front of the pawn to support its advance. However, there is no forced win in the case of a-pawns or h-pawns (which chess players refer to as rook pawns because they stand in front of rooks in the starting position) as long as the defending king has access to the potential queening square – and sometimes even when it doesn't.

This position is drawn whatever White tries.

| 1 | Ka6 | Kb8 | 2 | Kb6 | Ka8 |

Black simply shuffles the king between a8 and b8.

| 3 | a5 | Kb8 | 4 | a6 | Ka8 |

Now 5 a7 is stalemate.

In the example above, Black plays Kc7 and then back to c8. The white king is boxed in on a7 and a8. It is a draw.

127

GENERAL TIPS ABOUT PLAY

It is important to know the general etiquette and rules of chess. For example, what happens if you have a lapse of concentration and inadvertently make an illegal move? What do you do if a piece not quite on its square keeps catching your eye and distracting you? In both cases there is a formal procedure to follow.

Illegal moves

During the first few games you play, you can expect to make the occasional illegal move. If you or your opponent (or, in a formal chess competition, the arbiter) notices the illegality, the rule is that you should return to the position immediately before the illegality occurred and the player making the illegal move replace it with a legal one. However, the 'touch-piece-move' rule applies.

Let's suppose White has a complete aberration in this position and moves the bishop on c1 to f5. This is an illegal move. Either now or after a few moves, one of the players realizes that an illegal move has been played. The correct procedure would be for the position in the diagram be set up again and that White, having touched the bishop, is obliged to make a move with it. So White has five legal moves with the c1 bishop to choose from. Should an illegal move not be spotted until several moves after it was made, the original position before that move should be reinstated. It can be difficult if the move is not spotted immediately.

Right: Black tries to advance the rook-pawn but White calls a halt. Black's king is in check from the queen on b2 so, although the pawn has been touched, the king has to be moved instead in order to escape the check.

In the above position, Black tries to play the move 1...Bg4. This is illegal because his king is in check. Therefore, Black has to retract the bishop move and replace it with a move that gets out of check. If possible, Black is also obliged to move the bishop that has already been touched. As it happens, the move 1...Bd7 is possible with the bishop, to block the check, so that is the only legal move in this position. Rather luckily for Black, it is also a good move.

Black, to play, is oblivious to the check against the black king and tries to play 1...Qd6. This is illegal and must be replaced with a legal move, with the piece that was originally touched, if possible. Unfortunately for Black, the move 1...Qd7 is the only legal move using the touched queen. It must be played and no doubt White will capture the luckless queen.

In this position, White has just played the terrible move 1 Bb5+. In reply, Black plays the equally terrible 1...dxe4. But, luckily for Black, it is also illegal: Black is in check. When obliged to replace this with something legal, Black finds that no legal move of the touched d-pawn is possible to escape check. The touch-piece-move obligation becomes void, and Black is free to play any legal move to get out of check. Black finally notices that Black can improve on the previous try and plays 1...axb5!, winning the bishop. It may seem rather arbitrary that some illegal moves are positively rewarded while others harshly punished – but, as in life, crime on the chessboard can sometimes pay.

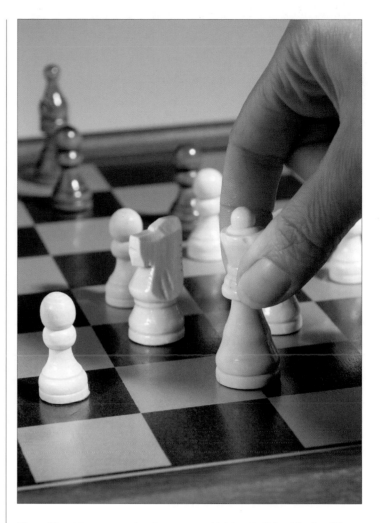

Above: The white queen overlaps two squares, which is potentially misleading. Either player on their turn can reposition the piece, but they must advise their opponent first.

Even in informal games, it is a good idea to observe the rule about the touching of pieces, so as to get into a good habit of thinking carefully before making decisions. In formal competitions, even among schoolchildren, the rule is strictly enforced. Note that it does not apply if you accidentally touch a piece, or knock a piece over.

Repositioning

Occasionally the situation arises when the pieces are not neatly set up on the board. For example, in making a move, a player may have put a piece on the border between two squares. This can sometimes make it difficult to know which square a piece is actually on. In such circumstances – so long as it is your turn to move – you should advise your opponent that you are going to adjust the positioning of a piece. You are then free to go ahead and reposition the piece without penalty. Chess players often do this by using the French phrase *J'adoube*, which means 'I adjust'.

CHAPTER THREE:

BEYOND THE BASICS

If you have read and absorbed everything in the previous chapter, you should now know enough to be able to play an enjoyable game of chess with your friends, read a chess book or article, or play through a published chess game, and understand what is going on. If not, it would be a good idea to play some games and perhaps read a newspaper column about chess before reading any further, to gain a bit of experience before embarking on this last lap of your journey. At this stage, you may find that you lose more games than you win. Don't worry. Now you are going to learn not just how to play, but how to win. One of the most enjoyable and rewarding ways to achieve chess prowess is by looking at games played by world champions. We shall be looking at some of their masterpieces in this chapter.

Right: After the queen, the rook is the second most powerful piece on the chessboard. Although called the 'rook' in English, it known as the 'tower' in French, German and Spanish.

PLAY BETTER CHESS

Now that we are through the basic rules of the game, the order in which you read this book is less significant. In fact, now is a very good time to browse later pages of the book that deal with expanding your horizons and choosing chess-playing software, or a chess computer. As the man in the street said to the lady who asked him 'How do I get to the Carnegie Hall?' – 'You gotta practise!' It is simply not possible to transmit the benefit of regular practice via the pages of a book. Playing and studying must go in tandem.

Digital opponents

Ideally, you need to be playing someone who is a bit further advanced than you are, but not too much. Playing a much stronger player would not be sensible in terms of competition or encouragement, although he or she might be persuaded to treat it as a tutorial and show you where you are going wrong. Computer software, or Internet play, is a good idea from the point of view of convenience, but it is inadvisable to play too often against computers. For one thing, playing with an inanimate (or remote) opponent is a bit lonely and unsociable. For another, bear in mind that the latest chess software programs play chess of a phenomenally high standard.

There are many inexpensive software programs available for purchase that are more than capable of holding their own with the world chess champion in a quick game, so they will be vastly too good for you and me. But don't be discouraged, because it is still interesting trying to figure out how the computer wins. Further, it is a wonderful experience when you play your first human opponent after a long series of depressing digital defeats – and you see this person make a mistake.

Below: Ten-year-olds play chess during their school chess lesson, in Stroebeck, Germany. Stroebeck has the only school in Germany where chess is a compulsory subject for every student. The tradition of playing chess at the school is nearly 200 years old.

Above: Chess is not only a game for all ages but is also one you can play almost anywhere, enjoying hours of fun in doing so. It can be very beneficial to play with a more advanced player – you may not win but you will learn more about the game.

Right: It may look small but modern-day software is so advanced that even a hand-held chess computer such as this can beat most players with ease. Even great chess masters have been beaten by today's computer software.

One peculiar advantage of chess software – that it does not snigger when it wins – is sometimes cited, but this is not strictly true. Be warned, some PC-based chess software is programmed to give verbal commentary during play. This usually consists of desperate attempts at humour and is valueless. It is advisable to find out how to switch off your computer's sound facilities during play.

Principle number one: there are no principles

Now that we have progressed beyond the basic rules and general principles of the game, here is another rule of thumb that is worth absorbing – be sceptical of general principles. That includes any such principles you may read in this book. General principles exist for guidance, but should not be slavishly adhered to. Much of the aesthetic beauty in chess occurs when general principles are turned on their head; for example, a position where a pawn is more valuable than a queen. General principles always have to be weighed against a pragmatic and objective assessment of the actual position on the board. The ability to judge

when general principles do not apply comes with experience and is the essence of chess wisdom. But it is a good idea to follow your instincts in playing moves right from the start. Your judgement may be wrong, but the resultant defeat will teach you a valuable lesson.

Time is a key factor in chess. Competition chess is played with clocks, but in informal chess you have as long as you like to think about your moves. However, it is usually a mistake to spend too long over these in your first games of chess – 20 or 30 seconds is plenty.

INTERMEDIATE OPENING STRATEGY

Although the keynote to many chess openings is the occupation of the centre, it can be just as useful to control the centre from a distance. Generally speaking, many of the openings that involve occupation of the centre were developed before the 20th century but, since then, chess masters have developed a more pragmatic approach to opening play. Here are various strategies for opening the game.

Previously, chess experts could be very dogmatic about the 'right' way to play the opening, but nowadays leading players often take the view that whatever seems to work in practice is good. Here is an example:

1	d4	Nf6
2	c4	g6
3	Nc3	Bg7
4	e4	d6
5	Nf3	0-0

If we survey the position, we can see that White has fully occupied the centre with pawns, and is controlling the d5 and e5 squares. Black, on the other hand, has sat back and apparently given White free rein in the centre.

You might conclude that this is a poor opening for Black. In fact, it is regarded as a very respectable one, and has been played by stellar players such as Bobby Fischer and Garry Kasparov. The reason is that, on the basis of many thousands of games played in this opening, White has never been able to prove that this central control necessarily leads to a tangible advantage. Black's pieces are set up rather passively, but there is no obvious way for White's pawns to advance, or for White's pieces to reach squares, such that an attack on the king or other advantage will accrue.

This opening is called the 'King's Indian Defence'. The word 'Indian' in this context is an allusion to the old Indian form of the game, where the pieces were characteristically positioned as in the part-diagram below, with the knight on f6 and the pawn moved to g6 to allow the bishop to come to g7. The 'King' component of the name indicates that the 'Indian' configuration is on the kingside of the board.

When a bishop is moved one square from its original position to one of the board's long diagonals (a1–h8 or h1–a8) in this way, it is referred to as a *fianchetto* (this term is used as a noun or verb). This is an Italian word meaning 'little flank'. There is a large family of openings in which one or both of the players *fianchetto* bishops – these are sometimes referred to as 'flank openings'.

Black's underlying strategy in this opening is to allow White to dominate the centre but then to launch a counter-attack from the flank. The black pawns are held in reserve, waiting for the right moment to strike. For White, the temptation is to push forward too far until a seemingly impregnable centre becomes overstretched. In some variations, Black probes on the queenside, starting with the pawn thrust c5. More often, Black looks to move the knight on f6 to e8 or h5, paving the way for f5 and a pawn storm if White castles kingside. Defence, in this position, can very swiftly turn into attack. Returning to the game position, one possible continuation could be as follows:

6 Be2 Nbd7

7 0-0 e5

8 d5 ...

The important thing to note here is that the central pawns are locked together, which rather restricts the movement of the major and minor pieces. This is referred to as a 'closed position'. Such positions usually require a long sequence of patient and subtle manoeuvring in order to open the position up for tactical action. As such, this sort of opening is not very suitable for play between beginners and elementary players. It is better to start with openings that allow more scope for the pieces, in order to learn and practise tactical chess. For now, it is enough to know that such openings exist, and that Black's passive-looking

Queen's Indian Defence

There is also an opening called the 'Queen's Indian Defence'. In it, Black *fianchettoes* a bishop on the queenside. Typical opening moves are:

1	d4	Nf6
2	c4	e6
3	Nf3	b6
4	g3	Bb7
5	Bg2	Be7

Note that both White and Black have *fianchettoed* a bishop (White on g2 and Black on b7).

opening strategy is by no means mistaken. However, looking again at the diagram after 8 d5, it is worth considering what Black's plan might be in this position. One idea is to play 8...Nc5, which attacks the white pawn on e4. After White defends it (with a move such as 9 Qc2), it would then be a good idea to play 9...a5, which prevents White from playing 10 b4 to chase the knight back to its previous position. Another idea for Black in this sort of position is to drop the f6 knight back with 8...Ne8, and follow up with 9...f5 to undermine the white pawn on e4.

THE RUY LÓPEZ

Perhaps the most famous of chess openings is the one that is named after the famous Spanish chess-playing priest Ruy López de Segura (*c.*1530–1580), who was one of the best players of his time and the author of an early book on the game. The opening is also sometimes referred to as 'The Spanish Game'.

The initial moves that give this opening its name are as follows:

1	e4	e5
2	Nf3	Nc6
3	Bb5	...

The last move played, 3 Bb5, is the signature move of the Ruy López opening. White threatens to capture the knight on c6 (4 Bxc6), thus removing the only defender of the pawn on e5 and allowing its capture with 5 Nxe5.

However, over the course of several hundred years, chess players have worked out that this threat is superficial. Black can usually recapture a pawn if White follows through with this rather crude threat. So, Black often plays a move designed to attack the bishop or to encourage it to capture the knight anyway.

3	...	a6

This is by no means the only move for Black in this position. Other possibilities are 3...Nf6, 3...f5, 3...Bc5, 3...d6 and 3...Nd4. All of these moves are respectable and lead to quite different positions from those that generally occur after 3...a6. It is important to know that chess openings are multi-layered – there are openings within openings (known as variations) – and

some of these variations have quite different sub-variations. It is not necessary to know all the variations and sub-variations in order to play an opening, but it is important to keep an open mind when your opponent appears to depart from what you might have read in books. Just because a move is unorthodox, it doesn't mean it is bad.

4	Ba4	...

This is the most common continuation in competitive chess. But some players prefer to capture on c6: 4 Bxc6 dxc6. Now it is a good idea to develop normally, with a move such as 5 0-0. However, it is a waste of time to play 5 Nxe5? because Black replies 5...Qd4, simultaneously attacking the knight and the pawn on e4. After White moves the knight, Black can recapture the pawn with 6...Qxe4+ and the position is equal. White, having the first move, should strive for something a little better than equality from the opening.

4	...	Nf6

5   O-O   ...

This time it is White's turn to allow the capture of a pawn. Once again, Black can take it or leave it: both variations are regarded as respectable.

5   ...   Be7

Black continues with a quiet, developing move. But 5...Nxe4 is perfectly playable. Then there follows something like 6 d4 b5 7 Bb3 d5 8 dxe5 Be6 9 c3 Bc5, when the material is level and both players have some open lines for their pieces. This is a good line for elementary and intermediate level players to try out.

6   Re1   b5
7   Bb3   d6

8   c3   O-O

9   h3   Na5
10   Bc2   c5
11   d4   ...

Quite a complex position has arisen, with pawns challenging each other in the centre. The position can become closed (if White soon opts to play d5, for example). If there is a major pawn exchange, the game can open up for the bishops and rooks to become active.

The possibilities and complexities of the Ruy López opening have fascinated chess players for many hundreds of years, and it has also been one of the most fashionable openings in top competition. One of its attractions is that it suits elementary level play as well as it does top grandmaster play. The ideas behind the opening are fairly easy to grasp and conform to most general principles. From White's point of view it offers a slight and enduring edge, while from Black's point of view it is solid and contests the centre of the board in a positive manner.

THE SICILIAN DEFENCE

Until perhaps 50 years ago, the most common reply to White's first move of 1 e4 was 1...e5, but in the modern era, the move 1...c5 has become more common. This is the move that gives the name to the 'Sicilian Defence' (often shortened to 'The Sicilian'). The name of the defence is taken from the homeland of a 17th-century player named Pietro Carrera, who first mentioned it in his chess writings. It was known and appreciated several centuries ago, but only really came into its own in the 20th century.

1	e4	c5

One of the significant aspects of 1...c5 is that it avoids the symmetry that can follow after 1...e5. The pawn on c5 controls the d4 square just as a pawn on e5 would do, but leaves the central situation slightly more flexible.

2	Nf3	...

This is by far the most common second move for White, just as it is against 1...e5. It is a good developing move. However, there are other reasonable options for White. One is 2 Nc3, often followed by g3 and Bg2. This is known as the 'Closed Sicilian', as play tends to be cagey after the pawns become locked. Another option is 2 c3, where White plans to advance 3 d4 and, if the pawn is captured (3...cxd4), replace it with another pawn (4 cxd4) in order to have a pair of pawns occupying the centre.

One of the attractions of the Sicilian for both colours is the sheer multiplicity of options available. After 2 Nf3, the Sicilian Defence subdivides into three major variations that themselves subdivide further into many different sub-variations. There is only room here to give a flavour of the possibilities, which will be

perfectly sufficient to play elementary chess. At the higher levels of the game, it becomes important to know some opening theory in depth, but at the lower levels it is not necessary to spend time memorizing specific lines.

2	...	Nc6

2...d6 and 2...e6 are very common and equally reasonable alternatives. In fact, 2...d6 is the most common move of all in this position. A common continuation is 3 d4 cxd4 4 Nxd4 Nf6 5 Nc3 g6 6 Be3 Bg7 7 f3 0-0 8 Qd2 Nc6 9 Bc4 Bd7 10 0-0-0.

This variation is known as the 'Sicilian Dragon' because it is thought that Black's piece configuration is similar in aspect to the constellation Draco. Let's look at how the game might progress after the move 2...Nc6.

3	d4

White could play 3 Bb5 (as in the Ruy López), but the n next move is the most common, seeking to open lines and uncover attacking possibilities. But, if Black then played 3...a6, 4 Ba4?? would be a blunder: 4...b5 5 Bb3 c4 and the bishop is lost.

3 ... cxd4
4 Nxd4 Nf6

5 Nc3 d6
6 Bg5 e6

It might appear that Black is playing slightly more passively than White. It is true that White has slightly more space (or freedom to manoeuvre) but the two black pawns on d6 and e6 still control important centre squares.

7 Qd2 Be7

White now decides to castle queenside, but this is not obligatory. 8 f4 is also possible. 8 Be2 may be not so good because Black could play 8...Nxe4 9 Nxe4 Bxg5 10 Nxg5 Nxd4 11 Qxd4 Qxg5 12 Qxd6 Bd7 13 Bf3 0-0-0 when the position may slightly favour Black.

Right: Geographical Map of Sicily by Pietro da Cortona. Homeland of the 17th-century player Pietro Carrera, the region gives its name to the Sicilian Defence, which Carrera was the first to mention in his writings.

8 0-0-0 0-0

This position is roughly equal but imbalanced because the players have castled on opposite sides of the board. This can be very significant in the middlegame. With the white king tucked away safely on the queenside, White can attack the black king on the kingside by advancing the pawns there without danger to his own However, Black can do the same thing – attack the white king on the queenside by advancing pawns, thus a6, b5 and then b4 to attack the knight on c3.

THE NIMZO-INDIAN DEFENCE

The name of the 'Nimzo-Indian Defence' (or 'Nimzowitsch-Indian Defence') is partly a tribute to a great chess player, and partly a misnomer. The Latvian player Aron Nimzowitsch (1886–1935) was one of the greatest-ever chess theorists and also a very fine player, being a close rival of the world champions of the 1920s and 1930s, José Raúl Capablanca and Alexander Alekhine. In 1925 he wrote a highly influential book on chess for advanced players, entitled *My System*, in which he exploded a few myths about chess strategy and set out his own pragmatic ideas for playing the game. Nimzowitsch was also an opening theorist of some renown.

The Nimzo-Indian defence, which we are going to look at here, was pioneered by Nimzowitsch. The 'Indian' component of the name is actually not correct because the opening does not involve a *fianchetto* (as in the King's Indian Defence).

| 1 | d4 | Nf6 |
| 2 | c4 | e6 |

Instead of playing 2...g6 and moving the bishop to g7, Black decides to use the bishop on the a3–f8 diagonal.

| 3 | | Nc3 |

If, instead, White plays 3 Nf3, play can develop down different lines. For example, Black could play 3...Bb4+, which is the starting point for what is known as the

'Bogo-Indian Defence' (partly named after another famous between-wars player from Ukraine called Efim Bogoljubow), when White often replies with 4 Bd2 Qe7 5 g3 Nc6 6 Bg2 Bxd2+ 7 Nbxd2 and a fairly even position results. Another possibility is 3...b6 4 g3 which, as we have already seen, are the starting moves of what is known as the Queen's Indian Defence.

3   ...   Bb4

The above position is the starting point for the Nimzo-Indian Defence. Black's bishop pins the knight to the king, so White cannot continue with 4 e4? because Black could simply capture with 4...Nxe4.

4   e3   ...

A slightly passive-looking move, but it is the most common move at this point. Other possibilities are 4 Bg5, 4 Nf3 or 4 a3, provoking the bishop to capture or retreat. 4 Qc2 is also possible and has the slight plus point that it allows the queen to recapture (after 4...Bxc3+) and avoid the doubling of the pawns. This is largely a matter of taste. The line with 4 Qc2 is known as the 'Classical variation', as it was the most popular line when the Nimzo-Indian was first played in the early part of the 20th century.

4   ...   0-0

Black could capture on c3 with 4...Bxc3+, but there is no hurry to play this. It would be a more or less equal

exchange: the small advantage of doubling White's pawns (on c3 and c4) would perhaps be outweighed by the loss of the (slightly more valuable) bishop for White's knight.

5   Bd3   d5

Black's move is designed to stop White playing the advance e4. Note that Black often plays 5...c5 here when play can follow 6 Nf3 d5 – reaching the same position as appears in the main line. This is a simple example of an opening transposition. The order in which the moves are played is sometimes not significant. However, there are other possibilities. For example, after 5...c5 6 Nf3 Nc6 7 0-0 d6 8 Qc2 Bxc3 9 bxc3 e5, play moves along very different lines.

6   Nf3   c5
7   0-0   Nc6

A number of pawn captures are now possible, but would result in a straightforward recapture.

Both sides have succeeded in developing most of their pieces, and both kings are tucked away on safe squares. This is a perfectly playable position for both colours. The only problem – and this applies to both sides – lies in how to develop the bishops that are currently still on their original squares.

Left: Born in Riga, Latvia in 1886, Nimzowitsch (left) settled in Denmark in 1922. His career as a professional chess player lasted for more than 30 years.

FLANK OPENINGS

All the openings examined so far involved either 1 e4 or 1 d4 on White's first move. Neither of these moves is obligatory, and there are other respectable ways of starting a chess game. These are known collectively as 'flank openings', as they do not involve a move of a central pawn on the first turn.

The first move 1 c4 begins what is known as the 'English Opening', so called because it was first championed by the great English player Howard Staunton, who used it in his 1843 match against the French player St Amant. We have already seen that 1...c5 (the Sicilian Defence) is a good move for Black against 1 e4, so it stands to reason that 1 c4 should be reasonable for White.

Despite Staunton's example, this opening was infrequently used until the mid-20th century, when it was taken up by top Soviet players such as world champions Botvinnik and Smyslov. Today, although still not played as frequently as 1 e4 or 1 d4, it retains a good reputation.

1	c4	e5

1...Nf6 is seen more frequently, with Black inviting White to transpose into the Nimzo-Indian or King's Indian after 2 d4. Another frequent response is 1...c5, where Black often strives to play symmetrically for a number of moves (e.g. 2 Nf3 Nf6 3 Nc3 Nc6 4 g3 g6 5 Bg2 Bg7 6 0-0 0-0, etc).

2	Nc3	Nf6
3	Nf3	...

3 g3 is another frequently played move when play can continue 3...d5 4 cxd5 Nxd5 5 Bg2.

3	...	Nc6
4	g3	d5
5	cxd5	Nxd5
6	Bg2	...

Note how similar this is to the Sicilian Defence, but with the colours the other way round. In fact, it is sometimes known as the 'Reversed Sicilian Defence'. It can be a little hazardous for Black to play openings designed for White because, if you think about it, White will always have an extra move by virtue of having started the game. However, in this specific line, it is not a problem. The downside of choosing a Black-style set-up if you have White is that such positions tend to be slightly more passive than can be achieved by playing conventional opening variations. Notice, for example, in the above diagram, White's rather limited control of the centre. Again, this tends to be a matter of taste, but if you like to play attacking chess from the beginning, you may find yourself temperamentally unsuited to playing flank openings.

Another flank opening starts with 1 Nf3, which is known as the 'Réti Opening', after Czech player Richard Réti (1889–1929), who, like Nimzowitsch, contributed radically new ideas to chess strategy after

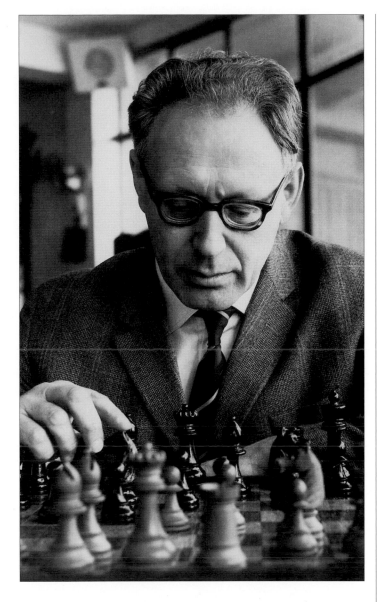

Above: Mikhail Botvinnik, seen playing in the 1961/62 Hastings International Congress. He played at the traditional British Christmas/New Year event three times, winning first prize in 1961/62 and 1966/67, playing 1 c4 in most of his White games.

World War I. In practice, 1 Nf3 and 1 c4 overlap to a considerable degree and often transpose.

| **1** | **Nf3** | **Nf6** |

The temptation to mimic White's opening moves is always strong, but there are other possibilities, such as 1...d5, 1...c5 (after which 2 e4 transposes to the Sicilian Defence) or 1...g6.

| **2** | **g3** | **...** |

2 d4 transposes into a standard Queen's pawn opening, or perhaps the Queen's Gambit (once White plays c4). 2 c4 transposes into the English Opening.

| **2** | **...** | **d5** |
| **3** | **Bg2** | **c6** |

3...c5 is perfectly playable, but 3...c6 is ultra-solid, with a view to blighting the g2 bishop's prospects on the long diagonal.

4	**0–0**	**Bg4**
5	**d3**	**Nbd7**
6	**Nbd2**	**...**

The above set of moves seems to restrict the scope of the c1 bishop, but White is concentrating on supporting a pawn advance such as e4 or c4 with this knight.

| **6** | **...** | **e5** |
| **7** | **e4** | **...** |

This is a very solid set-up for White, but is perhaps a little cagey and passive.

THINKING AHEAD AND CALCULATING 1

Strong chess players are often asked how far ahead they can see when calculating a move. The rather unsatisfying answer usually given is that it depends on the position. In fact, much depends on the complexity of the situation, with an extreme example of a simple one shown below.

Here, with White to play, a strong player would not calculate but simply count moves. Can the white pawn reach a8 before the black king arrives to stop it? White counts squares – a4 (the pawn moves two squares on its first turn), a5, a6, a7 and a8 = five. But the black king can only reach the b-file in five moves so it cannot catch the pawn. Thus the pawn queens. However, if it is Black to move, the king reaches b7 after the pawn gets to a7, saving the day and securing a draw with best play.

In the above position, White, to play, has a very much better position. One simple idea here is to win a pawn.

| 1 | Nxg3 | hxg3 |
| 2 | Qxg3 | Bf6! |

White is a pawn up, but Black's last move has secured the defence of the g7 pawn and the knight on e5.

It is likely that White might win at some point, but there is a long way to go. However, White has a much better move in the initial position.

| 1 | Bxe5! | ... |

White has removed Black's only defender of the key f7 square, but it involves sacrificing the rook on f1.

1	...	Nxf1
2	Rxf1	dxe5

In the game from which this was taken, Black played 2...f6, but that left Black at a material disadvantage of bishop and knight for the rook. White's well-placed minor pieces soon made short work of Black.

3	Qxf7+	Kd7
4	Qe6+	Ke8
5	Qxe5	...

White has a knight and two pawns for a rook, so in material terms, it is level. However, Black's king remains exposed, the g7 pawn is under threat and White's two minor pieces will soon swing into action. It is very definitely better for White.

Sometimes, even in a complex position, it is sufficient to calculate just a couple of moves to be satisfied that a big advantage will accrue.

White, to play, has a big advantage because the black king is very exposed. A move such as 1 Qf5 would put further pressure on the king, but there is something immediately decisive.

1	Nxd5+!	...

A fork with check, which also discovers an attack on the queen on c7.

1	...	Nxd5

Not a bad defensive move. Black captures the checking piece and also manages to provide a defender for the queen. 2 Qxc7 Nxc7 3 Rxc7 would leave White a pawn up in a good position – but there is something very much better than this.

2	Qe4+!	...

After this check, White will capture on c7 with the rook, winning easily. For example, 2...Kd8 3 Rxc7 Kxc7 and now White plays 4 Bxd5 after which he has a queen and pawn in return for a rook – a huge material advantage. If Black tries 2...Qe5 White can capture with the knight, 3 Nxe5, and White will have a material advantage of queen and pawn for knight. Having satisfied themselves that the moves 1 Nxd5+ Nxd5 2 Qe4+ would lead to a huge material advantage, most strong players playing White would soon make the move. That said, having made up their mind to play the move, they would probably go through their analysis two or three times to make sure they hadn't missed anything. This is particularly important when you are playing a complex sacrifice.

THINKING AHEAD AND CALCULATING 2

We have looked at some examples where careful calculation of the next few moves has brought rewards in terms of a cut-and-dried tactical solution. In some positions there may be one move that is markedly better than all the others (e.g. a move that leads to checkmate, material advantage, or simply a recapture or a logical developing move); but in many others, it may not be so clear-cut and it will be necessary to consider your options.

Before doing any thinking, it is necessary to look at the board and run through the options. For example, you may want to start by looking at the move you want to play. Does it work? If you are happy that it does work, should you play it right away? No – wait – have another look around to see if there is something better or more clear-cut. But first make a careful mental note of the move you think is good. If there is a snag to the move, try and concentrate on why it doesn't work. The basic idea behind the move may be promising. Perhaps you can play another move that will allow the idea to work perfectly a move or two later.

White, to play, notices that Black's king has no legal move, but that the intended checkmating move R1e6 currently fails because Black can reply Nxe6. However, that thought leads to another: the black knight is effectively tied to the defence of the e6 square so it is not really defending the b5 pawn.

1   Bxb5!   ...

Now if 1...Nxb5, White simply answers 2 R1e6 mate.

1   ...   Rxd5

This looks like a good answer, but White has another trick to play.

2   Bc4!   ...

2   ...   Rc5
3   Rf7 mate

This is rather a piquant finish. Although the black rook pins the bishop against White's king, the bishop still effectively defends the rook on f7 and helps it to checkmate. Black didn't have to move the rook on move 2, but any other move would have cost the exchange (i.e. rook for a minor piece).

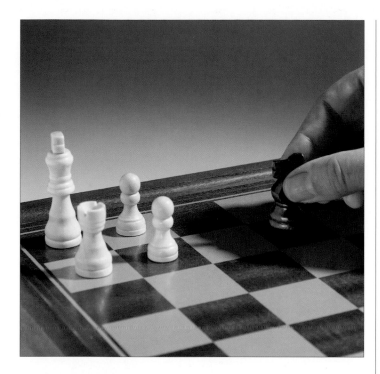

Left: Black is about to play the knight to c2, bringing about a 'smothered mate'. This term describes the situation where a king is completely hemmed in by its own pieces and cannot move out of check from a knight.

White, to play, looks around the board and decides that everything is defended and all is well.

1	Rd2??	f3!

Black's last move threatens mate (with Qxg2) and the capture of the white queen. There is no alternative other than to capture the pawn with the queen (the g2 pawn is pinned).

2	Qxf3	Rxc4

Black has won a bishop for a pawn. The 2...f3 move is called a 'deflecting sacrifice' because it forced the queen away from the defence of the bishop. Another way of looking at this is to say that the white queen was overloaded. It wasn't able to defend the bishop and also guard against the f3 move at the same time.

Instinct versus learning

Players often experience a dilemma when choosing between a move that looks impressive and another that looks like the sort of thing they have seen in textbooks. The most sensible course is to calculate as objectively as you can and play the move that makes the most sense. If you are still confused after a lot of thinking, play the instinctive selection. Even if it is wrong, you may learn something from what happens.

It is often worth spending the last moments doing some last-minute checking before you make a move. Ask yourself: 'Have I overlooked an obvious capture of one of my men?' Or: 'Have I missed an obvious chance to capture one of my opponent's pieces?' It doesn't take long to review each piece in turn and examine capturing possibilities. It is also a good idea to cast an eye over any obvious threats from your opponent.

PLANNING

It is always a good idea to have a plan. Obviously, the long-term plan is to deliver checkmate, but it is good to have something more achievable, particularly in simple positions where there are fewer tactical possibilities to calculate. A plan does not have to be too grandiose. It might consist of redeploying your worst-posted piece, improving the scope of a blocked-in bishop or ensuring a weak or backward pawn is supported.

Material is level (above) with Black to play. In general terms, it might be argued that, with bishop for knight and with Black having doubled pawns on g7 and g6, White stands better. However, in this specific situation, the doubled pawn on g6 is acting as a barrier to the white bishop and to any chance of a viable kingside attack.

Black has no immediate tactical possibilities in this position, and there are no serious threats to guard against. So it is necessary to think of a constructive plan. One idea here would be to play the knight to d5 to attack the pawn on c3. However, it seems more sensible to do something useful with the rook on f8, which is Black's worst-placed piece. It can only go to e8, where it would be not much better than on f8, so Black creates space for it to find a better square.

1 ... Rd7!

Now Black will have the choice of playing the f8 rook to c8 or d8 next move.

2 Bf1 ...

This retreat looks passive, but is actually quite sensible. White gets ready to challenge rooks on the d-file, should Black now play Rfd8.

2 ... Nd5

Black could have played Rfd8 or Rfc8 here, both of which look just as good.

3 Re4 Rc8

Black now has three pieces menacing the pawn on c3.

4 Rd4 ...

White sets a trap. If 4...Nxc3, White can play 5 Rxd7 Qxd7 6 Rxc3, winning a piece.

4	...	a6

This is a waiting move that also restricts the scope of White's bishop. There follows a series of cagey moves, during which the two players hope to exploit any inaccurate moves that may occur. The position is still roughly level, but Black starts to pressurize the weaknesses in White's position.

5	Qd3	Rcd8
6	Qf3	Rc8
7	Bg2	Qe5

8	Re4	Qg5	9	Ree1?	...

White starts to go wrong. 9 Rc2 looks a safer move.

9	...	Rdc7

Black may even have been able to play 9...Nxb4 here, since 10 cxb4 allows 10...Rxc1. However, the move played is also good.

10	h4	Qd2

It is a little risky placing the queen here, but the black queen can escape to a safe square if attacked.

11	Red1	Qb2

There is still a long way to go in the game, but this position can be seen as the culmination of Black's short-term plan initiated with 1...Rd7. Black has managed to bring no fewer than four pieces to bear on the weak pawn on c3 and will soon win it by force.

Most people playing the white side in this position would find it rather depressing and probably fold very quickly. But a grandmaster (or a powerful computer) could still put up a tough defence: 12 Rb1, and if 12...Qxc3 13 Qd3. Black is a pawn up, but White now has some counterplay against the knight on d5. For example, 13...Qxd3 14 Rxd3 Rc1+ 15 Rxc1 Rxc1+ 16 Kh2 Rc4 17 Bxd5 exd5 18 Rxd5 Rxb4. Although Black remains a pawn up, it could be hard to force a win.

ATTACKING CHESS

By the term 'attacking chess', chess players usually mean that play involves a direct attack on the opponent's king. This is by no means the only way to play a game of chess. Many chess players engage in 'percentage chess', which involves players paying closer attention to the material situation or to the safety of their army than to the ultimate aim of checkmating the opponent. However, attacking players enjoy the excitement of a checkmating attack and tailor their play to that end.

The first prerequisite of attacking chess is a suitable choice of opening. Not all openings are equally well suited for attacking chess. But the openings often preferred by elementary players (such as the Giuoco Piano or the Ruy López) can be a good choice for someone who enjoys attacking chess. They tend to provide more open lines, so that you can gain swift access to the opponent's king.

The downside to attacking chess is that it is easy to go wrong in a tactical melee. The result becomes something of a lottery. Consequently, a strong player will often prefer percentage chess against a weaker opponent, seeking to exploit their extra skill without excess risk. But it can be a good idea for a weaker player to indulge in attacking play against a stronger opponent, as the more complicated the position, the more chance that luck will play a part.

Here is a game between two junior players, showing how a game can get out of control very quickly and lead to a swift denouement.

| 1 | e4 | e5 |
| 2 | Nf3 | Nc6 |

Probably the commonest opening moves in all forms of chess – both professional and amateur.

| 3 | Bc4 | Nf6 |

Black's last move is the starting position of the 'Two Knights' Defence'. This opening is ideal for players of either colour who enjoy attacking chess. There are plenty of aggressive possibilities for both colours.

| 4 | Ng5 | ... |

White starts the fun going with the very crude threat of 5 Bxf7+ or 5 Nxf7, forking queen and rook. It is a good move. Instead, White could play 4 d4, which is aggressive, or 4 d3, which would be the choice of a more cautious player. 4 Nc3 is also possible, but then Black could try 4...Nxe4 and, if 5 Nxe4 d5, could win back the piece.

4   ...   d5

Black sensibly blocks the threat to the f7 pawn. It is by no means the only move available to Black. Some very aggressive Black players prefer 4...Bc5. This is a sacrifice, allowing a capture on f7. White can probably get away with either capture (5 Bxf7+ or 5 Nxf7), but Black often gets a powerful counterattack against the white king.

5   exd5   Nxd5?

This looks like a routine recapture, but it is regarded as a poor move by chess experts. White will get a big attack. Instead, Black normally plays 5...Na5 to molest the c4 bishop. Play continues 6 Bb5+ c6 7 dxc6 bxc6 8 Be2 h6 9 Nf3 e4 10 Ne5 Bd6. White is a pawn up, but is being relentlessly harried by Black. The result is that White is poorly developed. A strong player for White could hope to survive Black's counterattack, but a weaker one would be likely to go under.

Looking at the position above, it is not obvious why Black's last move is an error. It cannot be explained by reference to 'general principles'. Chess players over the centuries have worked out a very strong continuation for White in this position, and it is necessary to know this before playing the Two Knights' Defence.

6   d4   ...

An even more aggressive, but perhaps overly risky, alternative is 6 Nxf7, sacrificing a knight for a direct attack on the black king. Play can continue 6...Kxf7 7 Qf3+ Ke6 (the only move to defend the knight on d5) 8 Nc3 Ncb4 9 Qe4. White has a strong grip on the game and it will be hard for Black to withstand the threats with the black king so exposed.

6   ...   exd4
7   0–0   ...

continues on the next page ➡

Position after 7 0–0

Taking stock of the above position, it can be seen that Black has an extra pawn, but that White has considerable compensation in terms of better development. Black is still a couple of moves away from being able to castle on the kingside, while White is about to play Re1+ and perhaps bring the white queen to f3, where it would threaten both Qxf7 mate and Qxd5, winning a piece. White played d4 earlier in order to open up the e-file for the rook to give check. There is quite a lot for Black to cope with.

7   ...   Bd6?
8   Nxf7   ...

In fact, White could simply have taken the knight on d5 that had been left undefended by Black's hurry to develop pieces. But White's attacking instincts are right, and this move commences a fierce attack against Black's king.

8   ...   Kxf7
9   Bxd5+   Ke8

A poor choice. Black should invite the exchange of the powerful c4 bishop with 9...Be6. On e8, the king will be exposed to a check on the e-file.

10   Qf3   ...

Both players are finding it hard to sift through the many options available in this open position. 10 Re1+ Ne7 11 Qh5+ g6 12 Qh4 would work out as a stronger option for White.

10   ...   Rf8?

10...Ne5 is a more resilient move, blocking the e-file and keeping a defence on f7 as well as attacking the white queen. Even so, after 11 Re1 Qe7, followed by the surprising retreat 12 Qd1, White's powerful pin on the e-file leaves Black with major problems to solve. The knight on e5 is in great danger of White playing f4 to win it.

11   Qh5+   ...

White is trying to weaken the squares around Black's king and also to pick up the pawn on h7.

11   ...   g6

The move 11...Kd7 is answered by 12 Qg4+ Ke8 13 Re1+ Ne5 14 Qxg7, and White still has a strong attack.

12   Bxc6+   ...

If White plays 12 Qxh7, Black can reply with 12...Bxh2+ 13 Qxh2 Qxd5, which means Black has at least some chance of saving the game.

Instead, White simplifies the position. Although this means relinquishing the dangerous white-squared bishop, it has done its job, helping to puncture holes in Black's position. At best, Black is saddled now with doubled pawns on the c-file, but the black king is horribly exposed in the centre of the rank and vulnerable to a direct attack.

12 ... bxc6

13 Qxh7 ...

Not the best move. 13 Re1+ is hard to meet: 13...Be7 14 Qxh7 Qd6 15 Bh6 leaves Black in a hole.

13 ... g5?

After this, the game is over. 13...Qf6 gives Black a chance of holding the position together, although White stands better.

14 Qg6+ ...

Once again, White misses the most decisive move to end the game. After 14 Re1+, it is clear that Black cannot move the king but has to interpose a piece to escape check. But after 14...Be7, White simply plays 15 Bxg5 and Black has run out of good defences. If 15...Rf7 16 Qg8+ Rf8 17 Qg6+, then White will capture the bishop on e7 next move.

14 ... Rf7

14...Kd7 is a better move, but still loses after 15 Bxg5 when White is a comfortable two pawns up with a strong attack.

15 Bxg5 Qd7

If Black blocks the attack on the queen with 15...Be7, White pins the bishop with 16 Re1 and it will soon be captured.

16 Re1+ Kf8

Black is now at White's mercy. In fact there is a mate in three moves here. Can you see it?

17 Bh6+ Rg7

There is no choice.

18 Re8+! ...

An attractive rook sacrifice to force checkmate.

18 ... Qxe8
19 Qxg7 mate

This is a good example of aggressive chess. It is noticeable in the final position that White has not moved the queenside rook or knight. That is a little unusual. It is normally better to ensure that the majority of the pieces are in play before launching such an attack.

THE SACRIFICE

We have already seen some examples of sacrifices at various stages of a game. For example, a gambit is a pawn sacrifice that occurs during the opening stages of a game. This particular sacrifice is designed to gain momentum for an attack while the opponent expends valuable time rounding up the pawn. On the previous page, White finished with a rook sacrifice in order to create a mating finish.

The sacrifice is an important part of attacking chess. Very often, it is an inducement to the opponent to move a piece away from an important defensive role, or to allow lines to be opened up for an attack. Here is an interesting example of a pawn sacrifice being used to open the position up to an attack. Playing White was the leading English woman player, Harriet Hunt.

| 1 | e4 | c6 |

This is the first move of the 'Caro-Kann Defence', named after two 19th-century players. It is a good opening for Black, albeit slightly more sedate than the uncompromising Sicilian Defence.

| 2 | d4 | d5 |

The basic idea of the Caro-Kann Defence is for the c6 pawn to support the pawn on d5, so that if it is captured, Black can recapture with the pawn.

3	e5	Bf5
4	Nf3	e6
5	Be2	c5

Black seeks to open up the position. If this is not done, then White will have more room to manoeuvre, and Black's set-up will remain rather cramped. The disadvantage of opening up the position is that it gives White scope for her pieces.

6	Be3	Nd7
7	0–0	Ne7
8	c4	...

White seeks to open the position still further. White has developed a little quicker than Black. Notice that Black used two moves to move the c-pawn, first to c6 and then to c5.

| 8 | ... | dxc4 |
| 9 | Na3 | ... |

White could recapture on c4 immediately with 9 Bxc4, but prefers to play another developing move since the c4 pawn cannot be defended in any case.

| 9 | ... | cxd4? |

This looks like an error. Black should play 9...Nd5 with a view to playing Be7 and then 0–0. Black needs to get the black king to safety.

10   Nxc4!   ...

White avoids a mechanical recapturing move on d4, but instead plays something else first. This is sometimes referred to as an *intermezzo* move – an 'in-between' move used to improve the position before making an obvious recapture. White's move is also a sacrifice because Black can now play 10...dxe3, winning a bishop for a pawn.

10   ...   Nc6

Had Black played the greedy 10...dxe3, White's next move would have come as a shock – 11 Nd6 checkmate! The black king is surrounded and cannot escape. This is a nice example of a smothered mate.

11   Nxd4!   ...

This move offers another sacrifice. Both of Black's knights are threatening the e5 pawn and it is only defended by White's knight on c4.

11   ...   Ndxe5?

Black accepts the sacrifice, but it would have been better to decline with 11...Nxd4 12 Qxd4 Bc5 13 Nd6+ Bxd6 14 Qxd6, although White still has a better position because the black king is stranded on a central file.

12   Nxe5   Nxe5
13   Bb5+   ...

13...Ke7 14 Nxf5+ exf5 15 Qa4 leaves the black king at the mercy of White's pieces.

13   ...   Nd7
14   Nxf5   exf5

15   Re1   Black resigns

Resignation may seem premature, but Black has no hope of salvation here. White threatens a lethal discovered check 16 Bg5+. If 15...Be7, 16 Bc5 will win the bishop on e7.

QUEEN SACRIFICES

If you play chess on a regular basis – and that is the only way to improve – you will become used to playing (or see your opponent playing) pawn sacrifices. But a queen sacrifice is not something that comes along every day. They are regarded as aesthetically pleasing, perhaps akin to a 'hole in one' in golf. Nevertheless, it is worth knowing about some queen sacrifice themes that can occasionally be exploited in practical play.

Here is a very famous example played by Legall de Kermeur (1702–1792), whose other claim to fame was as the chess teacher of Philidor at the Café de la Régence in Paris. It occurs in the early stages of the game and is worth remembering.

Legall–St Brie, Paris 1750

1	e4	e5
2	Nf3	d6

These are the first moves of the opening known as 'Philidor's Defence', although it was first played and analysed long before the famous Frenchman's birth. Although solid enough, this defence has the disadvantage of restricting the development of Black's f8 bishop. This will have significant consequences.

3	Bc4	Bg4

One debatable principle of chess that is often quoted states that 'knights should be developed before bishops'. That is far from being a hard-and-fast principle, and 3...Nf6 would be poor here after 4 Ng5, when Black's only reasonable option is to waste a move playing 4...d5, having already played 2...d6. Black should probably play 3...Be7 and then Nf6 on the next move, when Ng5 can be answered by 0–0.

4	Nc3	g6?

Here, Monsieur Legall played a move so beautiful and surprising that the whole sequence has been known by his name ever since.

5	Nxe5!!	...

The white knight had seemingly been pinned against the queen by the bishop on g4, but Legall had seen further into the position. This is a fine example of an occasion when a strong chess player ignores the principles of the game to indulge in a piece of individual brilliance.

5	...	Bxd1

Black was not obliged to accept the sacrifice and could have continued with 5...Be6 6 Bxe6 fxe6 7 Nf3 when Black would have been only one pawn down. Legall's brilliant move would have been no less impressive for that.

6	Bxf7+	Ke7

The only move.

7   Nd5 mate

Black's king has been fatally encircled by White's three minor pieces.

Philidor's legacy

This example of a queen sacrifice occurs with surprising regularity – 'Philidor's Legacy' is named after Legall's distinguished protégé, although there is no extant example of him using it in play.

White, to play, appears to be in some trouble, being the exchange down (i.e. knight for rook). However White can force mate in four moves.

1   Nf7+   Kg8

1...Rxf7 allows 2 Qd8+, and it will be checkmate on the back rank in two more moves after the queen and rook have been interposed and captured. In similar positions in practical chess (rather than our composed example), it is often possible to make this Rxf7 capture

without being mated on the back rank, so the defending player may be able to survive at the cost of the exchange.

2   Nh6+   ...

Double check means Black must move the king again.

2   ...   Kh8
3   Qg8+!!   ...

A stunning coup. Note how the knight on h6 defends the queen on g8, forcing Black's next move.

3   ...   Rxg8
4   Nf7 mate

A beautiful smothered mate. This attractive concept is almost as old as modern chess itself: it was first recorded in 1497 in the writings of the Spanish chess player and writer Luís Ramírez Lucena.

CONSTRUCTIVE DEFENCE

As in most games and sports, nobody likes to have to defend. This aversion is reflected in the titles of chess books, where the word 'attack' or 'attacking' heavily outnumbers 'defence' or 'defensive', and also in chess puzzles, where the objective is nearly always to win rather than to escape with an ingeniously achieved draw.

At the highest level of chess, draws outnumber decisive results, and a grandmaster's defensive technique is as important as his or her attacking prowess. Good defensive skills can turn likely losses into draws, or, even into wins, if opponents overplay their hand.

The main barrier to good defence is the psychological one. Players become depressed playing a difficult position and tend to make more mistakes. The best idea is to adopt some sort of plan – perhaps to put up a long and dogged resistance in the hope that your opponent goes wrong, or perhaps to throw all your remaining pieces at your opponent's king in the hope of a surprise checkmate.

If you are material down, remember that there are some endgames to aim for where the player with more material cannot win by force. If, for example, your opponent has an extra bishop, and both sides have some pawns, you should aim to exchange all the pawns off to reach the endgame of king and bishop

versus king, which is a draw. The same applies to king and knight versus king – it is a draw. Even two knights and king are not enough to force checkmate against a bare king.

Below is an example of a combination leading to a forced draw.

Black is to play. The position looks hopeless. White has two connected passed pawns and there is every prospect that at least one of the pawns will be promoted in due course, after which the win will be simple. However, armed with a little knowledge of the endgame, Black found a way to draw:

1 ... Nxb5!

On a very surprising move, Black gives up the knight for one of the pawns, but White still has the a-pawn.

2 Kxb5 Kb8

Black's king heads for the corner. The nice thing from Black's point of view is that there was no need to think. It is sufficient to know that a bishop accompanied by a rook pawn (i.e. a pawn on the a-file or h-file) cannot force a win where the defending king reaches the queening square, and where the colour of the queening square differs from the colour of the squares on which the bishop can move. In this position, White has a dark-squared bishop, and the queening square is white. Hence, White cannot win because the black king cannot be forced away from the corner.

3 Kb6 Ka8
4 a6 Kb8
5 Be5+ Ka8
6 Ka5 ...

White's king has to give ground, or it will be stalemate.

Left: Black is facing a pawn onslaught on the queenside and has been pushed on to the defensive. It is not a pleasant situation to be in, but there's no reason to panic. With careful play, Black can hold firm and perhaps even win if White overreaches.

Here is the key to this position. As long as Black plays correctly, keeping the king in front of or alongside White's remaining pawn, any attempt by White to drive it from the corner will result in stalemate. There is no way White can force the pawn through to its queening square. Thus:

6 ... Ka7
7 Bd4+ Ka8
8 a7 Kb7
9 Kb5 Ka8

Any king move forward now brings about stalemate. The game must end in a draw.

Blocked pawns

As well as liquidating all the pawns, there are positions where having blocked pawns right across the board can also help the defender to escape with a draw.

The position above is an extreme but instructive example: White is two rooks down on material. Normally such a deficit would be ruinous, but here White has a safe draw. White simply moves the king around ad infinitum and there is no way that the rooks can force a way through the locked pawn barrier. Notice that it might be different if Black had, say, a light-squared bishop or a knight instead of one of the rooks: such a piece could capture on b5 or d5 to make a breach in the wall and open a file for a rook.

continues on the next page

Opposite bishop endgame

Another scenario that favours the defender is the 'opposite bishop endgame'. Where each side has a bishop (plus pawns), but the bishops move on different-coloured squares, it is often very difficult or impossible for the player with the advantage to force a win.

In this position, with White to play, Black's pawn is only two squares away from the queening square and White's king is a long way from the action. However, White can simply play 1 Bc5 or 1 Bh4. If Black advances the pawn, the bishop captures it and we are left with king and bishop versus king – which we already know is a draw. So long as White's bishop controls the f2 square, there is nothing Black can do to win the game.

Compare that with this position, which is the same except that Black's bishop is on g3 – so we have a same-colour bishop endgame. This is a simple win for Black. If White plays 1 Bc5, Black can use the black bishop to guide the pawn to promotion: 1...Bf4 2 Bg1 Be3 3 Bh2 f2, and the pawn promotes.

If the defending king is well placed, it is possible to defend an opposite-coloured bishop endgame against two (or even more) extra pawns.

White's defensive task is relatively simple. White needs to place the king on e3 and the bishop on f2 and then make moves with the bishop on the e1–h4 diagonal.

Perpetual check

Another useful weapon in the hand of a defender is 'perpetual check', when a player cannot escape from an infinite series of checks. When the player being repeatedly checked gets fed up trying to find a way out, it is normal for the players to agree a draw.

Here White, to play, is a pawn up and seems to have a reasonable chance of winning by promoting one of the far-advanced pawns on b6 and h6. Black's own pawn on e2 is well blockaded by the white king.

1	Rg7+	Kh8

Note that Black moves the king to a square where it will have no further legal moves. This is a clue that Black is hoping for a chance of stalemate.

2	b7?	...

This is a mistake after which Black can force a draw. White should play 2 Rg6, which leaves the king with a legal move (Kh7), thus avoiding stalemate tricks.

2	...	Rb1+!

Black gives up the remaining pawn and embarks on a series of checks.

3	Kxe2	Rb2+
4	Kd3	Rb3+
5	Kc4	Rb4+!

Black is happy to jettison the rook because, if it is taken, it is stalemate. White can run away with the king but Black will keep checking. In fact, the two players (both chess grandmasters) agreed a draw here because they could see that White could never escape the checks. There are a few tricks here that might ensnare a lesser player and it might be worth playing on to see if Black falls for a trick. For example:

6	Kd5	Rd4+??

A big mistake. 6...Rb5+ holds the draw.

7	Kc6	Rd6+

8	Kc7	Rc6+
9	Kb8	...

Now 9...Rc8+ would allow 10 bxc8Q+ to win, while after 9...Rxh6 10 Rd7, White will promote the b-pawn.

Opportunities to bale out for a draw quite frequently occur in the middlegame.

White, to play, is the exchange and a pawn down in material, but has a nice trick to escape with a draw.

1	Nf6+!	gxf6

Black has no choice – or the queen would be lost.

2	Qg4+	Kh8
3	Qh4+	Kg7
4	Qg4+	etc.

A CHESS MASTERPIECE

Playing through games played by masters can be an entertaining way of learning, and probably the most famous chess game of all time is Morphy versus the Duke of Brunswick. (Note that when referring to chess games, the name of the player with White is always placed first – often the two players' names are simply hyphenated.)

Paul Charles Morphy (1837–1884) was a true chess genius, and the best player in the world in the mid-19th century. He was born and lived all his life in New Orleans, but he made a spectacular chess tour of Europe in 1858 and carried all before him.

This game was not really a serious tournament encounter, being played in the Duke of Brunswick's box at the Paris Opera in 1858 during an operatic performance (of Bellini's *Norma*). The Duke (actually an ex-Duke, having been deposed in 1830) was no more than a keen amateur and played in consultation with Count Charles Isouard. They were no match for the world's best player, but the way in which Morphy won was spectacular.

1	e4	e5
2	Nf3	d6

2...d6 is the first move of Philidor's Defence.

3	d4	Bg4

This is definitely not one of the better moves in the position. The problem is that it causes Black to waste time after the coming capture on e5.

4	dxe5	...

Here, the two aristocrats must have noticed that, if 4...dxe5, White could play 5 Qxd8+ Kxd8 and, now that the knight on f3 is no longer pinned, White could simply play 6 Nxe5, winning a pawn. So Black is obliged to capture on f3 first, exchanging the valuable bishop for a knight and leaving the white squares vulnerable as well.

4	...	Bxf3
5	Qxf3	dxe5
6	Bc4	...

Morphy sets up the rather ungentlemanly threat of Qxf7 mate. Perhaps he was keen to get the game over with and listen to the opera. The most important thing to note here is that White now has two pieces in play whereas Black has none. The plan begun with 3...Bg4 has cost Black valuable time.

6	...	Nf6

Black should really have preferred 6...Qf6 here, as this move allows Morphy to play a double attack.

7   Qb3   ...

Paul Morphy has breached a couple of opening principles already. He has moved his queen out into the middle of the board (admittedly it was a more or less forced recapture) and he now moves the same piece a second time. However, he has created two powerful threats: one is to capture the unprotected b7 pawn and the other is to play Bxf7+, followed by Qe6 mate.

7   ...   Qe7

The two Black players realize they cannot defend both of the threats and play this move to deal with the more serious of the two. Another possibility would be to play a developing move such as 7...Bc5 and let the f7 pawn go after 8 Bxf7+ Kf8. However, Black's position is already critical, whatever he does.

8   Nc3   ...

An interesting choice of move by Morphy. He prefers

development of a piece to the mere capture of a pawn with 8 Qxb7, when Black can effect a queen exchange with 8...Qb4+. One suspects that Morphy was genuinely keen to get the game over with quickly rather than to opt for a queenless middlegame and long, drawn-out endgame. Another possibility would have been to play 8 Bxf7+ when 8...Qxf7 allows 9 Qxb7 and the capture of the rook on a8.

8   ...   c6

Black is more or less obliged to play this to defend the b7 pawn via the queen on e7. Another way to secure the b-pawn is to move it to b6 but, after 8...b6 9 Bg5 and now White is threatening Nd5, so Black has to play 9...c6 anyway. After 8...c6, everything is defended in Black's camp, but there are problems developing the pieces. The bishop is hemmed in on f8 so Black has difficulties in castling, while the knight on b8 cannot go to d7 because White has Qxb7.

9   Bg5   b5

Suddenly it looks like Black may have recovered some ground. Material is level and Black threatens to capture the bishop on c4 with the b5 pawn. The bishop seems to have little choice but to retreat to d3 or e2. But White – the best player in the world at the time – came up with something dramatic.

continues on the next page ➲

10   Nxb5!   ...

Morphy sacrifices his knight for two pawns. He has also seen that he will get a check with the bishop on the a4–e8 diagonal. Other significant plus-points in his favour are his lead in development (all his minor pieces are in play, whereas Black still has two on their original squares), and the fact that Black's queen is blocking the entry into the game of the f8 bishop. This, in its turn, means that Black is a long way from being able to castle kingside. And, once the pawns on b5 and c6 have disappeared, the king is unlikely to find refuge on the wide-open queenside.

10   ...   cxb5

If Black's objective had been to last as long as possible against Morphy, it might have been better to play 10...Qb4+ and exchange queens. But White would have emerged with two extra pawns after 11 Qxb4 Bxb4+ 12 c3 cxb5 13 Bxb5+ Nbd7 14 cxb4.

MORPHY'S OPPONENT

♛ ♝ ♞ ♚

Karl, Duke of Brunswick (1804–1873) inherited the duchy when he was 11. He ruled until 1830 when he was ousted in favour of his brother Wilhelm. Thereafter he seems to have divided his time between Paris and Geneva (to which city he left his fortune).

---

11   Bxb5+   Nbd7

11...Kd8 is unlikely to last long, since the king is too exposed. White plays 12 0–0–0+ (castling with check) Kc7 13 Rd3, and White is threatening to double rook with 14 Rhd1 or simply play 14 Rc3+.

12   0–0–0   ...

White gets his king to safety and simultaneously sets up the strong threat of Rxd7, which, at the very least, wins the queen. One of the features of this game is the number of times that Morphy plays moves that have a dual purpose.

12   ...   Rd8

Black tries to defend the d7 knight. 12...0–0–0 was not an option for Black because 13 Ba6+ Kc7 14 Qb7 is checkmate. If 12...Qe6, White has 13 Bxf6!, and if 13...Qxb3, 14 Bxd7 is checkmate.

13   Rxd7!   ...

White sacrifices the exchange, which means that he will be a rook for two pawns down in material terms.

13   ...   Rxd7
14   Rd1   ...

White now has all his pieces (except for his king and pawns) pointed in the general direction of Black's king and queen. Although White is a rook down, Black has a rook and bishop tucked away doing nothing on the kingside. This position demonstrates how fundamentally important it is to have all your pieces doing something useful. Black now tries to break the pin on the knight and find a way out for his blocked bishop on f8 and allow a recapture with the knight on d7.

14   ...   Qe6
15   Bxd7+   Nxd7

Now for the denouement. One likes to imagine there was a drum roll coming up from the orchestra pit at this point...

16   Qb8+!!

A stunning queen sacrifice. Black cannot move his king or interpose a piece, but he can capture the queen.

16   ...   Nxb8
17   Rd8 mate

A dazzling display of attacking chess, almost from the beginning of the game to the end. In the final position, White is materially down to the tune of queen and knight for a couple of pawns, but checkmate is the object of the game.

continues on the next page ➔

Pins

The Morphy–Duke of Brunswick game was a good example of the power of the pin in chess.

Many of Black's problems stemmed from his inability to shake off the vice-like grip exerted by Morphy's two bishops.

Bishops are often played to squares such as b5 and g5 in order to pin a knight against queen or king. A common way to try and break the pin is to move a pawn to attack the bishop and force it to move away or take the knight. Take or move away? This can often be a tricky decision. Here is an example in the Ruy López Opening, where the bishop moves away and gets into trouble.

| 1 | e4 | e5 | 3 | Bb5 | a6 |
| 2 | Nf3 | Nc6 | 4 | Ba4 | ... |

Typically, the bishop retreats to a4, but 4 Bxc6 is occasionally seen. It has been tried by players as distinguished as Bobby Fischer, so it must be quite a good move.

| 4 | ... | d6 |

A reasonable option for Black, although it brings about a pin of the knight against the black king (sometimes called a 'self-pin'). Now the best move is probably 5 c3,

although 5 0–0 and the delayed capture 5 Bxc6+ are also frequently played.

| 5 | d4 | ... |

This is a little risky, as we shall soon see.

| 5 | ... | b5 | 7 | Nxd4 | exd4 |
| 6 | Bb3 | Nxd4 | 8 | Qxd4? | ... |

A bad mistake. White should play the *intermezzo* move 8 Bd5 before recapturing.

| 8 | ... | c5! | 9 | Qd5 | ... |

At first sight, this position looks rather wonderful for White, who threatens mate in one on f7 and the undefended rook on a8. However, appearances can be deceptive and a nasty shock is in store.

| 9 | ... | Be6 |

With this single move, Black manages to defend against the threat of Qxf7 mate and also protect the rook on a8 (with the queen on d8). But it still looks promising for White after the next move.

| 10 | Qc6+ | Bd7 |
| 11 | Qd5 | ... |

White will have been expecting 11...Be6 when 12 Qc6+ Bd7 13 Qd5, etc, appears to lead to perpetual check. But Black is not interested in a draw.

| 11 | ... | c4! |

Calamity: White's bishop is trapped by the advancing pawn. The best White can do is get two pawns for the loss of the bishop. This opening trap is so old that it is known as the 'Noah's Ark' trap.

The bishop hits back

Sometimes, when the bishop is chased back in this way, it has the last laugh. This example comes from a match between the leading French and British players of the 1830s.

White, to play, wants to break the pin on the knight on f3. White is also a pawn down, having sacrificed a pawn to get an attack going in the opening.

| 1 | g4? | ... |

A very natural move, which works in some positions, but unfortunately not in this one.

| 1 | ... | Nxg4+! |

Black hits back with a knight sacrifice.

| 2 | hxg4 | Qxg4 |

Far from breaking the pin, White has actually made it worse with the introduction of the queen into the void that has now opened up in front of White's king. If White now moves the f3 knight, Black plays Qh4+ and then takes the queen with the bishop on h5.

| 3 | Be2 | Qf4+ | 5 | Bxf3 | f5! |
| 4 | Kh1 | Bxf3+ | | | |

Black's last move is a clever one. The intention is to play the rook up to f6, which will allow it to move to g6 or h6, where it will intensify the attack against the rather vulnerable white king.

| 6 | Bg2 | Rf6 | 8 | Bh3 | fxe4 |
| 7 | Qd3 | Rh6+ | | | |

This effectively ends the game. White's queen is attacked and has to give up the defence of the h3 bishop. In fact, White played 9 Nxe4 Rxe4 10 Bc1, and Black played 10...Re3!, which soon led to mate.

167

KING SAFETY

One of the great attractions of openings such as the Two Knights' Defence and the Giuoco Piano is the chance to attack the king by way of the f2/f7 squares. We have already seen this in the Two Knights' Defence, where White attacks f7 as early as move four. A king can often defend itself by castling.

In the instance above, the threat to f7 is met by playing d5. But, in positions where the bishop has already moved away from its original square, it would be more usual for Black to proceed by simply castling.

For instance, in the Giuoco Piano:

1	e4	e5
2	Nf3	Nc6
3	Bc4	Bc5
4	d3	Nf6
5	Nc3	d6

Some beginners like to continue as follows:

6	Ng5?	0–0

This is a mistaken plan by White. By castling, Black provokes two challengers for the f7 square. If White were to capture with either piece, Black would capture with the rook, e.g. 7 Nxf7 Rxf7 8 Bxf7+ Kxf7. White has given up two minor pieces (3 + 3) for a rook and pawn (5 + 1), so in material terms, it might seem like a fair deal, but in practice, the two pieces will be sorely missed by White as the middlegame struggle begins. Most strong chess players would prefer the two pieces. Of course, if White does not capture on f7, a move or two later Black will chase the knight away with h6 and the whole escapade will just be a waste of time.

Prevention is better than cure

Rather than suffering molestation from pieces that arrive on squares such as g5 or, in the case of White, g4, many players prefer to move a pawn to h6 or h3 to prevent the pieces from ever arriving on the square.

1	e4	e5	4	Nc3	d6
2	Nf3	Nc6	5	h3	...
3	Bc4	Bc5			

White plays h3 in order to prevent an awkward pin such as Bg4, and also to guard against a knight going to g4 and threatening the f2 square.

5 ... Be6

Since the bishop can no longer go to g4, Black decides to use it to neutralize White's useful bishop on c4.

6 Bxe6 fxe6

Black has accepted the disadvantage of doubled pawns. In compensation, Black has a half-open f-file that may be useful for a later rook attack on White's king.

7	d3	Nf6	9	Qe2	0-0-0
8	Bg5	Qe7	10	0-0	...

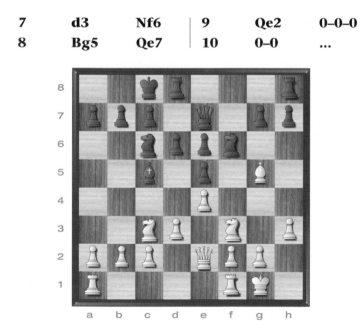

This seems unwise. White would probably have been safer to castle queenside. Now the white king is a potential target for Black's pieces, and the pawn on h3 can eventually be targeted by a pawn advance.

10 ... h6

This is the prelude to Black's kingside attack. The pawn attacks the bishop and gets ready to support its colleague in the advance to g5.

11	Be3	Bxe3	13	Nb5	...
12	Qxe3	g5			

White tries to work up an attack on the opposite side of the board, but Black can counter this easily.

13	...	Kb8	14	a3	...

White is planning something similar to Black's advance on the kingside but it is too slow.

14 ... g4

Black has completed the first stage of his attack. Whether White captures on g4 with the h3 pawn, or the knight moves away (allowing gxh3), Black has broken up the pawn structure in front of the king.

TRICKS AND TRAPS

Chess is full of tricks and traps, and there are many opening traps into which the unwary may fall. We have already seen the Noah's Ark trap (which costs White a bishop in one line of the Ruy López). Here is another, the 'Blackburne Shilling Gambit', named after British professional player Joseph Blackburne (1841–1924).

1	e4	e5	3	Bc4	Nd4!?
2	Nf3	Nc6			

The exclamation mark and question mark are often used in chess notation to denote 'an interesting move'. Here, it really means 'cheeky move'. Play this against an experienced player and they will probably just laugh and say: 'I'm not falling for that!' Nevertheless, many inexperienced chess players continue to take the e5 pawn.

4 Nxe5? ...

White's best moves are 4 0-0 or 4 Nxd4, gaining time because Black has moved the knight twice.

4 ... Qg5!

Black's queen swings into action attacking the knight on e5 and the pawn on g2. However, White now has a tempting capture on f7, which is attacked by bishop and knight.

5 Nxf7 ...

White could defend the double attack with 5 Ng4 but then Black has 5...d5!, attacking the bishop and also discovering a second attack on the knight. Note also that 5 Nf3 runs into 5...Qxg2, with a simultaneous attack on the rook on h1 and the knight on f3. Relatively best is 5 Bxf7+, but White will still have a problem with protecting or relocating the knight on e5 after the black king moves out of check.

5 ... Qxg2

Now White has to move the rook.

6 Rf1 ...

If 6 Nxh8 Qxh1+ 7 Bf1 Qxe4+ 8 Be2 Nxc2+, then White will have to take the knight with his queen because 9 Kf1 Qh1 is checkmate.

6 ... Qxe4+

7	**Be2**	**Nf3 mate**

The bishop on e2 is pinned by the queen.

Middlegame traps

It is usually only beginners and elementary players who fall for opening traps, but even the most exalted player can occasionally fall for tricks in the middlegame. The following position arose in the first game of the most famous chess match of all time: the 1972 world championship between Boris Spassky and Bobby Fischer.

It was Bobby Fischer's turn as Black. The position is level and most pundits expected a draw to be agreed within the next few moves. Spassky's h-pawn is *en prise* (open to capture), but nobody expected Fischer to take it because it is a familiar trap.

1	**...**	**Bxh2??**

Sensation – Fischer takes the pawn. Even amateur players were surprised that the world championship challenger should place his bishop in jeopardy in this way.

2	**g3**	**...**

The bishop is now trapped. It is no use playing 2...Bg1 because White plays 3 Ke2 followed by 4 Kf1 and the king will gobble up the incarcerated bishop.

2	**...**	**h5**
3	**Ke2**	**h4**
4	**Kf3**	**Ke7**

Fischer may have overlooked the fact that after 4...h3 5 Kg4 Bg1 6 Kxh3 Bxf2, White can play 7 Bd2!, and the bishop is trapped on f2.

5	**Kg2**	**hxg3**
6	**fxg3**	**...**

Fischer was now forced to give up his bishop for the pawn on g3. He came close to drawing the game, but eventually lost.

continues on the next page ➔

'Poisoned pawns'

Many traps involve a piece grabbing a pawn on the opposite side of the board and then finding itself cut off behind enemy lines. Here is a classic example of a queen that pays the price for devouring the rather dramatically named 'poisoned pawn'.

Black, to play, is tempted by a pawn on b2, which has been left undefended after White's last move, Be3.

1 ... Qxb2?

The opportunity for the queen to take a pawn on b2 occurs in quite a number of different chess openings, so it is useful to study this closely. Sometimes the queen can get away with it and return with her spoils. This is not the case here.

2 Nb5! ...

This is an equally familiar trap. As well as cutting off couple of escape squares for the queen (a3 and c3), White also threatens Nc7+ forking rook and king.

2 ... Nxd3

Black could try 2...Nba6, but then 2 Bxc5 Bxc5 3 a3 Bd7 4 Qd2 and next move White plays 5 Rfb1 to trap the queen.

3 Qxd3 Bd7
4 Nc7+ and White won.

Sometimes players think they are setting a trap themselves, only to find that the opponent has sprung a much bigger one.

| 1 | ... | Qa3 | 3 | d5 | Ne5 |
| 2 | Rb1 | 0–0 | 4 | Bb4 | ... |

The queen appears to have no escape square. On the face of it, the best that Black can manage is to play 4...Nxc4 5 Bxa3 Nxa3, but that wouldn't save the game.

4 ... Qf3!!

A thunderbolt. If White takes the queen with 5 gxf3, there follows 5...Nxf3+ 6 Kf1 (forced) 6 Bh3 mate.

A picturesque checkmate.

When is a pin not a pin?

Here is an example of an opening trap in the 'Queen's Gambit Declined'.

1	d4	d5	2	c4	e6

This very respectable move is the beginning of the Queen's Gambit Declined. It is actually more common than the 'Queen's Gambit Accepted' (2...dxc4).

3	Nc3	Nf6	4	Bg5	Nbd7

The move 4...Be7 is seen more often but this is also good, and sets a trap.

5	cxd5	...

OK, although 5 Nf3 and 5 e3 are more usual here.

5	...	exd5	6	Nxd5??	...

White falls headlong into the elephant trap. Like all the best chess traps, this move looks totally plausible. The knight on f6 is pinned against the queen by the bishop – so why not take the knight?

6	...	Nxd5!

So Black takes it anyway.

7	Bxd8	Bb4+!

Now the penny drops. White is in check and the only legal way to counter it is to interpose the queen.

8	Qd2	Bxd2+
9	Kxd2	Kxd8

The carnage ends, and the body count shows that White has lost a knight for a pawn.

173

MAXIMIZE YOUR PIECE POWER: ROOKS

Rooks are the second-most powerful pieces in most chessboard situations, but lose much of their firepower if they are blocked in, particularly behind pawns. They operate best on open files (i.e. files with no pawns) and can be deadly on the seventh rank (the rank on which the opponent's pawns stand in the starting position).

Looking at it from the defence point of view, the best way to defend against a strong rook on an open file is to place one of your own rooks on the same file (as long as it is adequately defended, of course).

In this position, with White to move, the best and most natural move is to grab the open file with the rook.

1   Rd1   ...

Black has no easy way to counter White's control of the d-file immediately, but with care it can be defended.

1   ...   Kf8

It is not possible to prevent the invasion of the seventh rank with 1...Re7??, because this allows a back-rank mate with 2 Rd8+ Re8 3 Rxe8 mate.

2   Rd7   ...

White is now threatening to take the pawn on c7.

2   ...   Re7

Black challenges the white rook with his own. After 3 Rd8+ Re8, White is no further forward, having either to exchange rooks or retreat down the d-file. In either case the position is about equal.

If the rook retreats, Black can play the king to e8 and then place the rook on the d-file, as it will be defended by the king. If it were Black to move in the original position opposite, play could proceed thus:

1   ...   Rd8

Of course, Black grabs the file while there is the chance.

2   Kf1   Rd2 | 3   Rc1   ...

The only way to save the c2 pawn.

3   ...   Rd4 | 4   Re1   ...

Black could play 4...Rd2, but after 5 Re2, White could hold the balance in the same way as in the first example, when White was to move first.

A partnership of rooks

Two rooks working together on a file or rank can often be an irresistible fighting force.

White has already doubled rooks on the d-file and now seeks to build more pressure.

1   Rd7   Bb6

If Black plays 1...Rxd7 2 Rxd7 Bb6 3 Kf2, now the black rook is tied to the defence of the f7 pawn. White will soon be able to capture the b-pawn with impunity.

2   Kf2   g5
3   Ke2   Kf6

Not the best move, but things are very difficult for Black.

4   R1d6+   ...

4 Rf1+ followed by a capture on f7 is perhaps more effective. Such is the stranglehold exerted by the white rook on d7 that Black can do little but wait for the inevitable. The pawn on b7 is vulnerable, and defending it with the rook on d8 would mean completely surrendering the d-file – not an appealing prospect.

4   ...   Kg7
5   Rd2   ...

White has not quite worked out the best way to win yet and plays a 'pass' move. White's advantage of the doubled rooks on the d-file (plus one of them on the seventh) offers the luxury of taking a bit more time.

5   ...   Kg6 | 6   Rxb7   Rde8

Black attacks the pawn on e3, but this is easy to defend.

7   Rd3   f5??

Black cracks under pressure. In practical play (from which this example is taken), it is often enough to establish a dominant position and create maximum problems for the opponent in order to win the game.

8   Rd6+ Rf6 | 9   Bf7+! ...

White exploits the fact that the f6 rook is pinned, in order to play this fork.

9   ...   Kg7
10   Bxe8+   1–0 (i.e. Black resigned)

MAXIMIZE YOUR PIECE POWER: BISHOPS

Like rooks, bishops also work well when used in tandem and can benefit from plenty of scope along diagonals. As you will see, their effectiveness is not just limited to rapier-like pins and skewers; it can be far more subtle but just as deadly. Keep an eye on your pawn structure, for it can render a single bishop all but useless.

In this example, Black has two bishops against White's bishop and knight. Although in strict material terms, they add up to the same value, the two bishops often confer a practical advantage. In this position, Black also has the advantage that White's pawns are in five groups, compared to Black's three. In particular, the f4 pawn is vulnerable, although it is currently defended by a bishop.

| 1 | ... | Kg7 |

A good plan. Black has kept the king safely in the corner, but the queens and rooks have gone from the board and now is a sensible time to use it actively. It is unlikely to be in too much direct danger from White's bishop and knight.

| 2 | Nf2 | Kf6 |

The black king continues its march up the board, eyeing up the isolated pawn on f4. You may ask what's to stop White from using his king in similar fashion, scuttling across the board to shore up the defences. It sounds sensible enough, but as the game unfolds, keep your eye on Black's two bishops and observe the impenetrable barrier they create. One of them already controls d1 and d3 and stops the white king's approach.

| 3 | Nh3 | Kf5 |

Black's plan is to apply more pressure to the f4 pawn. White has seen this coming and drafted a white knight in to support it further. The snag with this defensive plan is that Black will chase the knight away with the move Kg4 in due course and then gobble up the pawn, so White has to try and block the threat of capture on f4.

| 4 | Ng5 | f6 |
| 5 | Nh7 | ... |

Here, White might have tried a little trick: 5 Ne6, and if 5...Kxe6 6 f5+ Kxf5 7 Bxh6, in the hope that the opposite-coloured bishop endgame might yield a draw.

| 5 | ... | Bg7 |

Now White's knight is virtually a prisoner in the corner. In order to get it out, White has to surrender the defence of the f4 pawn.

6	Bb4	Kxf4
7	Nf8	Kf5
8	Nd7	Ke4
9	Nc5+	Kf3
10	Ne6	Bh6
11	Bd6	f5

The game is not completely over, but it is easy to see that Black has a big advantage: an extra pawn, and control of the important squares on the f-file, which should allow Black's passed f-pawn to promote, or force White to surrender a piece. One important component in Black's advantage was the bishop on e2. Although it did not move, it helped to stop White's king from coming across to aid the defence of the kingside. In this position, Black's two bishops are completely preventing White's king from entering the game.

Say no to bad bishops

It is often important to think about the scope of your bishops before making a pawn move. As far as possible, it is best to arrange your pawns so that they are not all on the same colour square as one of your bishops. Also, when you are trying to restrict the scope of your opponent's bishop, try to occupy the same colour squares with pawns – but always make sure they are readily defensible.

In this position, with White to move, you should definitely not play 1 c4, because it further restricts the scope of the d3 bishop. White, though, does just that.

1   c4?   Kd6

Black could also fix the weakness with 1...c5, but this is more active.

2   b4   c5

Now things are quite difficult for White. The knight will be able to jump around and eventually come to d4, where it could be a nuisance. But the white bishop is hemmed in by its own pawns on c4 and e4.

3   b5   Ne6
4   g3   Nd4

This is a classic example of what chess players call a 'good knight versus bad bishop' position. The move 1 c4 is what is sometimes referred to as a 'positional blunder'. It doesn't lose any material or allow mate (those are called 'tactical blunders'), but it leads White into a horribly passive position where the opponent is causing all the running. By thrusting forward the pawn White has trapped the white-squared bishop behind its own lines, effectively taking it out of the game. Going back to the position before 1 c4: had White played 1 Bc4+, White would have had a perfectly comfortable game, perhaps even a slightly better one.

MAXIMIZE YOUR PIECE POWER: KNIGHTS

Knights don't move along straight lines like bishops and rooks, but their power is also heavily influenced by the pawn structure. If a knight can be located in or near the enemy camp, on a square where it cannot be easily dislodged (particularly by pawns), it can be highly advantageous.

Here, both of Black's bishops are hemmed in, although at least the one on f8 is defending the g7 square. White's single bishop has more scope but it can be blocked effectively in due course. It is White's two knights that hold the key to what follows.

1   Nh5   ...

This was played in the hope that Black would make a weak move that would allow an entry somewhere.

1   ...   f6

This is what White hoped for, but it does block the scope of the white bishop. 1...Ne5 would have been better.

2   Nf4   ...

White spots an entry path into the enemy position via e6. Black will find it hard to evict the knight from there.

2   ...   Ra8?

The best defence was 2...Ne5!. After 3 Nxe5 dxe5, 4 Ne6? would be met by 4...Rxe6!. White cannot capture with the d-pawn without losing the queen. However, 4 Ne2 would still give White the edge because the knight is more valuable than either of Black's bishops.

White now has the knight firmly embedded in the heart of the enemy position.

3   ...   Qb8
4   Nh4   Qc8
5   Nf5   ...

In this position, White's knights totally dominate the board. One threat is to capture on f8 and then on d6, which wins at least a pawn. But it might be better to initiate an assault on the king with Qg3. If Black now plays 5...Ne5, White plays 6 Bxe5 dxe5 7 Nxf8 and Black must play 7...Kxf8 because of the threat of 8 Ne7+ forking king and queen. But after 7...Kxf8 8 Nxd6 wins a pawn and the exchange.

Knights like holes

As a defender, it is very important not to let your opponent have 'holes' that knights can jump into. In the following game, Black allowed just that and soon both knights were jumping over White like monkeys.

| 1 | ... | f6? |

This concedes the e6 square to the d4 knight.

| 2 | b3 | Rc8 | 4 | Bxb6 | Nxb6 |
| 3 | Ne6+ | Ke8 | 5 | Nxg7+ | ... |

White has netted a pawn.

| 5 | ... | Kf7 | 6 | Nd4! | Nc6 |

If 6...Kxg7 7 Rxe7+ followed by 8 Rxb7 and White will be a comfortable two pawns up.

| 7 | Ngf5 | Rc7 | 9 | Nbd6+ | Kg6 |
| 8 | Nb5 | Rd7 |

White can now try to weave a mating net.

| 10 | Re3 | h5 | 12 | Ne4! | ... |
| 11 | Rg3+ | Kh7 |

| 12 | ... | Rf8 |

Black would love to play 12...dxe4, but unfortunately there follows 13 Rxd7+ Nxd7 14 Rg7 mate.

| 13 | Nc5 | Rdf7 | 14 | Ne6 | ... |

The white knights relentlessly harass Black's rooks.

| 14 | ... | Rg8?? |

This is a blunder in a hopeless position. Even if Black defended with 14...Re8, White could play 15 Re1 and then play Nf4 to win the h5 pawn.

| 15 | Rxg8 | Kxg8 |
| 16 | Nh6+ | ... |

This move forked the king and rook. Black soon resigned. The key to White's success in this game was free access to squares such as e6 and d6.

EXCHANGING PIECES

Your opponent plays a move that allows you to exchange a piece of the same value or a pawn – what to do? Of course, every specific case must be judged on its merits. The fact is that sometimes it is a good idea to exchange (or 'trade' as North American players call it), and sometimes it isn't.

But there are still a few general principles that can help guide your decision. One is that, if you have a material advantage, you should seek to simplify the position by exchanging pieces (the obverse is, of course, true: if you are down in material, you tend to want to keep the pieces on). The process of exchanging pieces to realize a material advantage is sometimes referred to as 'liquidation'. The idea is that you remove most of the pieces from the board, and with them any prospect that your opponent could generate some sort of tactical come-back. You are effectively trying to transform as fast as possible from middlegame to endgame, which is when the benefit of a material advantage can usually be most easily realized.

As with all general principles, this one has to be treated with the utmost caution. Look, for example, at the following position.

White, to play, is a whole bishop up. Does White want to swap off all the pawns? Absolutely not! If all the pawns are exchanged, checkmate cannot be achieved with a solitary bishop. It might be satisfactory to swap off two or three pairs of pawns, but certainly not all of them. The basic strategy for White in this position is to use the extra bishop in conjunction with the king (it is high time it came out of hiding on g1) in order to outmanoeuvre the enemy king and win a pawn or two somewhere. Once White is sure of an extra, or a passed, pawn, then it may be time to swap all the other pawns off.

Above, White is a pawn up with very good prospects of winning. Does White want to exchange five pairs of pawns, leaving (say) the extra one on c4? The answer is a qualified 'yes'. If all the pawns except for the one on c4 were suddenly spirited from the board, the position would technically be a draw: the pawn could not be forced through. A good idea here would be to liquidate two pairs of pawns on the queenside, making the c4 pawn into a passed pawn. It can then be used as a decoy as the white king pursues the kingside pawns: a common strategy in king and pawn endgames.

Exchanging can be a useful ploy for reasons other than realizing a material advantage.

In the position bottom left, the material situation is level. But White, to play, has a much better placed king than Black. If the knight on d7 could be removed, then the white king could perhaps advance via c5 or e5, and capture the weak enemy pawns on b7 or f5. The answer is to try and exchange it.

1   Nc5!   ...

If Black accedes, the white king will be one square nearer the b7 pawn. Endgames with only kings and pawns tend to work in favour of the player with what previously had only been a slight edge. The second problem for Black is that, if the knight exchange is avoided, the white knight will take the b7 pawn with impunity. Strong players would consider this position as good as over for Black.

1   ...   Nxc5
2   Kxc5   Kd7
3   Kd5!

Crafty. Black had moved the king in order to defend the b7 pawn, but now the white king doubles back to go after the f5 pawn. It cannot be defended in time.

continues on the next page

Far Left: White takes the bishop on d4, but if Black is able to recapture White's bishop then neither side has gained an advantage. The pieces cancel each other out, so the material balance remains the same.

More on exchanging pieces

A common dilemma occurs in positions where rooks can be exchanged along a file.

In this position, with White to play, 1 Rxd8+ would be quite a serious error. Black would recapture, and White would not be able to challenge Black's control of the d-file. The black rook would come to d2 and harass the white pawns, and White would be put on the defensive. Instead, White should simply hold ground and leave the situation on the d-file unresolved. The same applies if it is Black's move: 1...Rxd1+ would be a serious positional error.

Here, White to play can exchange on d7 with Nxd7, or on c7 with Rxc7. Neither of these exchanges of pieces is a good idea. This natural move, doubling the rooks on the d-file, gets Black back into the game.

1	Nxd7?	Rxd7
2	Rxb5+	Ka6
3	Rc5	Rfd8

Black will regain the pawn previously lost by taking on d4.

If we now go back to the diagram before 1 Nxd7, the thing to notice is how much stronger the knight is than the weak bishop on d7, hemmed in by its own pawns. That is a big clue to the exchange being undesirable. 1 Rxc7+? Kxc7, 2 d5 is better than the 1 Nxd7 variation, but Black may be able to survive. The best move seems to be to avoid exchanges altogether and play 1 d5! when White is threatening to play 2 d6 and force the black rook to exchange on c5, leaving the bishop in peril on the following move.

Another situation where a player may not want to exchange pieces is where the opponent is in a very cramped position. Space on the chessboard is often a very important factor – the more room your pieces have to manoeuvre, the better their scope. By allowing an opponent with a cramped position to exchange pieces, you are allowing the rest of their army more room to manoeuvre.

The diagram at the bottom of the previous page shows just such a situation. Black's bishops, queen and rooks are hopelessly hemmed in by their own pieces, while the knights, though a little more mobile, have few squares to which they can usefully move.

White, to play, can play 1 Nxe5? to exchange a pair of knights, but after 1...Nxe5, Black's cramped position has been partially relieved by the exchange. However, if White plays 1 Nd4!, then the pile-up of black pieces in a confined space leaves Black with problems. Black needs to defend against 2 Ne6 forking queen and rook. The only way to do this is by moving the knight on d7. 1...Nc5 is no good because the knight gets chased back from whence it came by 2 b4!, while 1...Nb8 is a terribly passive move.

In this position, with White to play, it is obvious that the knight is a vastly better piece than the very restricted bishop. However, despite this, it is time to liquidate White's advantage, because White can make the transition into a winning king and pawn endgame.

| 1 | Nxd7! | Kxd7 | 2 | Kf6 | ... |

White is a pawn down but is able to win two pawns right away. Black is now in *zugzwang*, i.e. the compulsion of having to make a move causes Black to give ground.

| 2 | ... | e5 |

The best try. If White were to capture with either the d4 or f4 pawn, Black would at least have a passed pawn which could race down the board.

3	Kxe5	Ke7
4	Kxf5	Kf7
5	Ke5	Ke7
6	f5	...

Zugzwang again. Now Black has to give ground with the black king.

6	...	Kd7
7	f6	Kd8
8	Kd6	...

Now White wins the two remaining black pawns and triumphs easily. This is an example of giving up one advantage (good knight versus bad bishop) in order to simplify the win.

MORE BASIC ENDGAMES

We have already seen how to give checkmate with a single queen or rook left on the chessboard (besides the king), but it is also possible to give checkmate with a pair of bishops or a bishop and knight, as shown by the following basic examples. It's worth taking time to learn the underlying techniques.

This checkmate needs a bit of practice, but an experienced player can probably work it out without having to memorize any particular line of play. With a rook or queen, the idea is to drive the king to the edge of the board, but with the two bishops it is necessary to drive the king into one of the four corner squares. The following shows one example of how to mate with two bishops. Of course, it is not the only way.

1	Bh3	Kf3	4	Kc4	Ke5
2	Kb2	Kf4	5	Bg3+	Ke4
3	Kc3	Ke4			

Black's king has managed to stay in the middle of the board, but, now that the white king has arrived, White starts squeezing Black towards the edge.

6	Bd6	Ke3
7	Bf5	Ke2
8	Kd4	Kf3
9	Kd3	...

It is instructive to see how White cuts off Black's flight path in both directions. This sort of technique takes a little practice, but it will come with time.

9	...	Kf2
10	Bg4	Kf1
11	Ke3	Ke1
12	Bg3+	...

Once the defending king is driven to the edge of the board, the final phase of the process becomes relatively straightforward.

12	...	Kf1
13	Bh3+	Kg1
14	Kf3	Kh1
15	Bf4	...

15 Kf2?? would be a dreadful mistake – stalemate!

15	...	Kg1
16	Kg3	Kh1
17	Bg2+	Kg1
18	Be3 mate	

Mate with bishop and knight

Of the basic checkmates with minimal pieces and without pawns, the textbooks tell us that this is the most difficult. That is true, but it is not so difficult that it cannot be learned. Yes, the bad news is that you have to learn something more or less by heart – the good news is that it is only the last phase of the process that needs to be committed to memory.

The first part of the process is to get the black king to the edge of the board. This can be done with a bit of practice. Starting from the position above:

1	Nb3+	Kd5
2	Kb5	Ke5
3	Kc5	Kf5
4	Kd5	Kg5
5	Be2	Kf5
6	Nd4+	Kf6
7	Bd3	Ke7

8	Ke5	Kf7

At this point, there is something very important to know about this endgame. It is only possible to checkmate the king by driving it to a corner of the same colour as the bishop. Therefore, given that the bishop on d3 moves on white squares in this example, the place we are trying to drive the king to is either h1 or a8. This also influences the plan for the defence. Notice that, having been driven near the edge of the board, the black king now makes a move towards the h8 square – on which it can never be checkmated.

9	Ne6	Ke7
10	Ng5	Kf8
11	Kf6	Kg8

That is the end of the first phase. We have driven the black king to the edge of the board – but to the wrong corner. However, this is all part of the plan. First we drive the king to the wrong corner, and then to the right corner – and then to checkmate.

continues on next page ➡

Now for the final phase of the bishop and knight checkmate. The first thing to do is to study the above position for a while. Remember, we are trying to drive the black king from the wrong corner of the board (marked in red) towards one of the right corners (marked in green). The first part of the final assault is very logical. The black king must be kept out of the black square on h8. The white bishop will never be able to do that because it moves on white squares. So, by Holmesian deduction, it must be the white knight that does it from f7 or g6. So the right move has to be:

12   Nf7!   Kf8

That's it, we've forced the king out of the corner. Now the king must be shifted along the rank, towards execution on a8. So it must be deprived of the g8 square. This is easy.

13   Bh7   ...

So far, so logical. The bishop move stops the king from returning to g8. Now the king must walk one square further along the rank, towards doom on a8.

13   ...   Ke8 | 14   Ne5   Kd8

Everything is going smoothly. Note that the king could have tried to double-back here with 14...Kf8, but then White plays 15 Nd7+, forcing 15...Ke8 16 Ke6, and then the king is moving in the right direction.

15   Ke6   Kc7

It is at around this point that it becomes necessary to learn a trick or two by heart. It seems as if the black king has escaped its escort at this point and is getting ready for a sprint to a1, another square on which it is immune from checkmate. But the knight and bishop now have a couple of precise moves that stop the king from getting out of the net.

16   Nd7!   Kc6 | 17   Bd3!   ...

Two deft moves have thrown the net around the black king, stopping it coming to c5, b5 and b6. It can only go to b7 or c7.

| 17 | ... | Kc7 | 18 | Be4! | ... |

This pulls the net tighter. Black now has a choice of only c8 and d8.

| 18 | ... | Kc8 | 19 | Kd6 | Kd8 |

Obviously Black still hankers after one of the wrong-coloured corners, but this can easily be averted.

20   Bg6!   ...

20	...	Kc8	23	Kc6	Kb8
21	Nc5	Kd8	24	Kb6	...
22	Nb7+	Kc8			

Now the black king is completely boxed in and it becomes quite easy to trap it.

24   ...   Ka8

One last try for freedom. 24...Kc8, is rebuffed: 25 Bf5+ Kb8 26 Nc5 reaches the same position in the game.

| 25 | Nc5 | Kb8 |
| 26 | Bf5 | Ka8 |

27   Bg4!   ...

Not 27 Na6?? stalemate. White 'loses' a move (i.e. plays a meaningless move) with the bishop so that Na6 can be played next move with check.

| 27 | ... | Kb8 | 29 | Bf3 mate |
| 28 | Na6+ | Ka8 | | |

A very satisfying finish. To master the endgame, memorize the sequence between moves 12 to 18.

ENDGAMES: KINGS AND PAWNS

Pawns usually benefit from the support of the king when it comes to the final race through to promotion, but there are situations where they can look after themselves when the king is a long distance away. Usually it's a question of them supporting each other until the king can finally lend a hand.

Here, everything depends on whose turn it is to play. If it is White's turn, White wins, but if it is Black's turn, it is a draw (Black plays 1...Kc6, takes the c-pawn next move and takes the a-pawn soon afterwards). If it is White's turn...

1   a5!   ...

Black is left with a dilemma. If 1...Kc6 is played, then 2 a6! is played and if 1...Ka6 2 c6!. A capture on the following turn would allow the remaining pawn to promote. Let's look at one line:

1   ...   Kc6
2   a6!   Kc7

That's a nice try by Black. Now if White plays 3 a7??, Black can play 3...Kb7, capture the pawn and have time to get back to gobble up the c-pawn. However, White doesn't have to move a pawn.

3	Kg3!	Kc6	6	Kd4	Kc7
4	Kf4	Kc7	7	Kd5	...
5	Ke5	Kc6			

Now the win is very easy. It is interesting to see how the two pawns somehow defend each other despite being separated by one file. It is, of course, much easier if the pawns are on adjoining files.

This time it doesn't matter whose turn it is. Black cannot take the a5 pawn because it is defended by the b4 pawn, and Black cannot take the b4 pawn because the a5 pawn could no longer be stopped. In order to win, White simply needs to bring the king over to support the pawns, wait for the king to take a step backwards and then guide one of the pawns home.

Above White is to play but is doomed. When the black king captures f4, having used the h5 pawn as a decoy, it will be two files nearer the kingside and win the race to capture the pawns on a3 and b4 before White captures the black pawns on a6 and b5.

1   Kh4   ...

If White sits tight with 1 Kf3, Black plays 1...Kf5 2 Kg3 h4+ 3 Kf3 h3 4 Kg3 h2 and now White has to abandon the defence of the f3 pawn.

1	...	Kf5	3	Kg6	...
2	Kxh5	Kxf4			

It still looks like White has a chance of doing some damage to the black pawns, but it is an illusion.

3	...	Ke4	6	Kd6	Kb3
4	Kf6	Kd4	7	Kc6	Kxa3
5	Ke6	Kc4	8	Kc5	Ka4!

Now White must abandon the defence of the b4 pawn.

Who dares, loses

This looks dead level, and indeed it is. But the player whose move it is must tread carefully. Let's try White...

1   Kd5??   ...

The sub-heading was a big clue. Whoever tries to win the opposing player's pawn will lose this position.

1   ...   Kf4!

It is our old friend/enemy, *zugzwang*, again. White must move the king, Black takes the e4 pawn, and duly wins. If it had been Black to move, 1...Kf4?? 2 Kd5!, Black would have to abandon the defence of the e5 pawn and lose.

WINNING A WON POSITION

Chess players are very similar to fishermen in one respect: they are always bemoaning the 'one that got away'. The sentence usually starts with: 'I had a won position but...' – and then follows any one of a vast number of excuses for letting the win slip through their fingers. Complacency is the chess player's worst enemy.

An important general principle and one you can trust absolutely, despite the title of this section, is that there is no such thing in chess as a 'won position'. It's not over until the king has been checkmated. Disaster can strike at any time in the shape of a blunder or a stalemate. Perhaps it is reasonable to say that you have a 'winning position': the present tense implies that there is still some work to do to win. In contrast, the past participle 'won' somehow implies that the work has already been done. Therein lies the fatal delusion.

When your opponent is down to a king, or a few remaining pieces have no legal moves, remind yourself about the possibility of stalemate. It may be closer than you think.

Black is cruising to victory, but notices that White might be threatening perpetual check with Qc5+ etc, so plays...

1   ...   d3??

It must be admitted that it is very natural to play this move, which defends against queen checks on the f1–6a diagonal, but it needlessly squanders a win. A much better alternative would have been 1...Qe1+ 2 Kh2 Qxa5, winning another pawn. After that, Black can move the queen to b6 to defend all the pawns, and then push either the a-pawn or the d-pawn.

2   Qf2!!

A bolt from the blue. If Black plays 2...Qxf2, it is stalemate. However, any other move would cost the queen. So it has to be 2...Qxf2 and the game is drawn. The mistake here was down to Black not bearing in mind the reduced number of pieces that White had at his disposal, and thus not being extra wary about this sort of stalemate trick.

In this position, White has to move the knight on c4. It is a very difficult position for White since Black has a number of advantages. For one thing, the dark-squared bishop on g7 is vastly superior to White's weak bishop on b1. There is the threat of Nf4 in the air (White couldn't take it because of the undefended queen on e2), and there is the possibility of the black queen coming to a3.

1   Na5?   ...

The only move was 1 Nd2, although after 1...Rxc1 2 Rxc1 Nf4 3 Qe1 Nd5 4 Nf1 b4, the black knight will settle on c3 and harass the white position. After the white move, Black has to think about the various advantages of this position and see if they can be translated into a striking chance.

1   ...   Rxc1
2   Rxc1   Qa3!

Black spots a pleasant double attack on the rook and the knight.

3   Qe1   Bb2!

Black exploits the power of the bishop on the long diagonal. Suddenly, White finds that the rook cannot move. If it goes forward up the c-file, Black plays Qxa5!, exploiting the possibility of a back-rank mate with the rook if White captures on a5. If White plays 4 Rd1, Black still plays 4...Qxa5. Let's look at that position.

If White plays 5 Qxa5, the reply is 5...Rxd1+ and mate next move. If 5 Rxd8+, then Black simply replies 5...Qxd8 and remains a knight up on material. So a piece has been lost. After the previous diagram, the game continued:

4   Nc4   bxc4
5   Rxc4   ...

Black has a 'won position'. At such moments, it is all too easy to relax and make a mess of things. The important things to do are: to maintain the same level of concentration as if there were still everything to play for; and to try to find ways to simplify the position so that the win becomes trivial.

5   ...   Qa5!

Black once again exploits the fact that the back rank is exposed to a rook mate. The queen is untouchable.

6	Qf1	Qd5	10	Qe1	Ne4
7	Bc2	Nc5	11	Ra4	Nc3
8	g3	a5	12	Ra3	Be7
9	Qb1	Bf6			

Black will soon be a rook up in material. White resigned.

More winning techniques

The cliché 'and the rest is just a matter of technique' can be found in many chess game annotations, at the point where the writer thinks that the game is as good as won, and that there is no need to make detailed comments about the remaining moves. However, it is not very helpful to readers who have yet to acquire the necessary technique – which simply means 'playing a lot of good moves in succession'. This takes practice and concentration. One problem with chess is that you can play 99 excellent moves, but, if the 100th one is bad, it can cost you the game. The important thing is to maintain even concentration throughout the game, neither relaxing at any point (and playing the first thing that comes into your head), nor agonizing excessively over one move.

Overconfidence is a problem when you have a very good position. You think to yourself: 'I ought to be able to win this' and thereby start to put extra pressure on yourself. Here is an example.

This is undoubtedly a very good position for White, whose turn it is. White is a pawn up, with the opportunity to take a second one (on h7), but Black's king position is rather exposed. However, there is still a lot of material on the board, and some of Black's pieces have attacking possibilities.

| 1 | Bxb7 | ... |

This doesn't compromise White's position, but there were two better moves: 1 Rc3!, which attacks the queen and removes the rook from a square where it might get pinned against the king, and 1 Bxh7, which would have been the next move after 1 Rc3 anyway.

1	...	Qxb7
2	Qe6+	Kf8
3	Nb6?	...

Again, not a total disaster, but far from the best move. 3 Nd4 is much better, with a view to bringing more force to bear against the black king in due course. Notice that, if Black tries to discover an attack on the white queen with, for example, 3...Bxa3, White breaks through the defences with 4 Rxf6+! gxf6 5 Qxf6+ Qf7 6 Qh8+ Qg8 7 Rf3+ Ke7 8 Qf6+ Kd7 9 Nb6+, and White will soon checkmate the black king.

| 3 | ... | Rad8 |

White's advantage has diminished a little. White can no longer deploy the knight on b3 to d4 as before, but White is still a pawn up and generally better placed than Black.

| 4 | Nc4 | Qa7 |

Black pins the rook on e3 against the white king.

5   Ne5??   ...

White plays a rook sacrifice. In some ways it is very clever, but, objectively, it is a complete disaster because Black does not have to accept the sacrifice. White should have been content with the mundane 5 Kh1! which breaks the pin on the rook. After that, White could have claimed an advantage, but, after the move played, is struggling.

5   ...   Bd6!

If Black had accepted the rook sacrifice, Black would have lost: 5...Qxe3+?? 6 Kh1 and now the only way to deal with the threat of Qf7 mate would have been to capture the knight, leaving White with a queen and pawn for rook and knight – and a two-point material advantage.

6   Rxf6+?

White misses a chance of salvation. 6 Ng6+! secures perpetual check after 6...hxg6 7 Rxf6+ gxf6 8 Qxf6+ Kh8 9 Qh6+ and Black can never escape the series of queen checks.

6   ...   gxf6

7   Qxf6+   Kg8
8   Ng4   Bf8!

9   Kh1??   ...

A blunder. White could play 9 Qg5+ Kh8 10 Ne5, etc, and would still be in the game, though struggling.

9   ...   Rd1+

Black concludes the game with a back rank mate.

A CHESS BRILLIANCY

All chess players find chess brilliancies irresistible to read about in books and magazines. The following game is an attractive example of a queen sacrifice followed by a king hunt across the board. It is an unusual example of the power that bishops and knights can wield when attacking an exposed king.

Genuine brilliancies seldom occur in practical chess, and most professional players seek to play the percentages rather than deliberately striving for something aesthetically pleasing.

This game was played in London in 1912. White was Edward Lasker (1885–1981, but not to be confused with the then world champion Emanuel Lasker). Lasker became a US citizen and was a fine player, writer and teacher of the game. Black in this game was Sir George Thomas (1881–1972), an English baronet who won the British Chess Championship in 1923 and 1924. He was even more distinguished as a badminton player, winning the All-England Championships four times, and giving his name to one of the sport's most prestigious trophies.

	Lasker	Thomas
1	d4	f5

This is the first move of the Dutch Defence, which is a bold, counter-attacking defence for Black.

| 2 | e4 | ... |

Offering a pawn sacrifice. This is known as the Staunton Gambit, as it was used by the great English player Howard Staunton as early as 1847.

2	...	fxe4
3	Nc3	Nf6
4	Bg5	e6

These days most players prefer 4...Nc6 in this position. Now White can recapture the pawn.

5	Nxe4	Be7
6	Bxf6	Bxf6
7	Nf3	0–0

| 8 | Bd3 | b6 |

A reasonably balanced position. However, Black's kingside set-up is somewhat lacking in defenders, and White's group of minor pieces are pointing in the general direction of the h7 square.

| 9 | Ne5 | ... |

This leads to a brilliant victory, but objectively, is not the best move. Black should now simply play 9...Bxe5 to remove the attacking knight from the board. After 10 dxe5 Nc6, White has the menacing 11 Qh5, but then 11...Rf5 seems to be perfectly safe for Black. This a further warning against trying to win brilliantly. For every masterpiece you find in an anthology of chess brilliancies, there are probably another thousand flawed concepts that brought only ignominious defeat.

| 9 | ... | Bb7? |
| 10 | Qh5 | Qe7? |

This was Black's chance to stay in the game. 10...Bxe5 seems to keep Black's ship afloat, despite the gale-force wind that seems to be blowing around the h7 square. If now 11 Ng5 h6!, then White has no *coup de grace*.

One imagines Black carefully calculated various White tries in this position. 11 Nxf6+ is quite good, but after 11...gxf6 there is nothing decisive. 11 Ng5 is answered by 11...g6, and Black's position holds. White could even try 11 Nd6, but again 11...g6 12 Nxg6 Qxd6 13 Nxf8 Kxf8 seems reasonably safe for Black. However, Lasker found something unexpected:

11   Qxh7+!!   ...

In calculating all the candidate moves by the minor pieces, it was easy for Black to overlook this more drastic blow. Which of us in his shoes would have expected White to unleash such a fiendish sacrifice?

11   ...   Kxh7
12   Nxf6+   ...

Black is in double check, so must move his king. If he plays to h8, the end comes instantly – 13 Ng6 mate. There is only one other move.

12   ...   Kh6
13   Neg4+   Kg5
14   h4+   Kf4
15   g3+   Kf3

The black king has been forced further and further away from the safety of his own camp.

16   Be2+   ...

Not the quickest way to victory (16 0–0 and 16 Kf1 both set up unstoppable mate on the next move with 17 Nh2), but it is perhaps more aesthetically pleasing.

16   ...   Kg2
17   Rh2+   Kg1
18   Kd2 mate

A minor blemish: it would surely have been more piquant to play 18 0–0–0 mate.

RUBINSTEIN'S IMMORTAL GAME

Akiba Rubinstein (1882–1961) never became world chess champion but is universally acknowledged to be one of the finest players who failed to do so. For a number of years between 1907 and 1912, Rubinstein had the best record of any chess player in the world, including Emanuel Lasker. Here is his most famous game.

It is largely unremarkable for the first 19 moves or so, but then explodes into life with a veritable cascade of sacrifices. Rubinstein's opponent in this game, Gersz Rotlewi (1889–1920) was also Polish and a very promising player himself, but, sadly, he died young.

	Rotlewi	Rubinstein
1	d4	d5
2	Nf3	e6
3	e3	c5
4	c4	...

White starts with a Colle Opening, but now chooses to transpose into a Queen's Gambit. It is often possible to transpose from one opening system into another, and chess players often try to keep their opponents guessing in this way.

4	...	Nc6
5	Nc3	Nf6

The position is perfectly symmetrical. Notice that neither side has been in a hurry to exchange the pawns in the centre, but now White decides it is time to do so.

6	dxc5	Bxc5	9	Bb2	0–0
7	a3	a6	10	Qd2	...
8	b4	Bd6			

White has not made any tactical mistakes so far, but at the same time one cannot help feeling that he has played a little passively. It is usual for White to try and maintain the initiative in the opening and he has not done so here. Rather than 10 Qd2, White should perhaps play 10 Bd3 and then castle kingside.

10	...	Qe7	13	Bd3	Rd8
11	Bd3	dxc4	14	Qe2	...
12	Bxc4	b5			

White realizes that his Qd2 move was wrong (because of the potential danger coming from the rook on d8) and now relocates the queen to e2. But, in making one unnecessary move with his queen, he has lost time.

| 14 | ... | Bb7 | 15 | 0–0 | ... |

Note that the position is almost symmetrical again. However, somewhere along the line, Black has got in the useful developing move Rd8, and it is also his move now (whereas it was White's in the original position). Chess players talk about gaining a tempo when they steal a march on the opponent in this way; so here, Black has the advantage of two extra tempi.

15	...	Ne5	18	e4	Rac8
16	Nxe5	Bxe5	19	e5?	...
17	f4	Bc7			

White finally pushes his luck too far. He should play 19 Kh1 or 19 Rac

| 19 | ... | Bb6+ | 20 | Kh1 | Ng4! |

Black unleashes his first threat, which is Qh4 and mate on h2.

| 21 | Be4 | ... |

21 Qxg4 Rxd3, and Black threatens the knight on c3 and also Rd2, attacking the bishop and the g2 pawn.

| 21 | ... | Qh4 |
| 22 | g3 | ... |

This defends the mate threat, but leads to perhaps the greatest sacrificial orgy in chess history.

| 22 | ... | Rxc3!! |
| 23 | gxh4 | ... |

23 Bxb7 Rxg3! 24 Rf3 Rxf3 25 Bxf3 Nf2+ 26 Kg1 Ne4+ wins for Black.

Black has given up his queen for a knight and now has no fewer than three pieces *en prise*. His solution to this problem... is to put a fourth piece *en prise*!

| 23 | ... | Rd2!! |

Astounding. White has the pick of four captures, but all of them lead to ruin. For example, 24 Qxg4 Bxe4+ will lose White a rook and a queen to stop mate.

| 24 | Qxd2 | Bxe4+ |
| 25 | Qg2 | Rh3!! |

At this point, White resigned. There is nothing to be done about the threat of Rxh2 mate. For example, 26 Bd4 Rxh2+ 27 Kg1 Rxg2+ 28 Kh1 Rg3+ 29 Rf3 Bxf3 mate. It's not hard to understand why many consider this game to be Rubinstein's finest moment, nor to appreciate why grandmasters even today still study his games for insight and inspiration. A measure of his greatness is given by the lines named after him in the Sicilian, French and Nimzo-Indian defences.

CHAMPIONS IN ACTION

If you want to improve your chess, there are few better ways of doing so than learning from the masters. The following pages offer examples from play of all the world chess champions. It is instructive to note that each champion has an individual style of play. We begin with the first official world champion, Wilhelm Steinitz.

Wilhelm Steinitz: 1st World Champion (1886–1894)

The first player to be recognized as world champion was Wilhelm Steinitz. Early on, his chess style was mostly based on gambits and tactical play, but he gradually became more positional. This game was played in 1895 at a big tournament in Hastings, UK, against Kurt von Bardeleben, another strong master of that era.

Steinitz	von Bardeleben
1	d5!!	cxd5
2	Nd4	...

The pawn sacrifice 1 d5 clears the square for the knight, which exerts strong pressure on Black's position.

2	...	Kf7	4	Qg4	g6
3	Ne6	Rhc8	5	Ng5+	Ke8

Black seems to have everything defended, but he is in for a shock.

6	Rxe7+!!	Kf8!?

If 6...Qxe7 7 Rxc8+ wins and if 6...Kxe7 7 Re1+ Kd6 8 Qb4+ Rc5 9 Re6+ soon wins.

7	Rf7+!	...

White cannot capture the queen because it would allow a back-rank mate with Rxc1.

7	...	Kg8!	8	Rg7+!	...

The rook is immune to capture from the king because it would allow the queen to be captured with check.

8	...	Kh8	9	Rxh7+!	...

At this point, Steinitz announced to his opponent that he would force checkmate in 11 moves, starting with this one. But von Bardeleben put on his coat and left the tournament room without saying a word. Here is what Steinitz apparently had in mind: 9...Kg8 10 Rg7+ Kh8 11 Qh4+! Kxg7 12 Qh7+ Kf8 13 Qh8+ Ke7 14 Qg7+ Ke8 15 Qg8+ Ke7 16 Qf7+ Kd8 17 Qf8+ Qe8 18 Nf7+ Kd7 19 Qd6 mate.

Emanuel Lasker:
2nd World Champion (1894–1921)

Emanuel Lasker was an academic mathematician and philosopher, and dabbled in other games besides chess, so it was all the more remarkable that he should have managed to dominate chess for so long. His pragmatic approach, despite occasional long breaks from the game, demonstrated a superiority lasting many years.

Lasker was 66 when the following was played in a tournament in Moscow in 1935 – his opponent, Vasja Pirc (1907–1980) was only 28. Lasker was one of the few top players who maintained his chess strength well into his old age.

	Lasker	Pirc
1	e4	c5
2	Nf3	Nc6
3	d4	cxd4
4	Nxd4	Nf6
5	Nc3	d6
6	Be2	e6
7	0–0	a6
8	Be3	Qc7
9	f4	Na5

A fairly standard set-up in the Sicilian Defence. Black's last move intends Nc4, to harass the bishop on e3 and the pawn on b2. However, it wastes a lot of time when Black should really be ensuring the safety of his king.

10	f5	Nc4
11	Bxc4	Qxc4
12	fxe6	fxe6

| 13 | Rxf6! | ... |

Lasker sacrifices the exchange (rook for knight) in order to facilitate his attack on the king.

| 13 | ... | gxf6 | 14 | Qh5+ | Kd8 |

14...Ke7 keeps the queen from entering at f7, but loses to 15 Nf5+! exf5 16 Nd5+ Kd8 17 Bb6+ and White soon mates.

| 15 | Qf7 | ... |

If Black tries to save the rook with 15...Be7, White plays 16 Nf5 and the knight cannot be taken because the queen would be lost.

| 15 | ... | Bd7 | 17 | Qxh8 | Bh6 |
| 16 | Qxf6+ | Kc7 | | | |

The body count shows that White now has an extra knight and pawn, so Black tries this ingenious trick.

continues on the next page

18   Nxe6+!   ...

Much better than 18 Qxa8 Bxe3+ 19 Kh1 Bxd4 when Black is still in the game.

18	...	Qxe6
19	Qxa8	Bxe3+
20	Kh1	1–0

This game does not end in checkmate, but White has done just enough to ensure that his preponderance of material will win the game.

José Raúl Capablanca:
3rd World Champion (1921–1927)

The Cuban player Capablanca was a child prodigy with a wonderful natural talent for the game. He later turned into something of a playboy, and failed to work hard at the game. But, despite this, he remained one of the best players during the interwar years. His style was generally smooth and positional. Here is an unusual finish, from St Petersburg in 1914, against the great theoretician Aron Nimzowitsch.

Black is a pawn down, but his two rooks have strong pressure against White's queenside.

	Nimzowitsch	**Capablanca**
1	...	Rb4!

Threatening 2...Bd4, pinning the queen against the king.

2	Qg5	Bd4+
3	Kh1	Rab8

Now Black is putting heavy pressure on the b2 pawn and also threatening the knight on c3. Note also how difficult it is to move the knight to safety. Something has to give. White tries a drastic measure to relieve the pressure.

4	Rxd4	Qxd4
5	Rd1	Qc4
6	h4	Rxb2
7	Qd2	Qc5

Black is now winning comfortably. There is no hurry to finish White off.

8	Re1	Qh5	10	Kg1	Qh5
9	Ra1	Qxh4+	11	a5	...

Nimzowitsch would have been fully aware that the plan of advancing the a-pawn was a forlorn hope. Garry Kasparov described this idea as 'a little joke'.

11	...	Ra8	14	a7	Qc5
12	a6	Qc5+	15	e5	Qxe5
13	Kh1	Qc4	16	Ra4	Qh5+

17	Kg1	Qc5+
18	Kh2	d5

Black is being ultra-cautious: he doesn't want the knight to come to e4 after 18...Rxa7 19 Rxa7 Qxa7.

19	Rh4	Rxa7
20	Nd1	...

And White resigned at last. 20...Qxc2 forces an exchange of queens, and after that it is simple.

Alexander Alekhine: 4th World Champion (1927–1935, 1937–1946)

Alekhine still held the world championship title at his death in 1946, although he had not played a title match since regaining his title from the Dutchman Max Euwe in 1937. He was a forceful attacking player who devoted himself to chess.

Here, he plays White against the leading British player Hugh Alexander (1909–1974).

White has pressure along the long diagonal, but needs to get his kingside pieces into the attack.

	Alekhine	Alexander
1	e4!	Nxe4

A tricky defence.

2	Qc1	...

2 Bxg7? is not so good because of 2...Nxg5 3 Bxf8 Nxh3+ 4 Kg2 Rxf8 5 Kxh3 Nf6, and Black will win the d-pawn and have a bishop and two pawns for the rook.

2	...	Nef6
3	Bxf5!	...

If 3...gxf5 then 4 Nxf5, Black's queen is in a pickle. If 4...Qg6, 5 Ne7+ wins it, while if 4...Qf7, 5 Nh6+ wins it. If 4...Qh8, there follows 5 Nh6+ Kg7 6 Qg5 mate.

3	...	Kh8
4	Be6	...

Now that the f5 pawn has gone, the white bishop can join in the attack.

4	...	Ba6
5	Rfe1	Ne5
6	f4!	Nd3
7	Rxd3	Bxd3
8	g4	1–0

There is nothing to be done about the g-pawn going to g5, winning the knight and probably more besides.

continues on the next page ➡

Max Euwe: 5th World Champion (1935–1937)

Dutch schoolmaster and academic Max Euwe held the world title for only two years. Yet his achievement in winning it – he was an amateur player – remains one of the great fairytale success stories in chess.

This was the 26th game of Euwe's title-winning match against Alekhine in 1935. It was nicknamed 'the pearl of Zandvoort', after the town in which it was played.

White has two powerful pawns for the exchange.

	Euwe	Alekhine
1	Qe5	Qxe5
2	fxe5	...

Now the two pawns are connected passed pawns.

2	...	Rf5
3	Re1	...

It might have been better to play 3 Rg5 to exchange a pair of rooks.

3	...	h6
4	Nd8	Rf2
5	e6	Rd2
6	Nc6	Re8
7	e7	b5
8	Nd8	Kg7
9	Nb7	Kf6
10	Re6+	Kg5
11	Nd6	Rxe7
12	Ne4+	1–0

A classic example of the power of passed pawns.

Mikhail Botvinnik: 6th World Champion (1948–1957, 1958–1960, 1961–1963)

After Alekhine's death, a tournament was held to fill the vacancy at the top of chess. Mikhail Botvinnik won the five-player competition and became the first of several Soviet world champions. He lost his title twice, to Smyslov and Tal, but, on both occasions, was able to exploit an automatic rematch provision in the rules in order to regain it within 12 months. He was a hard-working player who prepared assiduously for every game he played and was a genius at identifying and exploiting tiny flaws in his closest rivals' games.

In this game he had White against the former world champion Capablanca in a tournament in the Netherlands, in 1938.

White is a pawn down but has powerful pressure against the king with a forceful pin of the knight.

	Botvinnik	Capablanca
1	Ba3!!	...

A superb sacrifice, deflecting the queen away from the defence of the king.

1	...	Qxa3
2	Nh5+!!	...

A second hammer blow. White has worked out he only needs the queen and e6 pawn to finish off the black king.

2	...	gxh5
3	Qg5+	Kf8

4	Qxf6+	Kg8

If instead the king goes to e8, White plays 5 Qf7+ Kd8 6 Qd7 mate.

5	e7	...

White finally stops checking. It is Black's turn to check the white king, But White has calculated that he can eventually escape perpetual check.

5	...	Qc1+	8	Kh4	Qe4+
6	Kf2	Qc2+	9	Kxh5	Qe2+
7	Kg3	Qd3+			

If Black plays 9...Qg6+ 10 Qxg6+ hxg6+ 11 Kxg6, then Black cannot prevent the pawn from promoting and giving checkmate.

10	Kh4	Qe4+	12	Kh5	1–0
11	g4	Qe1+			

Black cannot prevent the promotion of the pawn (after 12...h6 13 Qg6+ Kh8 14 e8Q+). So he resigned.

Vasily Smyslov: 6th World Champion (1957–1958)

Smyslov had only a brief reign as world champion, but remains one of the great stylists of the chess world. He is famous for his immaculate endgame play. Here, he defeats Mikhail Botvinnik in the 17th match game of the 1957 world championship.

The game was adjourned for the day after five hours' play. Overnight, Botvinnik realized that he could be doing worse here and offered a draw. But Smyslov sensed he could be winning and turned him down.

	Botvinnik	Smyslov
1	...	Kh6

This was the 'sealed move'. In other words, Smyslov had not played it on the board, but had written it on a piece of paper and sealed it in an envelope, handing it over to the match official for safe-keeping. By doing this, Botvinnik would not be handed the unfair advantage of extra time in which to analyse the actual position on the board until the resumption.

Black's plan is to win the h-pawn. White cannot defend it adequately because the knight has to cover the advance of the c-pawn.

2	Nc2	Be7	7	Nc2	Bd6
3	Kg3	Kh5	8	Ne1	Kh4
4	Kf3	Kxh4	9	Nc2	Kh3
5	Ne1	g5	10	Na1	Kh2
6	fxg5	Kxg5			

continues on the next page ➔

11	Kf2	...

White is trying to stop the king from infiltrating the position.

11	...	Bg3+	17	Ne1	Bd8
12	Kf3	Bh4	18	Nc2	Bf6
13	Nc2	Kg1	19	a3	Be7
14	Ke2	Kg2	20	b4	a4
15	Na1	Be7	21	Ne1	Bg5
16	Nc2	Kg3	22	Nc2	Bf6

Finally, after long manoeuvring, Black has achieved a *zugzwang*. If 23 Ne1 f4 24 exf4 Bxd4 25 Nd3 Ba7, then White has to give ground.

23	Kd3	Kf2
24	Na1	Bd8
25	Nc2	Bg5
26	b5	...

Otherwise the e3 pawn is lost, and Black's f-pawn will soon promote.

26	...	Bd8	28	Nc2	Ba5
27	Nb4	Bb6	29	Nb4	Ke1

Most players would play on here, but Botvinnik had seen enough and resigned. Either Black's king will sneak along the back row and win that way or (if 30 Kc2 or 30 Kxc3) he will go to e2 and win the e3 pawn.

Mikhail Tal: 8th World Champion (1960–1961)

Latvian star Mikhail Tal had a meteoric career as world champion, dazzling the world with his tactical wizardry at chess. Unfortunately, he paid little heed to his rather serious health problems.

Here, he has Black against Bukhuti Gurgenidze in Moscow, in 1957.

	Gurgenidze	Tal
1	...	Ng4

A casual-looking move that White underestimates. A move such as 2 Nf3 would leave White well placed.

2	h3?	Nxf2!

Tal does not need a second invitation to sacrifice.

| 3 | Kxf2 | Qh4+ | 4 | Kf1 | ... |

4 g3? Bd4+ would be bad: 5 Kg2 Qxh3+ leads to mate.

| 4 | ... | Bd4 |

Threatening mate. The position is now very sharp.

| 5 | Nd1 | Qxh3! |

White cannot take the queen with 6 gxh3 because 6...Bxh3 is mate.

| 6 | Bf3 | Qh2 | 8 | Ndc4 | ... |
| 7 | Ne3 | f5 | | | |

White should probably have tried to run away with 8 Ke2, but it was always hard to work out what was happening when playing Tal. His forte was to make the position as complicated as possible.

| 8 | ... | fxe4 | 9 | Bxe4 | Ba6 |

White is still a knight for two pawns up, but his position is probably beyond repair because of the various pins and the exposure of the king.

| 10 | Bf3 | Re5 | 12 | Bd2 | ... |
| 11 | Ra3 | Rae8 | | | |

White could have lasted longer with 12 Rd3.

| 12 | ... | Nxd5! |

Black brings the last attacking piece to bear on things.

| 13 | Bxd5+ | Rxd5 | 14 | Ke2 | ... |

Instead, 14 Nxd5 allows 14...Qg1 mate.

| 14 | ... | Bxe3 | 15 | Rxe3 | Bxc4+ |

White resigned. If 16 Qxc4 Qxg2+ 17 Kd1 Qxd2 mate, and if 16 Kd1 Rxe3 17 Rxe3 Qg1+ 18 Re1 Qf2 19 Kc1 Bb3! black wins.

Tigran Petosian: 9th World Champion (1963–1969)

Petrosian was a national hero in his native Armenia. He was a cautious and cagey player who avoided risk and tended to draw a lot of games. However, he could be a dangerous tactician on his day and was also a superb match player who finally ended the Botvinnik reign. He was also initially successful against the younger generation represented by Boris Spassky.

continues on the next page →

Here is a game from the 1962 world championship qualifying competition, from which Petrosian won the right to play Botvinnik in the final match. Petrosian has White against his old rival Viktor Korchnoi.

White, to play, has a good advantage in terms of development, and he wastes no time in exploiting it.

	Petrosian	Korchnoi
1	b4!	Qe5

If Black plays 1...Qxa3, 2 Nd5! leaves the queen stranded behind enemy lines.

| 2 | f4! | Qb8 |

Once again, Black cannot risk taking a pawn. If 2...Qxe3+, 3 Kh1, then White will play Rf3 next move to trap the queen.

3	Bxf7+!	Kxf7
4	Qb3+	Ke8
5	Nd5	...

Despite his reputation as a complacent player, Petrosian shows that he can play a vigorous and enterprising game here. Having driven Black's queen back into passive defence, he has sacrificed a bishop to open up the king.

5	...	Bd6
6	Ne6	b5
7	Ndc7+	Ke7

7...Bxc7 is best, but after 8 Nxc7+ Kd8 9 Rfd1, Black has not much chance of survival.

| 8 | Nd4 | ... |

Now White threatens the big fork Nc6+, winning the queen.

| 8 | ... | Kf8 |
| 9 | Nxa8 | 1–0 |

After 9...Qxa8 10 Qe6 Be7 11 Nc6, White is winning quite easily.

Boris Spassky: 10th World Champion (1969–72)

Spassky is generally remembered for his part in the famous 1972 world championship match in Reykjavik against Bobby Fischer, but he had been a world-class player for many years previously, after winning the world junior championship in 1955. Before 1972, he had never lost a game to Bobby Fischer and seemed to exercise a psychological advantage over the younger American. His style of play was often described as 'universal': he could play both bold, aggressive chess, and quieter, positional chess. This was Spassky's best game from Reykjavik.

White, to play, had lured Fischer into what is called the 'poisoned pawn' variation, where Black takes the pawn on b2 with the queen. Both players must have prepared this line thoroughly, but Spassky found some more incisive moves.

	Spassky	Fischer
1	Nb1!	...

A surprising return to its original square for the knight.

1	...	Qb4	2	Qe3	...

White avoids the queen exchange and also cuts off the possible return of the black queen to its own camp via b6. White threatens a3 followed by Nc3 to win the queen.

2	...	d5?

Analysts later worked out that Black should have played 2...Ne7, but this move was not so easy to find during the game.

3	exd5	Ne7
4	c4	Nf5
5	Qd3	h4?

Fischer is hoping to play 6...Ng3+! 7 hxg3 hxg3+, followed by a deadly check on the a7–g1 diagonal – but White has a move first.

6	Bg4	Nd6
7	N1d2	f5?
8	a3	Qb6
9	c5	...

Black's position is already beyond repair.

9	...	Qb5
10	Qc3	fxg4
11	a4	h3

Fischer's queen is lost. The surprise is that he doesn't simply resign. The rest of the moves may be passed over in silence.

12	axb5	hxg2+
13	Kxg2	Rh3
14	Qf6	Nf5
15	c6	Bc8
16	dxe6	fxe6
17	Rfe1	Be7
18	Rxe6	1–0

continues on the next page

Bobby Fischer: 11th World Champion (1972–1975)

Bobby Fischer raised the profile of chess by an extraordinary amount when he became world champion in 1972. It gave a huge boost to the game, particularly in places like the UK, where it had always been a minority interest activity. Sadly, Fischer failed to defend his title in 1975 and has not played since, apart from a return match with Spassky in 1992 that had no official status.

Here is Fischer's win against Spassky in the sixth game of the Reykjavik match.

Fischer	Spassky
1 **Bc4**	**Kh8**
2 **Qh3**	**...**

White uses his queen and bishop to pressurize the e6 pawn.

2	**...**	**Nf8**
3	**b3**	**a5**
4	**f5**	**...**

White plays to open up the f-file for his rooks and create a passed e-pawn.

4	**...**	**exf5**
5	**Rxf5**	**Nh7**

Setting a trap. If 6 Rf7?? Ng5! forks queen and rook.

6	**Rcf1**	**Qd8**

If 6...Ng5 now, White plays 7 Qg3 and then 8 h4 to drive the knight away.

7	**Qg3**	**Re7**
8	**h4**	**Rbb7**
9	**e6**	**...**

Now that Fischer is satisfied that the pawn cannot be attacked by the knight, he moves it to e6. He conducts the attack very calmly and precisely.

9	**...**	**Rbc7**

Black has run out of anything constructive to do. If 9...Nf6 10 Rxf6! gxf6 11 Rxf6, then White has too many threats.

10	**Qe5**	**Qe8**
11	**a4**	**Qd8**
12	**R1f2**	**Qe8**
13	**R2f3**	**Qd8**
14	**Bd3**	**Qe8**
15	**Qe4**	**...**

White now decides it is time to launch the final offensive. The threat is Rf8+!, followed by the capture of the knight and Qh7 mate.

15	**...**	**Nf6**
16	**Rxf6!**	**gxf6**
17	**Rxf6**	**Kg8**
18	**Bc4**	**Kh8**
19	**Qf4**	**1–0**

One impressive aspect of this attack was how unhurried it was. One watching grandmaster compared Fischer's performance to a Mozart symphony.

Anatoly Karpov: 12th World Champion (1975–1985, 1993–1999)

Anatoly Karpov qualified for a world title match with Fischer in 1975, and achieved a bloodless victory when Fischer failed to agree terms to defend his title. However, he then proved his worth by winning a large number of tournaments during the following ten years and also defending his title successfully, twice, against Viktor Korchnoi.

Karpov resembles Capablanca in that he has a huge natural talent for the game and also prefers to play positional (rather than tactical) chess for the most part. In his younger days, he was also known for the remarkable speed of his play, with good moves seemingly coming to him with a minimum of thought.

Here is one of Karpov's wins from his first match with Kasparov in 1984.

Black, to play, should be able to hold this level endgame, but he now makes a tiny slip.

	Karpov	**Kasparov**
1	...	**gxh4?**

Nine-hundred and ninety-nine times out of a thousand, White would automatically make the recapture 2 gxh4 here, but Karpov is no ordinary player.

| **2** | **Ng2!** | ... |

This is a temporary pawn sacrifice with the idea of infiltrating the kingside with his king.

| **2** | ... | **hxg3+** |

| **3** | **Kxg3** | ... |

White is a pawn down, but he will soon devour the h5 pawn. Equally importantly, he can now move his king into Black's position.

3	...	**Ke6**
4	**Nf4+**	**Kf5**
5	**Nxh5**	**Ke6**

Black has to retreat because White threatened to play Ng7, Ne8 and then Nc7 to attack the a6 pawn.

| **6** | **Nf4+** | **Kd6** | **7** | **Kg4** | ... |

Now the king moves up the board.

7	...	**Bc2**
8	**Kh5**	**Bd1**
9	**Kg6**	**Ke7**

If 9...Bxf3 10 Kxf6, White will be able to play Ne6, Ng7 and Nf5+ to force the black king to retreat in due course.

10	**Nxd5+**	**Ke6**
11	**Nc7+**	**Kd7**
12	**Nxa6**	**Bxf3**
13	**Kxf6**	**Kd6**
14	**Kf5**	**Kd5**
15	**Kf4**	**Bh1**
16	**Ke3**	**Kc4**

continues on the next page ➡

17   Nc5   ...

It is rather a long-winded process, but White is gradually establishing a winning endgame.

17	...	Bc6
18	Nd3	Bg2
19	Ne5+	Kc3
20	Ng6	Kc4
21	Ne7	Bb7
22	Nf5	Bg2
23	Nd6+	Kb3
24	Nxb5	Ka4
25	Nd6	1–0

Modern top-level chess can be a war of attrition. Such marathon games as this, even without the added pressure of competing for the crown of world champion, require intense concentration. Both Karpov and Kasparov were blessed in abundance with the ability to stay focused, which undoubtedly accounts for their domination of the game for so long. Though most believe Kasparov to have been the better player, Karpov holds the distinction of being the most successful tournament player of all time.

Garry Kasparov: 13th World Champion (1985–1993, 1993–2000)

Garry Kasparov is widely considered to be the best chess player of all time. Having won his title in a match against Anatoly Karpov, he defended it tenaciously against Karpov and others. His only significant setbacks were lost matches against the computer Deep Blue in 1997 and against Vladimir Kramnik in 2000, which cost him his unofficial (but prestigious) version of the world title. Kasparov is by nature an open, aggressive player but he quickly assimilated the art of positional chess in order to overcome Karpov in the 1980s.

Here, he plays White against Karpov in Spain in 2001, in a game which may yet prove to be the last major clash between the two giants.

Kasparov has stirred up a complex position in order to provoke his rival.

	Kasparov	**Karpov**
1	h6!	Nxc5

If 1...gxh6 2 Nd6+! there is a twin threat of Qxf7 mate and Bxh6+.

| 2 | Bf4 | Kf8 |

Kasparov thought 2...Qa5+ was better here, but it is very complex.

| 3 | hxg7+ | Kxg7 |
| 4 | 0-0-0 | ... |

White gets ready to switch the d1 rook to g1 and then attack the exposed king.

4	...	Kf8
5	Kb1	a6
6	Nc7	Rc8
7	Bxd5	...

7	...	exd5
8	Rxd5	Qxc7

If 8...Nd7 9 Ne6+ fxe6 10 Qxe6 sets up a lethal finish.

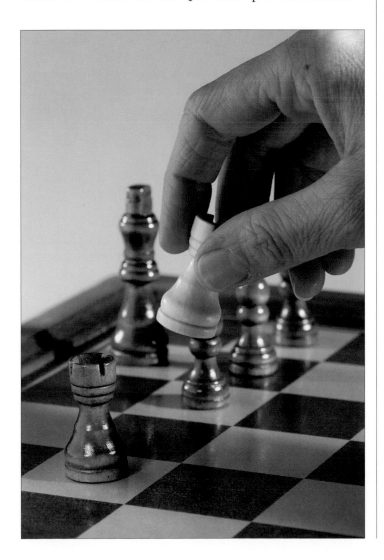

9	Bxc7	Rxc7
10	Rf5	...

Black has three minor pieces for the queen and two pawns. It is resignable.

10	...	Rd7
11	c3	f6
12	Rg1	Nd8
13	Qg4	Ke8
14	Rh5	Rf8
15	Rxc5!	Bxc5
16	Qh5+	1–0

A comprehensive victory that offers a fine example of Kasparov's relentlessly precise technique.

Left: White positions a rook deep in enemy territory, forcing Black on to the defensive. With such a powerful piece in the heart of his position, Black will have to be on the lookout for mating threats and vulnerable material.

COMMON TACTICAL PATTERNS

It is hardly surprising that you have to practise regularly in order to improve at chess, just as you would if learning to play any game, sport or musical instrument. One of the principal benefits of regular practice is pattern recognition. After awhile, you will be able to recognize various patterns that have occurred before. One or two of these are already becoming familiar from the pages of this book (e.g. the back-rank mate). This next position will help you spot a few of the most familiar patterns that recur with regularity in games of chess.

Material is level, and the position appears to be fairly balanced, but, in fact, Black (to play) has a way to force a win here. It involves an eight-move combination. Perhaps more surprisingly, if you showed the position to an experienced tournament player (not necessarily a master or grandmaster), you might be surprised to see him or her work it out in a matter of seconds. The reason experienced players can do it so quickly is not because they are brilliant at calculation, nor because they have seen the exact position before, but simply because they can recognize three or four patterns or elements in the position that they have come across before. Try imagining a familiar mating scenario and then quickly see a few moves that can get them to the desired conclusion. Here is the solution:

1   ...   Ng3+!

The first familiar pattern: the knight fork, with a difference, of course: this would be a winning king and queen fork but for the fact that the h2 pawn will snap the knight off in the next move. So is it a useless pattern here? Not quite: it achieves something by 'forcing' White's reply, which means that Black does not need to worry about what might happen after 2 Kg1.

2   hxg3   hxg3+

This is the next pattern – or perhaps two patterns in one: firstly, the creation of an open file (ideal for exploitation by rooks) and secondly the acquisition of a strong pawn on g3 (useful for imprisoning a king on the back rank, or supporting pieces on f2 and h2). Once an experienced player envisages these two tactical plus points, he or she next seeks a way to exploit the enemy's back-rank weakness, perhaps via the strong points at f2 and (particularly) h2. Using some imagination (something even the best chess-playing computers cannot do – yet), the player will ask themselves the question 'What if I could get my queen to h2?' – and then may see a way to achieve it.

3   Kg1   Rh1+!

Black jettisons a rook. The reason why will become clear soon.

4   Kxh1   Rh8+
5   Kg1   Rh1+!

Now the other rook is sacrificed the same way.

6   Kxh1   Qh8+

7   Kg1   ...

If you examine this position with a computer, it may suggest the move 7 Qh5 here. Of course, it doesn't help White's cause at all, because Black takes the queen and wins as before. The reason computers do such things is because they are programmed to stave off checkmate for as long as possible, and this move happens to make the game last a bit longer.

7   ...   Qh2+

There it is – the move that Black envisaged a few moves before. The reason for jettisoning the two rooks was to clear a path for the queen to achieve this objective. This is sometimes referred to as a 'clearance sacrifice'.

Below: White's queen moves in for the kill: Qg7#. Checkmate with the queen on this square, supported either by a pawn or bishop, is one of the common mating patterns used against the castled king.

8   Kf1   Qh1 mate

The lines show the queen's path to the mating square. An aesthetically beautiful finish, but to an experienced player – almost routine! One reason it is not so difficult to pull off is that all White's moves were forced. In real life, of course, such clear-cut opportunities do not come along all the time – but they do happen once in a while.

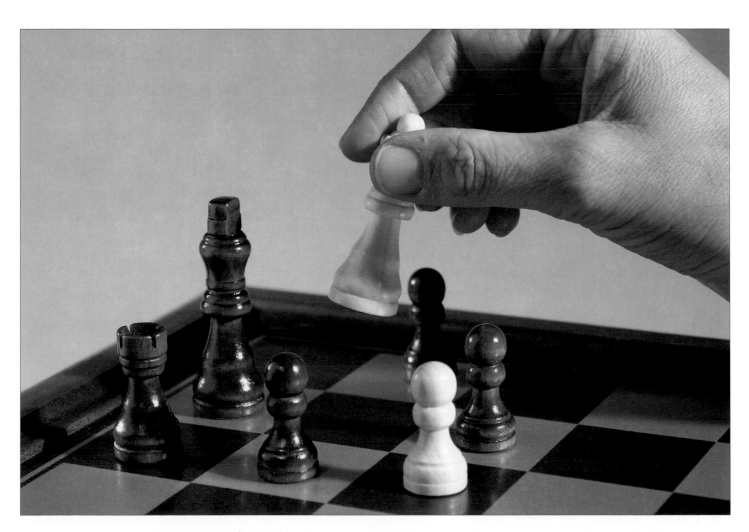

THE ENEMY KING'S DEFENCES

It is always worth spending a little time examining the enemy king's defences when it is your turn to move. For example, if you notice undefended squares around the king, or an absence of defensive pieces in the vicinity, it can often indicate that it is a good moment to start a direct attack on the king.

White is to play. An experienced player would note the following plus-points about this position: (a) Black's kingside pawn structure, with the pawn on g6, is a little weak, and could perhaps be exploited if White can establish an unchallenged queen, bishop or knight on f6 or h6; (b) White has three minor pieces to Black's two on the kingside; (c) Black is lagging behind in development (the b8 knight is still on its original square); (d) the white bishop on c4 is usefully placed on the a2–g8 diagonal (although threatening nothing at the moment).

There is only one negative point: the white e4 pawn is currently attacked by two enemy pieces and defended by only one. This last factor can easily be addressed, but such is the preponderance of strategic and tactical plus-points that White should first give serious thought to the possibility of a direct attack on the king. In fact, there is an immediate way to exploit White's development advantage and superior build-up on the kingside.

1   Bxg7   ...

A simple exchange of pieces, but it achieves the objective of removing Black's best kingside defender, the bishop on g7.

1   ...   Kxg7
2   Nf5+!   ...

This knight sacrifice serves to open up the g-file and allow the white queen to land on g5 with check.

2   ...   gxf5

If 2...Kg8 3 Qh6 Ne8 (to defend against mate on g7) 4 Ng5 and now 5 Qxh7 cannot be prevented. If 2...Kh8 3 Qh6 Rg8 4 Ng5, then the unstoppable threat is Nxf7 winning the queen. Notice that the well-placed bishop on c4 plays a vital part in this particular line.

3   Qg5+   Kh8
4   Qxf6+   Kg8

The first stage of the assault is over and material equality has been re-established. In visualizing this position, White would note the strength of the bishop on c4 (attacking f7 and covering the possible defensive idea of Ra6), and also the combination Ng5, Qh6 and Qxh7 mate. The two patterns (Bxf7 and Ng5/Qxh7) are both very common and would occur instantly to a strong player, making the next move very easy to find.

5   Ng5   Qc6

If Black's life depended on prolonging the game, the way to do it would be 5...Ra6, but then 6 Bxa6 Nxa6 7 Qxf5 f6 8 Ne6 would win even more material.

6   Bxf7+   1–0

6...Rxf7 7 Qxf7+ Kh8 when 8 Qxh7 and 8 Qf8 are both checkmate.

Here is another example of how to exploit similar weak squares around the king.

White, to move, has fixed a weakness around the black king and it is just a question of how best to exploit it.

1   Bg7!   ...

White might also be tempted to try 1 Bg5, with the idea of playing 2 Qh6 and 3 Qg7 mate. Black has two possible defences, however. One is 1...Bc7 when 2 Qh6 is adequately met by 2...Qf8!, and the other is 1...h5, which prevents the queen from reaching h6.

1   ...   Bc7

This loses immediately, but in fact there is little to be done other than give up a piece on f6 to stop the mate. 1...h5 2 Qg5, and the queen will reach the mating square via h6.

2   Qxh7+!   1–0

Black resigned. This is another clearance sacrifice – the queen gives itself up to clear a path for the rook to give mate – 2...Kxh7 3 Rh4+ Kg8 4 Rh8 mate. Once you have seen a few examples of such attacks, they will become second nature and will be easy to find in your own games.

CHAPTER FOUR:

COMPUTERS IN CHESS

Since the late 20th century, computers have had a profound effect on the way chess is played. With a performance level that is now on a par with world champions, they are formidable opponents to learn from and practise with, and are the means by which people all over the world can play chess with each other on the Internet. There are many affordable versions of chess-playing software, as well as dedicated chess computers, and these have become very popular. However, although computers are capable of winning chess matches against grandmasters, they still have not 'solved' the game. Most players would probably agree that, while computers are useful tools to improve chess strategy, nothing can match the pleasure of a game between human opponents.

Right: For true lovers of chess, the look and feel of a wooden chess set cannot be equalled by anything that appears on a computer screen.

CHOOSING A SILICON OPPONENT

Until a few years ago, chess-playing computers were despised by the best players. In 1968, the Scottish chessmaster David Levy made a bet with some computer scientists that no computer would beat him in the following ten years. In 1978, the boast was put to the test and Levy easily defeated the best chess-playing computer of the day. It wasn't until 1989 that a chess-playing program was developed that was strong enough to overcome Levy, and still more years passed before leading grandmasters and world champions began losing to computers with any regularity.

However, things have moved on swiftly in the 21st century, and now it is possible to purchase affordable chess-playing software, for a home computer, that is capable of playing grandmaster-level chess. In terms of playing strength, these programs are vastly stronger that any chess player (other than the world's elite) could possibly need. The main problem in playing against them is the feeling of depression that creeps over you after losing a long succession of games. However, take comfort in the fact that even professional players suffer similar results when they play quick games against computers.

Despite their huge chess-playing strength, these programs are still worth buying, even for beginners. They come with a large range of features. It is possible to set the level of play to suit your own playing strength and enable you to win some games and gauge your rate of improvement. Other facilities of the latest titles include: speech and sound (with supposedly humorous commentary that soon becomes tiresome); 3D-style board designs; training and tuition; hints and advice as you play; games databases (hundreds of thousands of grandmaster games that you can play through and analyse with the help of the computer); and you can add your own games and have the computer analyse and comment on them, although this can sometimes be humiliating.

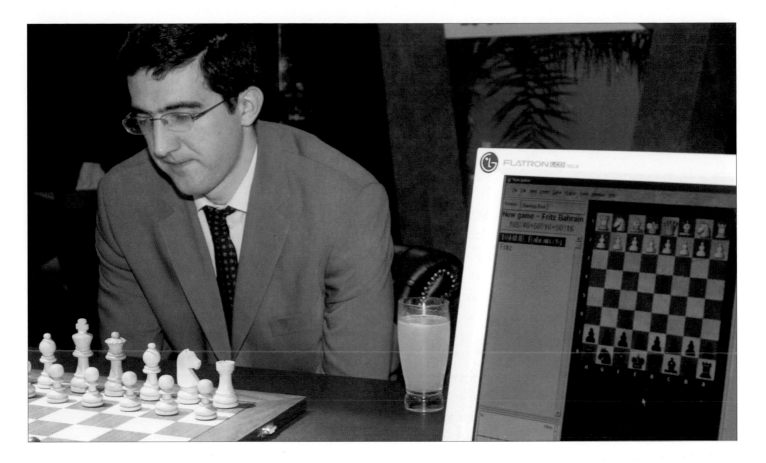

If you don't own a computer, there is another solution – buying a dedicated chess computer. These vary in style and size: they can be handheld devices (which you can carry in a coat pocket), desktop models (which can be carried in a briefcase), or deluxe models (including a beautiful wooden chess board and pieces, which allow moves to be entered simply by making the move on the board). These are more expensive than the former option. These dedicated computers play strong chess (although not as strong as their PC equivalents) and also come with many other useful facilities, such as teaching modes and handicap levels. Competition chess players tend not to use dedicated chess computers these days, mainly because they prefer to travel with a laptop loaded with chess-playing software, and because dedicated computers don't come with databases or allow you to store your own games or analysis.

The availability of good-quality handheld computers now means that it is possible to load some versions of PC-based chess-playing software on to a gadget that is not much bigger than a mobile phone. This development has caused some disquiet in the chess world, as it means that there is the possibility of cheating if players surreptitiously consult their 'pocket grandmaster' during play.

Above: World chess champion Vladimir Kramnik of Russia contemplates his first move during the final game of his eight-game match against computer software program Deep Fritz, in Bahrain in October 2002. Kramnik and the computer each won two games and four were drawn, making the match score 4–4.

Far left: In the 1950s, a research scientist at Manchester University, UK, set one of the university's computers a chess problem to solve. The computer took 15 minutes to respond but achieved checkmate in two moves.

WHERE TO BUY

♕ ♗ ♘ ♔

Among the top-selling and best-quality chess-playing software titles on the market, the author's favourite is Fritz (now up to its 10th version), although several others are as good, if not better. The other big names are Shredder, Junior, Hiarcs and the Eastern European program Rybka, which is now very popular among Russian grandmasters. As regards dedicated computers, the Mephisto Exclusive Senator is the top-of-the-range model, with other good ones being Excalibur Grandmaster, Novag Obsidian and Mephisto Master, with the best dedicated handheld chess computer being the Novag Star Ruby. Be sure to buy from a specialist chess shop and ask for advice on your exact needs.

PLAYING CHESS ON-LINE

In the last few years there has been a massive boom in people playing chess on the Internet. Of course, this coincides with the explosion in broadband availability and flat-rate monthly charges, rather than pay-as-you-go.

The advantages

Playing on-line has some tremendous advantages. You play when you want to play, you can nearly always find an opponent of the right standard, you can play quick games or slow games, you don't have to travel anywhere and, as long as you are courteous about it, you can stop playing at any time if everyday life intrudes.

The disadvantages

One disadvantage is that not everyone finds it easy to play via a two-dimensional board representation, or to use a mouse. It is also not very sociable (you can 'chat' by typing messages, but sometimes the chat is a little off-putting), you don't always know whether you are playing your opponents or their computer software (yes, people do cheat) and (like other computer-based activities) it is a little addictive and perhaps, if you play too often, bad for the eyesight.

On-line or not on-line?

Some chess players have fallen head over heels in love with Internet chess, whereas others find it completely repellent. Whatever opinions people may hold, there seems little doubt that Internet chess is here to stay, and it will undoubtedly improve in terms of presentation (which is already very impressive) and facilities.

It is unwise to play on the Internet until you have first had a reasonable amount of experience of playing traditional chess, preferably with someone who can give you a bit of advice and instruction as you develop your skills. Playing on-line too soon could put you off the game almost before you start.

Even experienced chess players find it quite hard to adjust to chess in two dimensions, and to all the different functions and choices that confront you when first loading up the software. One other negative aspect of chess on-line is that most on-line players opt for speed chess, where the players only have a very limited time in which to choose their moves before they are timed out or, as chess players put it, 'lose on time'. Speed chess is fun and has its place, but it is not good for developing good chessboard skills and habits – it is like trying to run before you can walk.

Where to play

Let's assume you have now put in the necessary time practising your game and are sufficiently competent to play on-line. Which site is best? One of the oldest and most reliable, and with about 30,000 members (of whom you can expect to find 2,000 on-line at any one time) is the Internet Chess Club (www.chessclub.com). You can have a free trial, become a guest member

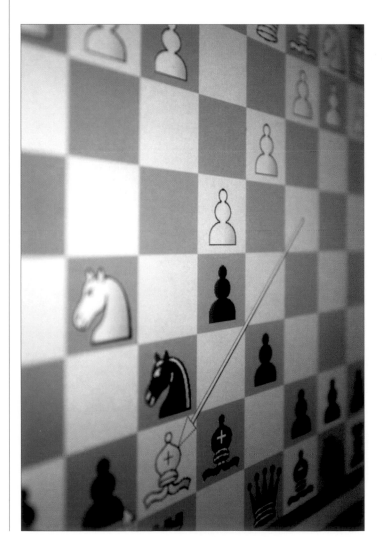

Right: Playing on-line is very different in several key respects to playing against a 'real' opponent. Primarily, you will have to accustom yourself to playing in two rather than three dimensions.

Above: Garry Kasparov considers his next move against one of 30 junior chess players. The game took place on-line on his own Internet chess site.

Left: As well as playing on-line, it is worth investing in a portable chess computer. They can be a great boon, particularly as a way of passing the time on a long journey.

(which is free) or opt to pay per year for full membership. To play, you download an interface that is fairly intuitive and straightforward to use, and which provides you with everything you need to find opponents and play a game.

Another equally good site can be found at www.playchess.com. Here, you can download playing software in the same way or, if you purchase chess-playing software such as Fritz, you can use Fritz itself to play on-line. These two websites are probably the most popular with the chess elite (with many grandmasters playing and giving lessons on-line), but there are plenty more Internet options, including websites such as www.worldchessnetwork.com and www.itsyourturn.com, which all have their own dedicated followers.

As well as playing chess, chess fans often like to watch top players in action on-line. Many top-level tournaments are broadcast live on the above websites and servers, and thousands of people watch them and exchange comments with each other. The 2006 World Championship match between Vladimir Kramnik and Veselin Topalov had around 100,000 spectators for each game.

KASPAROV AGAINST THE COMPUTER

Most chess players expected that the computer would eventually get the better of humankind when it came to playing chess, but it still came as a shock when, on 11 May 1997 in New York, Garry Kasparov lost the final game of his six-game match against the IBM computer known as Deep Blue, which meant that he had lost the match by 2½–3½. Kasparov had played Deep Blue the previous year, losing the first game but going on to win three of the remaining games and drawing two to triumph 4–2. The 1997 rematch, for which Deep Blue had been significantly upgraded, saw a reversal of fortune. Kasparov won the first game but then lost the second, thereafter becoming obsessed with the notion that the IBM programming team in charge of his silicon opponent (which included a chess grandmaster) had manually interfered with the move selection in that second game.

By the time he sat down for the sixth and final encounter, Kasparov was already a beaten man. He played the last game as if he had forgotten how to play chess. He had the black pieces and played a defence that was unfamiliar to him and totally unsuited to his playing style, and then committed an error on move seven, of which a club player would have been ashamed – and one that was instantly exploited by the computer. From as early as move eight, he was a dead duck and never looked capable of escaping defeat.

It is hard to convey the enormity of what had occurred. Until 1997, Kasparov had scarcely suffered any calamitous results and, whenever he had been under pressure, he had always fought tenaciously and

Below: In 1997 Kasparov lost to the computer Deep Blue. The computer was able to calculate 200 million moves a second, something no person could ever emulate. It came as a shock to the chess community that such a thing could happen, and years passed before Kasparov could get his revenge on the silicon chip.

Above: Garry Kasparov (left) began his first game against the world champion computer chess program Deep Junior in New York on 26 January 2003. In this, his fourth attempt to beat the computer, the match was drawn 3–3.

nearly always achieved his objective. He was unbeaten in match play. He went from all-conquering hero to dispirited zero in the space of eight moves.

What happened to Kasparov?

In truth, 11 May 1997 was not the day when computers became stronger chess players than humans; it was simply the day when Garry Kasparov proved he was a human being. He had allowed his concentration to wander on to what had happened in game two, and had failed to psych himself up for the final game.

It also proved that humans and computers are not really compatible chess opponents. Humans can only maintain a reasonable energy level for a few hours at a time, and need various breaks for food and sleep; whereas computers can go on as long as the electricity supply lasts. Human chess is replete with human emotions and psychology – hope, despair, confidence, disappointment – and the two players can display and decipher elements of body language during play.

Kasparov had always been a grandmaster of psychology as well as chess, with the swagger of a champion boxer as he came to the board, and a number of other mannerisms that had often intimidated other players. His psychological weaponry was completely useless against Deep Blue.

In one important respect, Deep Blue cheated. Its disk banks stored records of every top-level competitive chess game ever played to that date, plus it had access to a huge database of carefully sifted opening moves that had been prepared by grandmasters and tailored for the job of defeating the specific opponent. Of course, Kasparov also had, by human standards, a vast database of opening information too – but in his head. He has a superlative memory for such detail, but no human brain could replicate the perfect memory of a computer. If Kasparov had arrived with his complete chess library and a computer database of his own, he would have been disqualified for making use of notes during the game – one of the rules of the competition.

Thankfully, Kasparov soon recovered, and in 2003 he played a 3–3 drawn match with another computer, called Deep Junior.

BEATING THE SILICON MONSTER

The first thing to say about beating the silicon monster is that it has become a very hard thing to do. Even widely available software titles such as Fritz, Rybka and Chessmaster now play phenomenally strong chess that is good enough to beat grandmasters. The honest truth is that you are unlikely to be able to beat them on their highest levels.

So the first simple piece of advice is don't try to play them on their highest level. Fortunately, the latest PC-based software titles have a whole host of different playing levels, identified by names such as 'Handicap' or 'Friendly', which are cleverly programmed to create a more level playing field between the computer and the human player, while at the same time providing the player with a reasonable challenge. Even experienced players would do well to use these facilities, as losing a long string of games is bad for morale. As well as allowing you to win a few games (this is done in a subtle and not patronizing way), the computer can generate a handicap rating for you, rather like a golf handicap, which you can use to measure your progress.

Right: The latest chess-playing software also gives the player access to online chess-playing sites such as the Internet Chess Club and playchess.com, where it is possible to play against other humans as well as computers.

Below: It is possible to play on the computer with 3D-style display, in which the board and pieces can be moved as if on a three-dimensional chessboard.

Style of play against a computer is very important. Before considering this, it is worth noting that computers do not learn from their mistakes as they play games (i.e. they are not true 'knowledge-based systems', as IT experts would define them). While chess programming techniques have certainly improved over the past 30 years, most of the extra strength of the latest chess-playing software is due to the massive increase in hardware speed that has been achieved with every new generation of the microchip. The computer can sift through millions of different moves in a matter of seconds – obviously far more than the strongest human player could hope to emulate.

Avoid tactical melees

This advantage in calculation speed translates into a phenomenal strength in tactics – in other words, calculation of what happens when the two enemies are at close quarters. No human chess player – even Garry Kasparov – can now rival a good piece of chess software in this aspect of the game. This leads to the next piece

Notation | Table | Training | Score sheet | Openings Book | Reference

Saunders,JC 2144 - Yeo.Michael J 2120 ½-½
A04 Loft, g/30min rapid (3) 03.06.2000

1 Nf3 Nc6 2 g3 e5 3 d3 g6 4 Bg2 Bg7 5 0-0 d6 6 c3 f5 7 e4 Nf6 8 Nbd2 0-0 9 exf5 gxf5 10 Qa4
Kn8 11 Ne1 Bd7 12 Qb3 Rb8 13 a4 Qe8 14 Qc2 Qh5 15 Ndf3 Rg8 16 Nh4 14 17 Bf3 Bg4 18 Qe2
Rbf8 19 Bxg4 Nxg4 20h3 Nf6 21 Qxh5 Nxh5 22 g4 Bf6 23 Nf5 Ng7?? 24Nh6 Ne6 25 Nxg8 Rxg8
26Kh2 Nc5 27b4 Ne6 28Bb2 d5 29Rd1 e4 30 b5 Ne5 31 c4 dxc4 32 Bxe5 Bxe5 33 dxc4 f3+
½-½

Left: Many expert players now use chess databases to study the game (particularly the opening phase). These often have more than a million games, from the 15th century right up to the present day, as well as photos of thousands of competition players and much other relevant information that enables players to compile dossiers on each other's play.

of fairly obvious advice – avoid complicated tactics. Easier said than done, of course. Even strong grandmasters playing computers occasionally open up the position too readily to a tactical battle, and there is usually only one result possible.

Find a long-range strategy

However, it can be possible to take on the monster in a tactical battle, when the possibility of the tactical denouement can be seen from afar and judged to be in your favour. Computers are not so good at seeing a long way ahead in most positions; this is sometimes referred to as the 'horizon effect'. They usually concentrate on analysing the next few moves to the nth degree, and this is where experience, judgment and pattern recognition can come to the human player's aid.

Keep it simple

Generally speaking, it is a good idea to keep the position simple, with not too much hand-to-hand fighting to be calculated. For this reason, computers tend to play the endgame significantly worse. That said, this deficiency is gradually being eradicated from computer play. Also, when the material on the board is reduced to two or three men each, the computer can benefit from what is known as a 'tablebase'. These reduced-material positions have been exhaustively analysed out by computers, and the absolute best moves recorded on computer databases. If the computer finds that it has the exact position on the board in its database, it will stop calculating its moves in the normal way, and simply look up the right move in its in-built database. Now that really is cheating, isn't it? If you, the human player, sat down to play a tournament game and consulted an endgame manual during play, you would be disqualified. But that is exactly what some chess-playing programs do.

How not to play

Here's an example of how not to play against a computer. Playing White was a Dutch grandmaster, but he makes the mistake of allowing the position to become tactical quickly. Computers play a different sort of chess from humans (with a heavy emphasis on tactics), which can lead players to adapt their playing style to combat the computer. This can backfire, simply because the human is playing against their natural instincts. Something of the sort is at work here.

	Human	**Fritz SSS (Netherlands 2000)**
1	c4	Nf6
2	Nc3	e5
3	e4	...

This was intended as an 'anti-computer' move, but White does not follow it up accurately.

3	...	Bc5
4	g3	0-0
5	Bg2	Nc6
6	Nge2	d6
7	d3?	...

continues on the next page

Only a tiny error, but it is enough for the computer to start on the offensive. White should play 7 0–0.

| 7 | ... | Ng4 |
| 8 | 0–0 | f5 |

Black threatens to play fxe4 and attack the f2 pawn with a third piece (the rook on f8).

9	Na4	Nxf2!
10	Rxf2	Bxf2+
11	Kxf2	f4

The main idea behind Black's double capture on f2 was to draw the white king into the line of fire of the black rook on f8, and facilitate Qh4+ (should White play 12 gxf4). But there are a whole host of tactical problems that add up to insurmountable difficulties. For example, Black threatens to play Bg4 followed by Nd4, putting pressure on the e2 knight. The white king cannot move away from the f-file because f3 would fork two pieces. White plays the best move, but it is not good enough.

| 12 | gxf4 | exf4 |
| 13 | Ng1 | ... |

13 Nxf4 g5 loses a piece for two pawns.

13	...	Qh4+
14	Kf1	f3!
15	Nxf3	Qxh2

This position may not look so terrible, but the Dutch grandmaster decided to resign. It is just the sort of position that computers play brilliantly. The computer threatens Bh3 or Nd4, and then the whole White edifice crumbles.

How to beat the computer
Here is the way to win. Another Dutch grandmaster is playing White against the same computer.

	Human	Fritz SSS
1	c4	e5
2	g3	Nf6
3	Bg2	Nc6
4	Nc3	Bb4
5	a3	Bxc3
6	bxc3	0-0
7	e4	a6
8	a4	d6
9	d3	Bg4
10	f3	...

White is playing to keep the position blocked. This is a well-known anti-computer ploy.

10	...	Bd7
11	Ne2	Qc8
12	h3	b6
13	f4	Be6
14	f5	...

Blocking the position. 13...Be6 is poor: it shows that the computer does not understand the position.

14	...	Bd7
15	g4	Ne8
16	Ng3	Qd8
17	g5	Bc8
18	h4	f6
19	Qh5	...

White has a huge attack on the kingside. This is easily visible to the human eye, but the computer does not appreciate the long-term implications of its passivity.

| 19 | ... | Na5 |

| 20 | Ra3 | ... |

Safety first. The threat of Nb3 may have done nothing, but White doesn't want to give the computer the merest hint of counterplay.

20	...	Qe7
21	Nf1	Nc6
22	Ne3	Qd7
23	g6	h6

White had been expecting this attempt to close down the position and that was what his previous knight manoeuvre had been designed to refute.

| 24 | Ng4 | Ra7 |
| 25 | Rg1 | 1–0 |

The computer sees what is coming and resigns. White will play Bf3 followed by Bxh6 and it will be over.

Remember that these games were played in 2000. Human brains have not made much progress in the last six or seven years, but computers have. I doubt that this sort of strategy would work as well against current chess programs.

Even today, it is usually a good idea to play for blocked positions against a computer. The fewer the open lines available to the computer's pieces, the less chance that it will be able to exploit its awesome tactical power against you. You can see that the human player in the final position of the above game had a little more space to manoeuvre behind the pawns. This small advantage became a key factor in winning the game.

CHAPTER FIVE:

CHESS TODAY AND TOMORROW

As we enter the 21st century, chess is played as a professional sport in many countries in the world, and its leading practitioners are known as grandmasters. What does it take to become a grandmaster? How are chess competitions organized? What does the future hold for the game? Who will take over the mantle of Fischer and Kasparov? These are some of the questions examined in this section. One thing is for certain – whatever the future of professional chess, the game will continue to be played and loved by millions of people. There are many types of chess competition, and it is unlike other sports and games – it knows no barriers of distance, incapacity or competence. However busy, remote or disabled the player, there is a way to find a chess opponent.

Right: The knight is symbolic of chess – it makes light of barriers when it moves. In some languages and cultures it is known, more accurately, as 'the horse'.

So You Want to be a Grandmaster?

One of the things that many people know about chess, even if they don't play it, is that it is played by people known as grandmasters. The word has overtones of wizardry or freemasonry about it, and has done wonders for the image of the game. However, in reality, there is no magic, trickery or secret vows behind the word: a grandmaster is simply someone who has scored sufficiently exalted scores in some top-level chess competitions to be awarded the title by the World Chess Federation (known as FIDE or Fédération Internationale des Échecs).

The first grandmasters

The title of grandmaster first came into frequent use in chess when Tsar Nicholas II conferred it upon the participants of the 1914 St Petersburg chess tournament. The five players – world champion Emanuel Lasker, future champions José Raúl Capablanca and Alexander Alekhine, plus Siegbert Tarrasch and Frank Marshall – were the leading players of their day and fully deserved the honour. The title continued to be applied unofficially to elite players until the World Chess Federation devised a system for awarding the title shortly after World War II. About one hundred players qualified for the title until the system changed again in the early 1970s and was based on a newly devised rating system. This rating system was based on one that had previously been employed by the United States Chess Federation. International chess ratings are usually called FIDE ratings, or sometimes Elo ratings, after the man who devised the US precursor, Professor Arpad Elo.

The rating system

FIDE Ratings are published every three months, with more than 50,000 active chess players worldwide now appearing on the list. Over the course of time, there is a degree of statistical inflation in the system. In the early 1970s, Bobby Fischer was the world's top player with a rating of around 2780, but in recent years three players have cleared the 2800 barrier: Garry Kasparov, who has dominated the rating list since 1985, Viswanathan Anand of India, and Veselin Topalov of Bulgaria, who has led the rating list since Kasparov's retirement. In order to become a grandmaster, a player must record three tournament performances of 2600 standard, and also achieve a published rating of 2500. To receive a lesser title – international master – a player must achieve three performances of 2450 standard and have a published rating of at least 2400. Titles are conferred for life, but players' ratings tend to decrease after the optimum age for professional chess playing, which is around 35 to 40. The inflationary effect of the rating system has seen a large growth in the number of grandmasters: this figure recently topped one thousand. This has had the effect that the title means rather less than it did when the Tsar first conferred it in 1914. In those days it was confined to a small group of players with genuine world championship aspirations. Today a player of the calibre of Garry Kasparov could take on four or five lesser grandmasters in a simultaneous display and defeat them all quite easily.

That is not to belittle the achievement of modern grandmasters. It takes a great deal of dedication and talent to reach grandmaster status. It would be almost impossible to get to that level without starting very young. Most professional players start playing chess before their teens and in most cases they will be in their twenties before qualifying for the title. Given the numbers of players now competing for a limited amount of cash prizes and appearance fees, most do not earn a living that is commensurate with the work they put in. So – do you still want to be a grandmaster?

Right: Frank James Marshall, one of the five original 'grandmasters', and the US Chess Champion from 1909 to 1936. Today's grandmasters, who number in the hundreds, qualify according to the strict rules of the FIDE rating system.

Below: Emanuel Lasker (right) held the title World Champion of chess for a record 27 years, until defeat by Capablanca (left) in 1927. Lasker was noted for his 'psychological' chess playing, which took account of his opponent's style as well as the objective challenges posed by the board.

Left: Tsar Nicholas II of Russia, who presided over the great St Petersburg tournament of 1914 and was the first person to confer the title of 'grandmaster' on leading chess players.

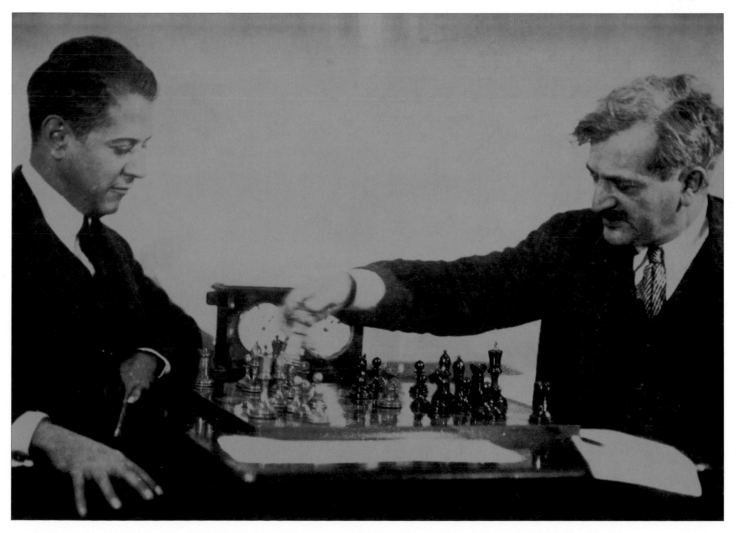

21ST-CENTURY CHAMPIONS

Chess has one phenomenon in common with music and mathematics – the infant prodigy. It is possible to reach a very high level of competence at chess at astonishingly early ages. Paul Morphy, José Raúl Capablanca, Sammy Reshevsky, Bobby Fischer and Judit Polgar were the most famous cases in chess history, but brilliant young players have continued to emerge in the 21st century.

Young grandmasters

Since Bobby Fischer, the age at which a player reaches the grandmaster title has always been used as the yardstick by which a player's achievement has been measured. In some ways, this is not an entirely satisfactory yardstick because there is no doubt that it has become easier to qualify as a grandmaster (or GM) in recent years. Bobby Fischer was 15 years, 6 months old when he became a GM in September 1958, and he did it by qualifying for a world championship decider between eight players who would play off for the right to play the world champion. Effectively, he became a grandmaster by qualifying for the world top nine. In recent years, 16 players have qualified for the GM title at a younger age than Fischer, but none of them simultaneously launched themselves into the world elite in quite the same way that Fischer did. Becoming a GM these days means joining the world's top 1,000. Fischer's was actually the greatest achievement and may never be equalled.

However, that is not to disparage the achievements of teenage (and, incredibly, pre-teen) players of recent years. Judit Polgar had the honour of breaking Fischer's age record. She became a GM in 1991 at the age of 15 years, 4 months. Another Hungarian, Peter Leko, broke the 15-year barrier, qualifying as a GM at 14 years, 4 months in 1994. In 1997 the record was broken

Above: Magnus Carlsen (right), the world's youngest grandmaster, gives a simultaneous display in Spain. The 13-year-old Norwegian played 25 simultaneous games against challengers who ranged from internationally rated adults to children from the Extremadura region. He won 22, drew 2 and lost only 1.

Left: The first child to become a GM, Bobby Fischer from Brooklyn, New York, competing in a tournament at the Manhattan Chess Club, aged 13. Bobby learned to play at the age of 6 and became a GM in 1958, aged 15.

Below left: Top French player Etienne Bacrot took up chess aged 4 and became a grandmaster at the age of 14. He is currently ranked world no.18.

twice: French player Etienne Bacrot broke Leko's record in March (aged 14 years, 2 months), and Ruslan Ponomariov of Ukraine broke it again in December (14 years, 0 months). Bu Xiangzhi of China broke the 14-year barrier: he was 13 years, 10 months when he became a GM in 1999. Finally, the current record-holder, Sergey Karyakin of Ukraine, qualified as a GM at the age of 12 years, 7 months and 0 days. No fewer than 16 players (14 male and 2 female) have now become grandmasters at a younger age than Bobby Fischer.

Interestingly, the leading contender for the title of 'world's best-ever player' – Garry Kasparov – was a venerable 16 years, 11 months when he became a grandmaster and never broke the age record. But this was only because the old Soviet Chess Federation liked to keep its 'secret weapons' to itself. The 14-year-old Garry Kasparov was capable of achieving everything that recent prodigies have achieved.

The next world champion will be...

Between 1993 and 2006, two rival championship systems ran in parallel following Garry Kasparov's split from the World Chess Federation over the terms of his 1993 match with Nigel Short. Finally, in October 2006, reunification was achieved when the two rival champions, Vladimir Kramnik and Veselin Topalov, met in a match. The winner was Kramnik, and he thus became the undisputed world chess champion. Towards the end of 2007 Kramnik lost his title in an eight-player world championship tournament in Mexico to Viswanathan Anand.

It will be equally interesting to see which of today's teenage stars will eventually inherit the crown. Possible contenders are Sergey Karyakin (b. 1990, from Ukraine), Teimour Radjabov (b. 1987, from Azerbaijan), Magnus Carlsen (b. 1990, from Norway) and Parimarjan Negi (b. 1993, from India). Another exciting prospect is Hou Yifan (b. 1994, from China). Aged only 12, she has been scoring well in adult competitions in 2006, and might be the first female player to conquer the world title.

CLOCKS AND THE TIME ELEMENT

For all competition chess, the amount of time you have to think about your moves is strictly regulated. This wasn't always the case. Before the middle of the 19th century, there could be agreed restrictions in the amount of time a player would take to make a move in top-level matches (though it is not clear whether these intervals were monitored in any rigorous way, or whether the agreed financial penalties were ever imposed), but there is no record of time restrictions being imposed in lesser competitions. If opponents were slow to move, you would just have to wait.

Of course, players became frustrated with the slowness of some of their opponents, and the ingenious Victorian mind was set to work to come up with solutions. In the 1860s, a form of double sandglass clock was brought into use: a player would have to make a number of moves before their sandglass ran out and, on moving, set their sandglass to the horizontal while that of their opponent was set to run again.

Eventually, in the 1890s, the modern chess clock came into being: a double clock with, for example, two hours allowed to each player for 40 moves. White's clock would be started with a button or lever and, when the player moved, he or she pressed a button to stop the clock and start the opponent's, and so on. The clock would be set to show four o'clock and, if it reached six o'clock with fewer than 40 moves played, the player would lose the game. For the sake of precision, a small flag was set into each clock face. It would be raised up by the minute hand as it approached the hour, and drop at the exact moment the minute hand reached the hour.

Ever since, tournament chess has involved the use of chess clocks. In recent years, digital chess clocks have been introduced, which have more facilities. One undesirable feature of chess played with

Below: The clock on the left of the back row is an old 1950s model; the two smaller clocks on the right were the most familiar style of clocks from the 1960s to 2000. In recent years the digital model (front, left) has become more popular.

Above: The 1967 World Junior Chess Champion, Julio Kaplan, from Puerto Rico, is seen in play at the 1967/68 Hastings, UK, Christmas tournament. The clock in use is of an older, larger and rather elegant wooden design.

mechanical clocks has been the problem of time trouble. Some players have the habit of thinking too long about their moves, and getting into the situation where they have only a few seconds left but still, for example, 15 moves to play. This can be exciting to watch for spectators. As soon as the player with more time left makes a move, the player in time trouble only has seconds to think of a move and play it.

Many a chess game has been ruined in such situations (which are known as 'time scrambles'). Curiously, 'time trouble' is infectious: very often the player with more time is infected by the panicking of the fast-moving opponent and is the one to make a big mistake. To alleviate this, the makers of digital clocks have introduced an ingenious time setting that works as before (for example, so many hours for so many moves) but also adds on a fixed amount of time (for example, 30 seconds or 1 minute) to a player's allotment after a move is made. This has the effect that a player never has less time to play one move than the value of the time increment (30 seconds or 1 minute or whatever the increment). Thus, the introduction of digital clocks has largely removed the time trouble element from the game.

Chess clocks are available from specialist chess retailers. They can be used for other two-player board games such as draughts and checkers. Use of a chess clock is not a priority for beginners but, once you have played for a few months, they can be used at home to speed up play, and to get a feel for tournament chess. They are also beneficial if you intend to play Internet chess, since this is nearly always played to specific time limits.

FAST CHESS: RAPIDPLAY AND BLITZ

People who don't know about chess sometimes dismiss it as a 'terribly slow game'. It is true that if you don't play with a clock, it can be, but competition players would never submit themselves to such torture. Competition chess is always played with a clock – and some competitions can be staggeringly fast. The faster you can play, the more fun it gets.

Competition chess players hardly ever play informal chess without a clock, except when they are engaged in teaching. Assuming the reader of this book to be a beginner – you are not ready for time-limit chess until you have had plenty of practice just moving the pieces around. You don't want to take too long over the moves, but at the same time the presence of an unfamiliar timepiece can be a little discouraging in the early stages of learning chess. When you are fully conversant with the rules, and perhaps are on the point of playing in your first competition, it is time to start playing with a clock. When you first begin to play chess with a clock, it would be a good idea to allow a time for a game. I would suggest 25 or 30 minutes. This means that each player has 25–30 minutes for all of their moves. If you run out of time, you lose the game – if the flag on your clock falls just as you are about to play checkmate, you have lost. Don't worry, sooner or later you will be in a terrible position and your opponent will run out of time. Don't believe anyone when they say there is no luck in chess – there is plenty, good and bad. However, don't make excuses. It's just part of the game.

Rapidplay chess

The reason 25 or 30 minutes is best is because this is a commonly used time limit for what are known as rapidplay (or quickplay) tournaments. Typically held on a Saturday or Sunday, they are five- or six-round tournaments held from about 10am to 6pm in the evening.

Below: For the first time in chess history, the 2006 world chess championship was decided by rapidplay games after the 12-game match was tied at 6–6. Vladimir Kramnik (right) went on to defeat Veselin Topalov in a four-game rapidplay decider, thereby becoming the undisputed champion of the world.

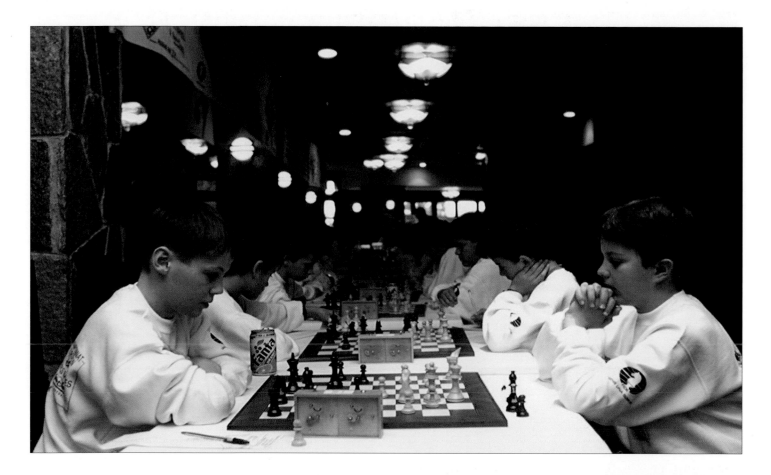

Each game takes up to an hour and is followed by a break of 5–10 minutes while the officials do the pairings, and there might be an hour's break for lunch. It is a good way of getting a tournament played in one day. Even if you lose, you get to play in every round and are paired to play someone on a similar score to yourself. It is one point for a win, half a point for a draw and zero for a loss. The winner and perhaps second and third place win a cash prize and go home with a sense of achievement. Normally, tournaments are divided up into sections, with beginners and unrated players grouped together. Rapidplay tournaments are almost the ideal entry into the world of competition chess.

Here is a website where you can find a list of rapidplay (and other) chess tournaments held in the UK – www.bcmchess.co.uk/news/events.htm

Blitz chess

An even faster form of chess than rapidplay is blitz chess. Typically, you have five minutes on your clock to make all the moves in the game. Does that sound ludicrously fast? It is, if you are a beginner. But, after a year of regular practice, your chess reflexes could be ready for some informal blitz chess with a friend.

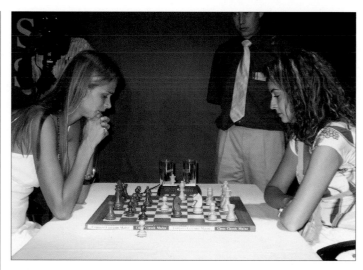

Top: The European Speed Chess Championship, which took place in 1993 in France. Junior speed chess is played at all levels, and many schools and clubs hold junior speed chess tournaments.

Above: The Estonian supermodel Carmen Kass (b. 1978) is a keen chess player who has been president of the Estonian Chess Federation. Here, left, she is playing a rapidplay game against the 2004 women's world chess champion Antoaneta Stefanova of Bulgaria.

Most competition chess players love playing blitz chess – it is fast and fun, and not too serious. You can chat with your opponent as you play. This is an incentive to practise hard and become good at chess. Blitz is the most fun you can have on a chessboard.

SLOW CHESS: CORRESPONDENCE CHESS

Not everyone takes to fast chess. Some players prefer to take their time over their moves. Here are a few other impediments to playing conventional club, tournament or even informal chess: you don't live close to anyone else who likes playing chess, or plays at your standard; you are too busy to travel to clubs and tournaments; or you suffer from a disability that means that you cannot easily get to a chess club. The Internet is an answer to some of these problems, but perhaps you don't use (or prefer not to use) the Internet.

Well, the good news is that there is still a way to play chess, even if one or all the above scenarios are true. You can play correspondence chess (or CC, as it is widely known, as opposed to 'over-the-board', or OTB, chess). In correspondence chess, moves can be made by post, telephone, email or fax. It is a very well-established form of chess playing, going back three centuries or more, but only becoming popular in the first half of the 19th century. Hundreds of thousands of CC players enjoy tournaments and compete in championships in this specialized form of the game.

If you join a postal chess club, you are then paired with an opponent, or a number of opponents. It is possible to have several games of postal chess in progress at the same time. The White player starts the game by writing the first move on a chess score sheet and sends it by post to the player playing Black, who posts back a reply. The game continues in the usual way. There are usually time limits (measured in days), so that you normally have to reply to a move within a day or two, and games usually last for a matter of weeks or months.

One significant difference between CC and OTB chess is that when playing CC you are allowed to consult books and computers in playing your moves. Books were always allowed in the past, which meant that players could consult opening manuals at the start of the game, and endgame manuals for the final moves of the game. However, the advent of powerful chess-playing software now means that, if they are so minded, players can simply play moves that the computer suggests, right through the game. Many people regard this as the death-knell of CC but, in fact, things are not so simple in real life. Not every move

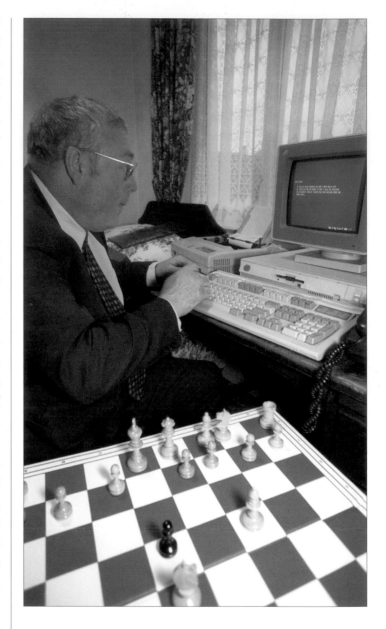

that a computer suggests is necessarily the absolute best one, and a good CC player will still exercise his or her own judgement in certain positions. But it cannot be denied that it takes some of the fun out of CC. When you play, you don't really know whether you are playing the opponent or the opponent's computer.

Incidentally, although CC now permits the use of computer software, it is still regarded as unsporting to consult another human for advice. Obviously, it is impossible to police such a rule, and it relies on proper conduct on the part of the players. The good news is that CC players rank well above the average (and their OTB equivalents) in this important respect.

Recently, there has been an explosion of interest in e-mail chess. It works on exactly the same principle, but there is no need for stamps and stationery, and on-line interfaces make it very easy to keep track of your games.

One word of warning: CC is not really for the absolute beginner. You need some OTB practice before trying correspondence chess. However, once you know the rules and want some practice, it becomes a very attractive option, particularly if you are nervous about your early chess steps being too public. CC allows your entry into (and possible exit from) competition chess to be made very discreetly.

Right: The scoresheet of a correspondence chess game played in 1977. Note that, as well as the moves (in old-fashioned 'descriptive' notation), the players have noted the day on which the move was posted to the opponent.

Below: British chess player John Walker posting his latest move to American life prisoner Claude Bloodgood, in 1999. Walker played CC with the notorious inmate for 30 years (although it is said he never won a game). A formidable opponent in more ways than one, Bloodgood, a convicted murderer, was at one point juggling some 2,000 games by correspondence.

Left: When they began playing in 1970, Walker and Bloodgood exchanged moves by post, but the Internet has brought radical changes to the virtual chess world. It is no longer necessary to wait days between moves, and easier to track your progress.

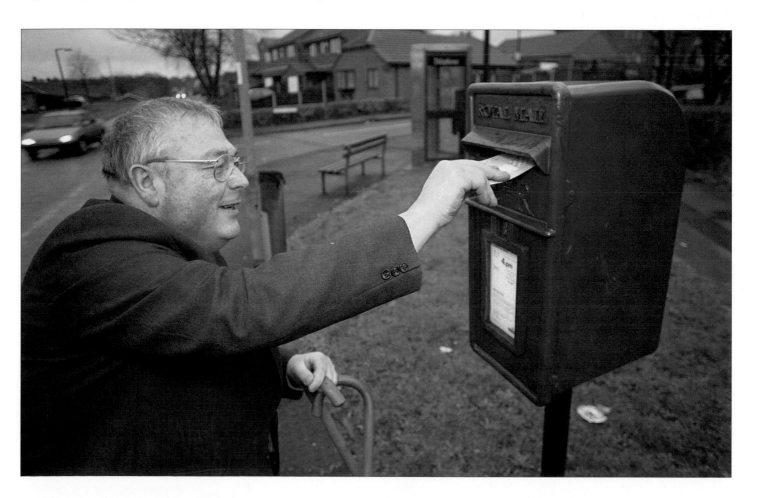

239

CHAPTER SIX:

EXPANDING YOUR HORIZONS

Assuming you have read the book to this point, you will have learned all the rules, gone away and played some practice games, come back and learned a little more about strategy and tactics, and also absorbed a little of the history, background and culture of chess – you are now a knowledgeable chess player. That may be all you want to know about chess – in which case, farewell, reader, go forth and enjoy the game. However, if you now want to raise your chess skills a notch or two further, this chapter supplies you with some advice on what to do next. Chess has a rich cultural heritage, with a vast literature stretching back hundreds of years. This chapter helps you to learn more about what interests you in the world of chess.

Right: You have now learned all the rules and absorbed much about the strategy of the game, plus its history and culture. This is more than enough if you simply want to enjoy a social game with friends. However, if you've decided to take your game further, this chapter helps you get ready for competition chess.

How to Teach Yourself

Unquestionably the best way to teach yourself chess is to practise. There are some wonderful resources available for learning chess at all levels, to supplement the experience of actually playing the game. These are worth using to develop your strategy.

The written word versus software

At one time, there was only one way to teach yourself chess, and that was to read a book. The computer age has lead to the introduction of major alternatives: teaching software, playing software and teaching websites. Before suggesting any specific titles or sources, it is best to consider which aspects of chess need to be studied.

There are several different types of chess book or software title. The book you are currently reading is an introduction to chess, covering the rules, elementary strategy, openings, middlegame and endgame, plus some background on the history, personalities and general culture of the game. You will not be surprised to know that each of these components is itself the subject of many chess books in their own right.

Useful books

Although it is difficult to prove, it has been asserted more than once that more books have been written about chess than all other games and sports combined. This is not hard to believe. Chess has been played in its current form for hundreds of years, and the fact that chess games can be transcribed in notation makes it very compatible with presentation via the written word.

This presents the reader with a problem: what sort of book is best to read? If the goal is to improve as a player from elementary to intermediate (and

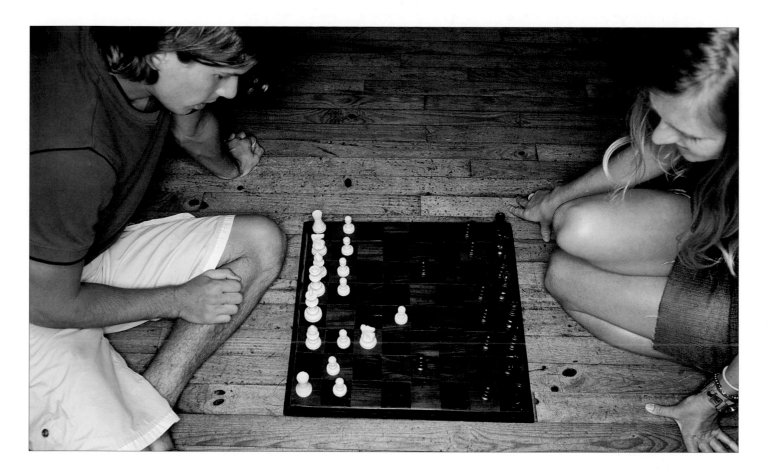

Above: The only way to learn how to play chess is by playing, as often as you can. Don't seek out chess 'experts': you'll learn more by playing opponents at your level, or from a parent or elder sibling, who can teach you and enjoy the game at the same time.

Left: A class of girls listens to their teacher Lucy Anness give a lesson on the game of chess at a school in Kent, England, in 1948. Miss Anness was proud to be headmistress of the only girls' school in Britain to teach chess as part of the curriculum.

ultimately further), the following types of book are appropriate in descending order of priority:

• Books teaching middlegame tactics and strategy: look for books that have plenty of examples from the play of amateur or intermediate-level players. Just as it is important to practise against players of a slightly higher standard, it is useful to play through examples taken from ordinary games. When reading such books, it is usually a good idea to set the games and positions up on a board and play through the examples.

• Puzzle books: typically, chess puzzle books have a number of diagrams on each page and invite you to find the next move in a given position. Usually the move will be surprising or spectacular. Working through tactical puzzles is good practice for visualization and just good old-fashioned fun. You don't need a board and pieces to do puzzles, so this makes them useful books to carry when travelling.

• Opening books: there are hundreds of these to choose from, but at this stage you only need a basic overview of available openings and perhaps the rudiments of a repertoire. Small is beautiful.

• A basic book on the endgame might be useful – nothing too heavy.

Books to avoid (for now) are: collections of games, or even instructional books, by famous world champions. These are for more advanced players – and world champions don't write beginners' books. When checking out the credentials of an author, it can be more useful to find out if they have a track record as a teacher rather than a player. Don't be too impressed by the quantity of books they have written.

Computer programs

By all means, play your computer on a friendly level (even one where it evens up the score between you), but don't overdo it. Playing chess in two dimensions can make it hard to adapt to play on a conventional board. Also, always remember that computers play chess in a slightly different way from humans, and you may find human versus human chess difficult to adapt to – though you will also find some humans much easier to beat.

WHERE TO PLAY COMPETITIVE CHESS

In all probability, you will start playing chess against a friend or relative who already 'knows the moves' (as we like to say). This is the best way for most people, unless that person happens to be a high-level competition player. Obviously, it is good to have a strong chess-playing friend from the point of view of learning how to play, but it would probably take too long for you to catch up with him or her in strength so that the games become genuinely competitive. There is only even a point in playing people of approximately the same standard. It may happen that you and your original partner happily go on playing informal chess from now until the end of time. However, for the purposes of this section, let's assume that you decide to take the plunge and involve yourself in the wider world of competition chess.

The first thing to be aware of is that some players at the bottom of the pyramid that represents the world of competition chess are not too far above the beginner level themselves. Someone of average intelligence who practises frequently and does a bit of chess reading can bridge the gap between beginner and low-level competition player in a few months. So there is no

Below: Twenty champion players gathered in 1930 for an international chess tournament in San Remo, Italy. On the left is Hans Kmoch from Austria, and on the right is Karl Ahues from Germany.

Above View of the 1989 Aubervilliers chess tournament in France, with its line-up of playing competitors. In this tournament around 800 competitors played – in some the number of competitors runs into thousands.

need to entertain the notion that everyone at a tournament or in a chess club is some sort of chess-playing genius. Nor are they freaks, geeks or nerds. Men and women, who are rich, poor, young, old, introvert or extrovert can all play chess. Sadly, though, there is a gender bias, with only about 5 per cent of the world's competition players being female. This situation is gradually improving, however.

Your first question is probably: club or tournament? Of course, you can do both in due course. Most reasonably sized towns in the UK and US have chess clubs, which usually meet one night during the week , or afternoon during the weekend, for matches and competitions. You can make contact either by turning up on a club night or contacting a club official. A few addresses are given in the 'Useful List' at the back of this book. Chess clubs always welcome new members and are generally friendly, usually meeting in church halls and community centres, and sometimes at their own premises or in plush rooms in hotels.

As regards tournaments, there are two main types. We have already mentioned rapidplay tournaments, which take place on Saturdays or Sundays, where five or six games are played in the course of one day. Each game lasts no more than one hour. Longer

tournaments can stretch from Friday evening to Sunday afternoon, again with five or six games played, but each individual game can last more than four hours. This may sound gruelling, but there is a tendency for the games of lower-level players to be shorter than that – which means there is time to socialize between games, or perhaps browse a bookstall (chess competitions very often have chess bookstalls) or have a meal or snack. It is usually not expensive to enter tournaments, and many award cash prizes of varying amounts. Your chances of winning might be better than you think – players are grouped together in sections of approximately equal strength, and relative beginners sometimes walk away with decent prizes.

Several chess calendars listing upcoming tournaments can be found on the Internet. A good place for European tournaments is eurochess.org, and for the USA, uschess.org.

Chess tournaments are often held in coastal resorts and holiday destinations during the summer, and they can offer an enjoyable way to combine an ordinary holiday with some chess.

PLAYING AT A CHESS CONGRESS

Playing chess at a congress or in a chess club is a little different from playing informal chess with friends, and takes a bit of getting used to at first. That is not to say that informal chess is not played at chess clubs. On your first visit to a club, you will probably be paired to play a few informal games that are not part of any competition and are more a way of breaking the ice – people will be casting an eye over you, to see if you are any good. These games will be much the same as you play with your friends. Some of the rules may be relaxed for the duration.

Bending the rules

The rule that you must move a piece that you have touched or moved may, for example, be waived. If it is just a friendly game and you play a ridiculous move that loses instantly, the polite enquiry 'Can I take that move back?' will probably be answered in the affirmative. You may also notice that other people are playing friendly games and talking incessantly during games, including teasing each other and making derogatory comments about each other's play. In this respect, chess club meetings can differ quite markedly from each other. Some have an atmosphere like a working man's club, with plenty of chat and people drinking alcohol as they play. At others, chess is played in library-like silence as if the result of the world chess championship were at stake.

However, if a formal match or tournament is in progress, the game is played by the rulebook. Silence is observed in the clubroom, even if some of the games being played are not part of the competition. During a competitive match, a request to take a move back would be met by total incredulity.

Team chess

One of the most enjoyable and sociable ways of playing chess is team chess, with clubs developing their own camaraderie. Many clubs run second, third and other subsidiary teams, and players of all standards can find their niche in such line-ups. Club team chess is usually confined to weekday evenings, fitting in with players' work patterns. Team chess is very popular in schools throughout the world. Teams may compete within a school and between schools. In the USA, for example, there are high-school championships.

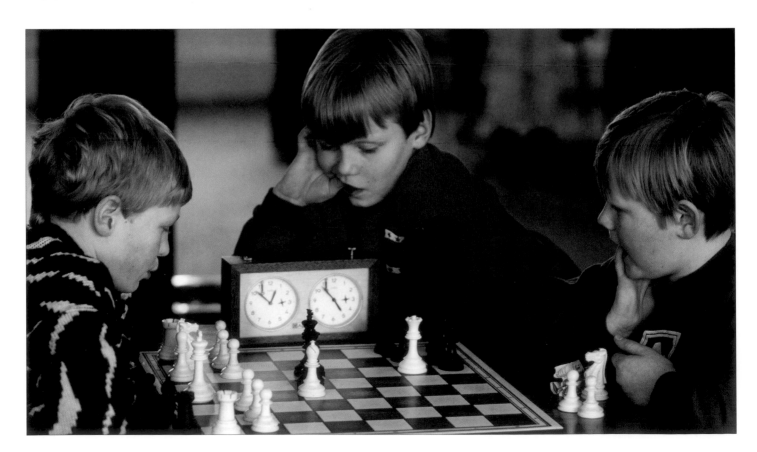

Tournament chess

Played in line with the formal rules of the game and using chess clocks, you should not ask for any relaxing of the rules when playing in a tournament. An arbiter is present to ensure fair play. However, that does not mean it is unfriendly or unsociable. Between games, players will chat with each other and – if it is not your turn to move – it is perfectly proper to walk around, obtain refreshments, and perhaps chat with a friend

Below left: Young boys from the Reykjavik Chess Club concentrate on a game. Many schools run chess clubs and members need not be budding Kasparovs to take part in mini-tournaments and inter-school games. While it is widely recognized that chess encourages concentration and mental agility, it can also be a very sociable activity.

Below: There are almost as many players watching as playing in this depiction of a 19th-century French salon. Chess spectators are sometimes called 'kibitzers' – a Yiddish word meaning people who watch (and even offer advice) while others play.

(as long as you do not disturb people in play). As well as using the clock, you will be expected to keep score of the moves. This is extremely useful, and you should spend time going through the game afterwards, particularly if you lose. Tournament chess is also played at junior level. Information about tournaments at any level can usually be found on the websites of the many chess federations that exist around the world, such as the US Chess Federation, the English Chess Federation and the Australian Chess Federation.

Most such tournaments take place at the weekend (they are known as weekend congresses), normally over four to six rounds. In most, players are usually divided into a number of sections, according to playing strength. Players play in all five games, and winners are paired against each other.

CHESS PROBLEMS AND STUDIES

One branch of the game that beginners sometimes find hard to grasp is the composition of problems and studies. There are several different types of composition, although there are some similarities among all of them. The idea is to compose a chess position where one of the sides has an unusual, hard to find and/or aesthetically pleasing way to win (or sometimes draw) available.

The popularity of chess problems in the 19th century led to several composers becoming famous. Probably the most well-known was the US composer Sam Loyd (1841–1911). He created a great many ingenious and entertaining chess puzzles, including the Excelsior, published in 1861.

Chess problems

The most common type of chess problem has a caption stating: 'Mate in x moves', where x is often 2, 3 or occasionally a larger number. Let's assume x is 2: this means that White is to play and make a remarkable or surprising move and, in reply to any move by Black, will reply with a second move that is checkmate (the second white move could be clever or quite obvious).

Over many years, conventions have grown up around chess problems and, in trying to solve the problem, you can be fairly sure of the following: 1) the first move will not be a major capture (and probably not a capture at all); 2) it won't be a checking move; 3) it will be something quite counter-intuitive in the context of practical chess (e.g. a queen being placed *en prise* to a pawn).

Chess problems often have quite outlandish positions that are unlikely to arise during a normal game. However, they use all the rules of chess and it can be quite useful to work through them. One important point: be sure to check all Black responses very carefully because there is often a surprise resource for Black that makes a nonsense of your proposed solution. Black is simply trying to extend the game beyond White's second move in order to invalidate a proposed solution.

Chess problem composing and solving are two different specialisms and there are chess competitions that test both skills. It is said that comparing the normal playing of chess to problem composition is like comparing prose and poetry: composition is about subjective considerations such as ingenuity, aesthetics, originality and taste. Solving problems involves skills such as visualization and clarity of thought, which play a vital part in chess-playing itself.

Here is a typical example of a chess problem. This particular problem dates from 1880.

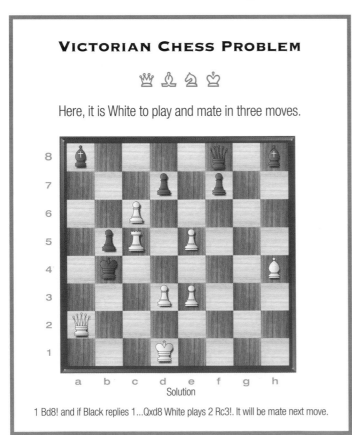

VICTORIAN CHESS PROBLEM

Here, it is White to play and mate in three moves.

Solution

1 Bd8! and if Black replies 1...Qxd8 White plays 2 Rc3!. It will be mate next move.

Mate in Two

The solution is 1 d4! – after that, all Black replies will be answered by checkmate in one move, e.g. 1...bxc4 2 Rxe5 mate, 1...Kxe4 2 Qh1 mate, 1...exd4 2 Qxd4 mate, 1...Qxc5 (don't forget to look at outlandish replies), 2 dxc5 mate, etc.

Chess studies

Studies are composed endgame positions resembling situations that arise in practical chess, with the caption 'win' or 'draw'. The solver is thus challenged to find a winning or drawing line by White (who usually plays first). The 'clever' part of the solution may come at any point of the winning/drawing sequence, or may even be every move of the sequence. As with problems, it must be assumed that the defender finds the very best defence. Here is an example of a study with a difference. White is to win – however, Black moves first and the challenge is to find the best try to avoid the loss. Only then is White tasked to find the way to refute Black's ingenious drawing attempt. The big problem for Black is how to stop White queening the pawn and then routinely winning.

Below: Composed problems are as old as competitive chess, and appeared in many old chess books alongside instruction and advice on how to play the game.

Black's clever starting move is 1...Be8!!. That may look like madness, but 2 fxe8Q is stalemate and if 2 f8Q? Nd7+! forks the king and queen so that, after 3 Nxd7, it is stalemate again. It is no good underpromoting to a rook because the same thing will happen. But after the astonishing 2 fxe8B!! – i.e. pawn takes bishop and promotes to a bishop – Black must make a knight move, and the knight will be lost. White will be left with the technical task of winning with the bishop and the knight – and, having reached a theoretically won position, the study is deemed to be solved.

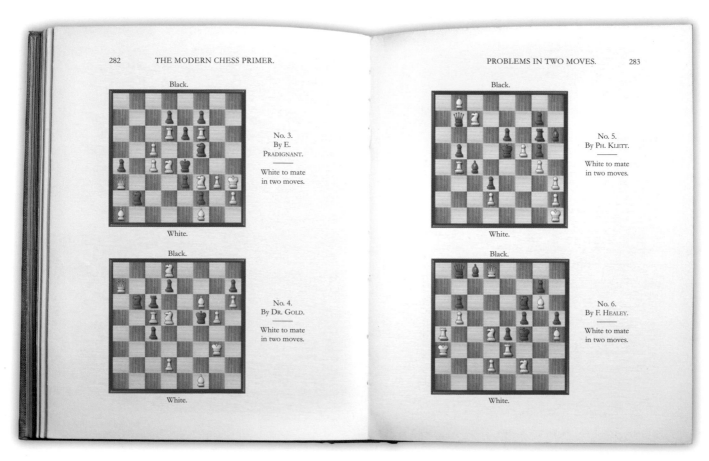

282   THE MODERN CHESS PRIMER.

Black.

No. 3.
By E.
Pradignant.

White to mate
in two moves.

White.

Black.

No. 4.
By Dr. Gold.

White to mate
in two moves.

White.

PROBLEMS IN TWO MOVES.   283

Black.

No. 5.
By Ph. Klett.

White to mate
in two moves.

White.

Black.

No. 6.
By F. Healey.

White to mate
in two moves.

White.

GLOSSARY

algebraic notation Chess notation in which each square of the board is given a unique identifier from a1 to h8, where the letter identifier signifies the file and the number the rank.

attack A move that threatens the advantageous capture of a piece or pawn on the following move, or gives check (q.v.) to the opposing king.

backward pawn A pawn that cannot be defended by another pawn or readily advanced without support from another pawn.

Black The player moving the black chess pieces is usually referred to as 'Black'.

blindfold chess A form of chess where one or both of the players plays without sight of the board and pieces. Moves are communicated verbally.

block To interpose a piece between the opponent's attacking piece and a more valuable piece.

board The chessboard of 64 squares on which the game is played. In the context of a team chess match, games are referred to as boards, e.g. 'board one', 'top board', etc.

castle Or 'castling'. A special combined move involving the king and a rook on the same turn. Note: beginners sometimes refer to the rook as a 'castle' but competition players never do so.

centre The four squares in the middle of the chessboard (in notation: d4, e4, d5, e5).

check A position where the king is attacked, or 'in check', but has means of escaping it. The player making the attack is said to 'give check' or play 'check' or a 'checking move'.

checkmate A position where a king is attacked (or 'in check') and has no legal move to escape the check. A player whose king is thus attacked loses the game. More often simply referred to as 'mate'.

closed position A position where the pieces of both sides have limited scope as the result of pawns blocking most of the lines for manoeuvre.

combination A sequence of moves by one side with a specific tactical purpose (e.g. checkmate or winning a piece).

defend, defence A piece is said to be 'defended' (or 'protected') if its capture can be immediately met by capturing the piece used to take it.

deflecting sacrifice An opposing piece is lured away from the defence of a major piece by the offer of a lesser-value one.

development The process of moving as many pieces as possible into useful positions during the opening phase of the game.

diagonal A line of same-colour squares running obliquely across the board. The lines of squares between opposite right-angles of the chessboard (in chess notation, a1-h8 and h1–a8) are known as the 'long diagonals'.

diagram The two-dimensional representation of a chess position as shown in a chess book or article.

discovered A 'discovered attack' is where a move of a piece effects an attack by another piece of the same colour which had previously been blocked. A 'discovered check' is a move which uncovers an attack by another on the opponent's king.

double check A move that attacks the opponent's king and at the same time discovers (q.v.) an attack by a second piece on the king.

doubled pawns Two or more pawns of the same colour on the same file.

draw A chess game can conclude in a draw, typically where the players agree to do so, or stalemate occurs.

en passant A pawn attacking a square crossed by an opponent's pawn that has advanced two squares on its initial move may capture the opponent's pawn as though it had only advanced one square. It is said to capture *en passant*.

en prise A piece that may be captured on the opponent's next turn is said to be *en prise* (usually pronounced 'ahn preez').

endgame The phase of a game in which only pawns and a greatly reduced number of other pieces remain on the board, leading to a change of strategy. Not all chess games reach an endgame. Also known as the 'ending'.

exchange Usually refers to the capture of one piece of equivalent value by each of the players on successive moves. For example, White uses a bishop to capture the opponent's bishop, and Black takes the bishop on the following turn.

fianchetto A move by a bishop to an adjacent square in front of the adjoining knight (b2, g2, b7, g7) in the opening phase of the game. A bishop so placed is sometimes referred to as a 'fianchettoed bishop'. From an Italian word meaning 'little flank'.

FIDE Stands for *Fédération Internationale des Échecs*. Also commonly referred to as the World Chess Federation, this organization is responsible for drafting the internationally-recognized laws of chess and organizing world championships.

file A column of eight squares between White's side of the board and Black's. In chess notation, the eight files of a chessboard are lettered a to h.

flank the side of the board (normally in reference to the a, b, g and h files)

fork A move that makes a significant or dangerous attack on two or more opposing pieces.

gambit An opening (q.v.) in which a player invites the capture of pieces (or more often pawns) in order to expedite the disposition of the pieces with a view to a quick attack.

grandmaster Title awarded by FIDE (q.v.) to an expert or professional chessplayer who has achieved a number of big scores in major competitions.

intermezzo An intermezzo move (also often referred to as a *zwischenzug* – German for 'in-between move') is a move played in between a sequence of exchanges.

isolated pawn A pawn that cannot be defended or supported by another pawn of its own colour on an adjoining file.

kingside Refers to the side of the board on which the kings stand as the game begins, i.e. the 32 squares on White's right-hand side.

major piece A queen or rook.

match A formal series of games between two opponents, with one point awarded for a win and half a point for a draw. Also refers to a team chess encounter, where players representing a club or country each play a game or games against an opposing team. NOTE: chessplayers never refer to a single game of chess between two players as a 'match'; it is always a 'game'.

mate Short for 'checkmate' (q.v.).

material Describes a player's pieces in terms of their overall values (q.v.). A player with an extra pawn, or a rook versus the opponent's bishop, is said to have a 'material advantage'.

middlegame The phase of a game after opening moves have been made and many of the pieces are deployed in the centre of the board or in close proximity to the enemy forces.

minor piece A bishop or knight.

move The turn to play. References to a number of moves invariably mean 'moves by each player'; thus, 'a game of 30 moves' means 30 moves by White and 30 by Black.

opening The initial moves of the game. Many standard openings have formal names and are played from memory by experienced players. Note: not all openings are 'gambits' (q.v.).

outpost An outpost is a square on the opponent's half of the board which is easily defensible by pawns but cannot be attacked by enemy pawns.

passed pawn A pawn is referred to as 'passed' if there is no enemy pawn ahead of it on the same file or on adjoining files.

perpetual check A series of checks that do not lead to checkmate but cannot be evaded by the opponent. Normally the game will conclude at this point as an agreed draw or a threefold repetition (q.v.).

piece Loosely used to refer to any chessman (e.g. king, queen, rook, bishop, knight, pawn); however, in many contexts this term is used more specifically to refer to chessmen *other than* a pawn.

pin A move that attacks an opposing piece which stands in front of a more valuable piece on the same line of attack is said to 'pin' the piece.

position The arrangement of all the pieces on the board at any one time.

problem A composed chess position in which one side can force an outcome (usually checkmate) in the stipulated number of moves. 'Mate in two' means White plays a move, Black replies and then White gives checkmate on the second move.

promotion A pawn that reaches the rank furthest from its starting position is 'promoted' – i.e. removed from the board and replaced by a queen, rook, bishop or knight of the same colour.

queenside Side of the board on which the queens stand as the game begins, i.e. the 32 squares on White's left-hand side.

rank A row of eight squares laterally across the board.

repetition of position *See threefold repetition.*

resign A player who judges that the opponent is ultimately certain to deliver checkmate is entitled to cut the game short by resigning. This is sometimes signified by turning the king on one side, and in tournaments by offering a handshake.

sacrifice A move that deliberately allows a valuable piece to be captured, with a view to achieving checkmate or a longer-term advantage.

simultaneous display A chess exhibition in which a strong chessplayer plays games concurrently against a number of opponents, often arrayed in a square or circle. Often abbreviated to 'simul'.

skewer A move that attacks a high-value piece which stands on the same line of attack as a less valuable one behind it (which will be captured when the more valuable piece moves away).

smothered mate Where a knight gives checkmate to an enemy king which is prevented from escape because it is surrounded by its own pieces.

stalemate A position where the player to move cannot move any of the pieces but is not in check. The game ends immediately as a draw.

strategy Long-term planning, often in positions where there are few immediate attacking possibilities.

tactics Short-term calculation, required in complex or close combat positions where there are many attacking possibilities.

tempo A move which, for example, involves moving a piece to a square and then back to its previous square to no effect is said to 'lose a tempo' (i.e. is a waste of time).

threefold repetition Where the same position occurs three times in a game, with the same player to move on each occasion, a player can choose to claim a draw 'by threefold repetition'.

tournament A formal competition in which players meet a number of other competitors in successive rounds. A number of different tournament formats are used for chess, including all-play-all and (less commonly) knock-out.

value, valuable As a rough guide, pieces other than the king are said to have 'relative values' (e.g. queen 9 points, pawn 1 point). Hence a queen is considerably more valuable than a pawn. The king is of infinite value.

White The player moving the white chess pieces is usually referred to as 'White'.

zugzwang A German word meaning 'compulsion to move'. Refers to a position in which the player to move is not in immediate danger but where any move involves spoiling the position in some way. Since in chess a player may not 'pass', a move has to be played resulting in the ruination of the position. A player in this position is said to be 'in *zugzwang*'.

USEFUL CONTACTS

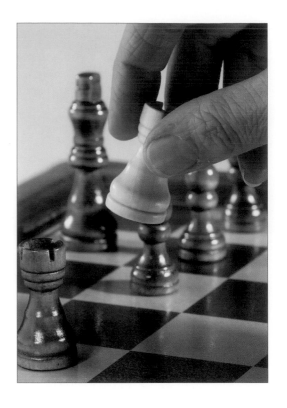

Beginners' book and software recommendations:
www.bcmchess.co.uk/chessbooks/beginners.html
A comprehensive list of chess books and software titles for beginners, kept up to date by this book's author.

Chess calendars:
BRITISH CHESS MAGAZINE: **www.bcmchess.co.uk/news/events.htm**
ENGLISH CHESS FEDERATION: **www.bcf.org.uk/calendar/index.html**
WELSH CHESS UNION CALENDAR:
www.welshchessunion.co.uk/html/calendar.html
CHESS SCOTLAND CALENDAR:
www.chessscotland.com/membership/cswebcalendar.htm
ULSTER CHESS UNION CALENDAR: **www.ulsterchess.org/events**
IRISH CHESS UNION CALENDAR: **www.icu.ie/events**
WORLD CHESS FEDERATION: **www.fide.com**
US CHESS FEDERATION: **www.uschess.org/news/calendar.html**
HARMEN JONKMAN'S CHESS CALENDAR: **www.chess-calendar.nl**

National federation websites and phone numbers:
ENGLISH CHESS FEDERATION: **www.englishchess.org.uk**,
tel: 01424 775222
WELSH CHESS UNION: **www.welshchessunion.co.uk**, tel: 01443 474730
CHESS SCOTLAND: **www.chessscotland.com**, tel: 0141 221 6464
ULSTER CHESS UNION: **www.ulsterchess.org**, tel: 028 9029 6734
IRISH CHESS UNION: **www.icu.ie**, tel: +353 1 878 2436
WORLD CHESS FEDERATION: **www.fide.com**
US CHESS FEDERATION: **www.uschess.org**
CHESS FEDERATION OF CANADA: **www.chess.ca**
AUSTRALIAN CHESS FEDERATION: **www.auschess.org.au**
CHESS IN NEW ZEALAND: **www.nzchess.co.nz**
EUROPEAN CHESS UNION: **www.eurochess.org**

Correspondence chess (UK):
BRITISH CORRESPONDENCE CHESS ASSOCIATION, tel: 0121 707 3850
NATIONAL CORRESPONDENCE CHESS CLUB, tel: 0121 321 3816
SOCIAL CORRESPONDENCE CHESS ASSOCIATION, tel: 01642 824301
POPULAR POSTAL CHESS CLUB, tel: 01923 823251
INTERNATIONAL CORRESPONDENCE CHESS FEDERATION: **www.iccf.com**
US CHESS ON-LINE: **www.uschess.org/cc/**
CORRESPONDENCE CHESS LEAGUE OF AMERICA: **www.chessbymail.com**
CORRESPONDENCE CHESS LEAGUE OF AUSTRALIA:
www.auschess.org.au/ccla/

Top: Though at its most basic it is a board game played between two people, chess is also an organized sport with international and national leagues.

Bibliography and Further Reading

Averbakh, Yuri, *What You Need to Know about Endgames* (Caissa Commerce, 2006)

Basalla, Bob, *Chess in the Movies* (TPI Wonderworks, Iowa, 2005)

Brady, Frank, *Bobby Fischer* (Batsford, London, 1974)

Chandler, Murray, *How to Beat Your Dad at Chess* (Gambit Publications, London, 1998)

Chandler, Murray and Milligan, Helen *Chess for Children* (Gambit Publications, London, 2004)

Fox, Mike and James, Richard, *The Even More Complete Chess Addict* (Faber & Faber, London, 1993)

Golombek, Harry (ed.), *The Encyclopedia of Chess* (Batsford, London, 1977)

Hartston, William, *The Guinness Book of Chess Grandmasters* (Guinness Publishing, 1996)

Hooper, David and Whyld, Kenneth, *The Oxford Companion to Chess* (Oxford University Press, Oxford, 1996)

Kasparov, Garry *Fighting Chess: My Games and Career* (Batsford, London, 1983)

Seirawan, Yasser, *Winning Chess Strategies* (Everyman Chess, 2003)

Silman, Jeremy, *The Amateur's Mind* (Siles Press, 1999)

Silman, Jeremy, *How to Reassess Your Chess* (Siles Press, 2003)

Silman, Jeremy, *The Reassess Your Chess Workbook* (Siles Press, 2001)

Sunnucks, Anne, *The Encyclopaedia of Chess* (Robert Hale, London, 1970)

Ward, Chris, *Improve Your Opening Play* (Everyman Chess, 2000)

Periodicals:

British Chess Magazine Despite its name, it covers chess worldwide, is read all over the world, and is the oldest magazine in continuous publication in the world (since 1881). It also has a website: www.bcmchess.co.uk

New in Chess Another chess magazine, published in The Netherlands, which covers chess worldwide. Its website can be found at: www.newinchess.com

Chess Life It is mainly confined to the USA, though it is accessible via its website: www.uschess.org

Left: Chess can now be played on the Internet, on chess computers and by correspondence. However, it is still mostly played on a traditional chessboard with the standard Staunton chess pieces.

INDEX

PICTURE CREDITS

The publisher would like to thank the following for kindly supplying photographs for this book: **AKG** 16 (l), 17; **Alamy** 220, 221 (b); **Ancient Art and Architecture** 43 (b); **Art Archive** 12, 13 (t), 14, 38 (l); **Bridgeman Art Library** 11 (r), 15, 34, 35 (l), 38 (r); **Corbis** 10 (l), 11 (r), 12 (t), 13 (b), 16 (r), 21 (bl), 23 (t), 24 (b), 25, 27, 32 (l), 37 (b), 39 (r), 40 (l), 41, 43 (t), 46, 47 (b), 73, 78, 111, 139, 140, 143, 218, 219, 222, 223, 230, 231, 232, 233, 235, 237 (t), 238, 239 (b), 242, 243, 244, 245, 246, 247; **Empics** 22, 132; **Getty Images** 221 (t); **iStockphoto** 133; **British Chess Magazine** 18, 19, 20, 21 (r), 23, 24, 26, 28, 29, 30, 31, 32 (r), 33, 42, 43 (t), 76, 77, 234, 236, 237 (b), 239 (t); **Kobal Collection** 35 (r), 36 (t and c), 37 (t); **Photos.com** 47 (t); **TopFoto** 40 (r)

All other images by Andrew Perris

Every effort has been made to obtain permission to reproduce copyright material, but there may be cases where we have been unable to trace a copyright holder. The publisher will be happy to correct any omissions in future printings.